06-08-07

Loving Arms

Loving Arms

British Women Writing the Second World War

KAREN SCHNEIDER

THE UNIVERSITY PRESS OF KENTUCKY

Copyright © 1997 by The University Press of Kentucky

Scholarly publisher for the Commonwealth,
serving Bellarmine College, Berea College, Centre
College of Kentucky, Eastern Kentucky University,
The Filson Club, Georgetown College, Kentucky
Historical Society, Kentucky State University,
Morehead State University, Murray State University,
Northern Kentucky University, Transylvania University,
University of Kentucky, University of Louisville,
and Western Kentucky University.

Editorial and Sales Offices: The University Press of Kentucky
663 South Limestone Street, Lexington, Kentucky 40508-4008

96 97 98 99 00   5 4 3 2 1

Library of Congress Cataloging-in-Publication Data

Schneider, Karen.
    Loving arms : British women writing the Second World War / Karen
Schneider.
        p.   cm.
    Includes bibliographical references and index.
    ISBN 0-8131-1980-4 (alk. paper)
    1. English literature—20th century—History and criticism.
    2. World War, 1939-1945—Great Britain—Literature and the war.
    3. Women and literature—Great Britain—History—20th century.
    4. English literature—Women authors—History and criticism.   5. War
stories, English—History and criticism.   6. World War, 1914-1918—
Women—Great Britain.   I. Title
PR478.W67S36   1996
820.9'358—dc20   96-5744

Manufactured in the United States of America

Contents

For
Minnie Katherine Schneider
and Robert D. Schneider

Abbreviations

AW	*Arms and the Woman*. Cooper, Munich, and Squier
BA	*Between the Acts*. Woolf
BC	*Bowen's Court*. Bowen
BL	*Behind the Lines*. Higonnet, et al.
CE	*The Collected Essays of Virginia Woolf*. Woolf
CI	*Collected Impressions*. Bowen
CS	*The Collected Stories of Elizabeth Bowen*. Bowen
CV	*Children of Violence*. Lessing
D	*The Diary of Virginia Woolf*. Woolf
FF	*Feminine Fictions*. P. Waugh
FGC	*The Four-Gated City*. Lessing
FM	*The Female Malady*. Showalter
GN	*The Golden Notebook*. Lessing
GWMM	*The Great War and Modern Memory*. P. Fussell
H	*The Holiday*. Smith
HD	*The Heat of the Day*. Bowen
L	*Letters*. Woolf
Ll	*Landlocked*. Lessing
"LSM"	"Liberty, Sorority, Misogyny." Marcus
MA	*Me Again*. Smith
MF	*Male Fantasies*. Theweleit
MM	*The Mermaid and the Minotaur*. Dinnerstein
MQ	*Martha Quest*. Lessing
MT	*The Mulberry Tree*. Bowen
NYP	*Novel on Yellow Paper*. Smith
OF	*Over the Frontier*. Smith
P/K	*Power/Knowledge*. Foucault
P&C	*Pictures and Conversations*. Bowen
PM	*A Proper Marriage*. Lessing
PS	*Postscripts*. Priestley
RS	*A Ripple from the Storm*. Lessing
SN	*Swastika Night*. Burdekin
"SPV"	"A Small Personal Voice." Lessing
SPV	*A Small Personal Voice*. Schlueter
SW&A	*Seven Winters and Afterthoughts*. Bowen
TG	*Three Guineas*. Woolf
War	*Writing War*. Hanley
WBE	*Writing beyond the Ending*. DuPlessis
WD	*A Writer's Diary*. Woolf
WW	*Women and War*. Elshtain

Acknowledgments

I must begin by acknowledging the intellectual generosity of my teachers at Colorado State University and Indiana University, without whose faith and encouragement I would never have become a scholar. Those to whom I owe a particular debt include Pattie Cowell and Jon Thiem, the late Cynthia Jordan, Ray Hedin, Susan Gubar, and Jim Naremore—exemplary mentors all. I am also grateful to the American Association of University Women for its generous dissertation fellowship, which got this project off the ground. Additional thanks go to my colleague and friend Catherine Green for her unfailing generosity and excellent editorial skills.

Earlier versions of Chapters 4 and 5 appeared in the *Journal of Modern Literature;* I am grateful to Morton P. Levitt for support of my work and for the necessary permissions. I also gratefully acknowledge permission to include "Making Peace," by Denise Levertov, granted by New Directions Publishing Corporation, New York.

Finally, I would like to thank Kevin Ryan for his irresistible puns (including this book's title) and his sustaining companionship.

Introduction

Narrating War

This story shall the good man teach his son,
And Crispin Crispian shall ne'er go by,
From this day to the ending of the world,
But we in it shall be remembered—
We few, we happy few, we band of brothers.
For he today that sheds his blood with me
Shall be my brother. . . .
And gentlemen in England now abed
Shall think themselves accursed they were not here,
And hold their manhoods cheap whiles any speaks
That fought with us upon Saint Crispin's Day.
　　　　　　　　　—*Henry V*, Act IV, sc. iii, l. 56-67

[It] is much less significant that men's History is made of wars than
that men's wars are made of stories.
　　　　　　—Nancy Huston, "Tales of War and Tears of Women"

My father was not quite old enough to see action in World War II, but
he had a war story, and a telling one at that. Eager to do his part, he cajoled my reluctant grandfather into allowing him to join the navy when he
was just seventeen. Concerned that the war was winding down, he volunteered for submarine duty and every other high-risk assignment he
thought would ensure combat. But it was too late; V-J Day smashed his
hopes. While others cheered, my father and his buddies, feeling irrevocably
cheated, wept.

Only recently have I learned to appreciate the full, paradoxical
dimensions of my father's story and his attitude toward it. My own response to his tale was, from the onsct, acutely ambivalent. On the one
hand, I thought, "How inane! They should have been glad to have escaped
the necessity of killing, the possibility of dying, glad the war was finally
over." But, cued by the story's ending, I also thought, "What a pity to have
missed all the excitement, the glory, the pathos." My father obviously felt

1

quite ambivalent as well. He admitted to tears with a somewhat abashed pride; at the same time he viewed the whole incident with irony, exclaiming over his youthful "stupidity." Such ambivalence characterizes modern war stories in general, which manage to represent war as ugly and awe-inspiring, deadly and exciting, repulsive and attractive all at the same time.

In reconstructing my father's story, I can now appreciate that my initial—and enduring—ambivalence toward war and its stories was inevitable, as my later response to the war in Vietnam clearly illustrates. Although I passionately opposed the war, I found myself perversely wanting to see "action" the only way a woman could, as a nurse stationed in a combat zone. I tried to rationalize this desire by attributing to myself the virtues of compassion and caregiving. But, as I had to admit even then, what I really craved was the war experience—the intensity, the life-and-death drama, the test of my character and courage. To a lesser degree—and in shameful secret—I shared my father's earlier disappointment, for traditional war fictions had powerfully shaped my consciousness in ways I could not completely resist. The editors of *Arms and the Woman,* a recent anthology of essays on war, gender, and literary representation, observe that such seemingly irrational ambivalence is rooted in the fairly universal "mythic attraction war holds *for both sexes*" (16, emphasis added)—an attraction not only evidenced but recreated by the stories we tell.

This point begins to illustrate the war story's far-reaching potency as an ideological force. In *Writing War: Fiction, Gender and Memory,* Lynne Hanley explains that, especially for the vast majority of us who have never experienced war directly, war fictions are "particularly potent in shaping our imagination, indeed our very memory, of war" (4). As my father's and my own war stories demonstrate, the rhetoric and narratives of war play a vital role in the ability of what Jean Bethke Elshtain quite aptly calls the "seduction of war" (*WW* 3) to form a cultural memory. But the seduction goes well beyond tenacious romantic notions of war as noble enterprise, personal testing ground, or even simple adventure. For at the heart of the war's "mythic attraction" lies the construction and manipulation of our psycho-sexual identities, our very subjectivities, if you will. In this regard, war and its representations seduce us because they validate and secure idealized notions of masculinity and femininity—notions of difference, privilege, and complementarity that, as we shall see, simultaneously underlie and reaffirm the broader "truths" with which we make sense of reality.

This brings me to the second paradox in my father's tale. The most striking detail of his story—men's tears—awakened me to his assumption that participation in the war was so important to my father and his friends that missing this "opportunity" made it acceptable for (almost) grown men to cry. In part because my father's story came to me filtered through the enormous cultural catalogue of war stories I had already absorbed, I understood that war was special to men, that being/becoming a man was hastened and/or guaranteed by combat, a potentially honorable and heroic (if deadly) endeavor. The ostensibly essential manliness and apparent nobility of wanting to fight added to the frustration of having that desire thwarted justified the tears and belied their usual association with femininity and weakness.

Furthermore, in a fundamental sense, the fact that he had the authority to tell a war story at all assured not only his maleness but his privileged masculinity. For, paradoxically, even this war story tacitly acknowledges and re-authorizes the mutually constitutive relation between war as a phenomenon and masculinity as an ontological condition—the very point on which King Henry relies when exhorting his men to battle at Agincourt. As Cynthia Enloe has observed, militarism plays a foundational role in the "ideological structure of the patriarchy because the notion of 'combat'" is central to the "construction of concepts of 'manhood' and justifications of the superiority of maleness in the social order" (*Khaki* 12-13). Because my father's story reinforces war's essential role in the maintenance of socio-cultural gender difference and its corollary, male privilege, it served (as war stories often do) as both narrative substitute and compensation for actual experience. Significantly, the narrative guarantees a validation that combat may or may not deliver.

To be sure, the mutually causal relationship among masculinism, militarism, and patriarchy is hardly a recent discovery (as I will discuss more fully in chapter 1). But in the last few decades, women and men from various disciplines have found contemporary feminist theory enormously useful for excavating the deeply rooted ways in which a "persistent system of gender relationships" informs war and our thinking about it (*BL* 34). At the same time, they have similarly uncovered how the ways we represent war inform and reinforce the sex-gender system as a whole. As Susan Jeffords has observed in *The Remasculinization of America*, "study of the structural relations between warfare and gender reveals them to be intimately connected, so much so that *one does not survive without the other*" (xv, emphasis added). Indeed, she adds, "the crystallized formations of masculinity in warfare . . . enable gender relations in society to survive."

Jeffords specifically anatomizes the "gendered structure of representations of the Vietnam War," which she identifies as "emblematic" of contemporary "ideological production" in America (xv). If the specific formulations she scrutinizes are unique to post-Vietnam American culture, the reciprocal relations between the production of gender-encoded ideology and representations of war decidedly are not. Thus, both how war is narrated and by whom are matters of no small importance—especially when we consider Lynne Hanley's admonition that "how we imagine (or remember, or forget) war has a great deal to do with our propensity to make war" (*War* 4).

To relate a traditional war story—even an antiwar story—is perhaps inevitably to reinscribe its assumptions, to affirm (even if with regret or repugnance) the abstractions that war concretizes: opposition; hierarchy; dominance and submission; the efficacy and, thus, the necessity of force; and, ultimately, conflict as the essence of human relations (not to mention of narrative itself). In war stories widely defined and accepted as such—men's stories as a rule—male epistemological and ontological privilege are tacitly assumed and thus naturalized, while the ideological foundations for such privilege remain largely invisible. However, as Elshtain aptly remarks, "[W]ars are not men's property. Rather, wars destroy and bring into being men and women as particular identities by canalizing energy and giving permission to narrate. Societies are, in some sense, the sum total of their 'war stories' . . . for war structure[s] identities that are continually reinscribed" (*WW* 166). The women whose war narratives prompted this study were sensitive to the very issues Elshtain touches on here: war's longterm and immediate role in the (en)gendering of identity; the way in which war as it is generally perceived and narrated obscures "the active presence of women *as subjects* in the discourse of war" (Schweik 533); and the ways in which those authorized to tell stories inscribe and guarantee social reality. Accordingly, the writers with whom I'm concerned laid narrative claim to war not primarily as a geopolitical event or even as a personal experience—although these both remain integral to the whole—but as a pan-political blueprint, an ideological mechanism, an objective correlative for humankind's penchant for "loving arms" as we do. As such, war is communal property and gives women and men alike "permission to narrate" it.

The assumption that war literature is properly written by and about men stems from the widespread if not altogether accurate identification of war as an essentially male activity and aggressive masculinity as an ontological condition.[1] As William Broyles somewhat pridefully declares in "Why Men Love War," war is not, properly speaking, merely the condition of the twentieth century, but "the enduring condition of *men*, period" (56, emphasis added). By his account, the best war story is one that relates almost nothing, for its purpose is "not to enlighten but to exclude," to put the "listener in his place. I suffered. I was there. You were not" (61). By these criteria, women are necessarily and rightfully excluded from the fraternity of war raconteurs.

However, to stake a claim for women's place in "combat zones" as such—no matter how appropriate—is quite beside the point. For women's absolute centrality to considerations of war extends far beyond whether or not they experience war in a conventional sense. As many women-authored war stories insist, war is not the condition of men but the condition of humanity, beginning with relations between the sexes. A close reading of Broyles's own analysis of the appeal of war for men speaks volumes about the ways in which the ideological significance of war for women, men, and the sex-gender system as a whole are inter-formative. This astounding and painfully honest account of why "men love war, though they hate it" yields up a catalogue of conceptual links between loving war and loving. Above all, in his identification of heterosexual romance and/or sex as life's defining conflict, the war of wars, Broyles inadvertently underscores the far-reaching implications of the time-honored "trope connecting love and war" (*AW* 10)—a trope many British women writing about World War II explored and often exploited to their own ends.

Claiming to find in sex an escape from geopolitical warfare, Broyles instead unveils a conceptual congruence between sex and war in which phallic aggression simultaneously defines and enables both male (sexual) victory over the female and life itself: "Sex is the weapon of life, the shooting sperm sent like an army of guerrillas to penetrate the egg's defenses—the only victory that really matters" (62). Perversely, then, sex is war. Inversely, moreover, war is sex, for, as he unhesitatingly admits, the "collective power" generated by the activity of war and its homosocial bonding "heighten[s] . . . sexuality" and makes "[w]ar . . . a turn on." When Broyles speaks of the "seduction of war," he finds the "beauty" of its phallic weaponry ("incredible guns like giant hoses washing down from the sky, like something God would do when He was really ticked off") inseparable from an erotics of deadly power. "Men loved their weapons . . . more—not less—because [their] function [was] to destroy, to kill." War, Broyles concludes, is the inevitable result of the "union, deep in the core of our being, between sex and destruction . . . love and death" (61).

In one tautological stroke, Broyles claims the discursive field of war for men, thus silencing women; posits a "natural" adversarial relationship between the sexes, in which women are doomed to defeat; constructs a causal relationship between male dominance/authority and the life force itself; and justifies war as both necessary and inevitable. At the same time, however, his rather naked version of the quite conventional use of love and war as interchangeable metaphors betrays a conceptual reciprocity between the "politics of gender" and the "politics of war" (J. Scott 26)—a congruence signified by the punning trope "loving arms." Broyles thus unwittingly confirms that if we are to know an "other" story of war—if we are to denaturalize the gender-encoding implicit in war and its stories, if we are to consider their ideological power for individuals, cultures, and humanity at large, and, finally, if we are to understand without illusions the seduction of loving arms, then we must hear the war stories women tell.

To read women's stories of war as war stories, therefore, is not only to redefine the parameters of war literature as a genre but, more importantly, to "reconceptualize aspects of . . . war's political history" and to "move the inquiry to a new terrain" (J. Scott 25). For, as Margaret R. Higonnet and Patrice L.-R. Higonnet have observed, women-authored war stories typically exceed the topical, temporal, thematic, and topographical limits of conventional war literature, shifting the focus away from "the militarized front . . . [and] public and institutionally defined areas, to include the private domain and the landscape of the mind" ("Double Helix" 46). In war literature by women, war tends to be enlarged (not transformed) from a discrete event to a more or less perpetual state of mind within which men and women love and do battle. Accordingly, the World War II literature we will examine identifies the psychic, domestic, and discursive battlegrounds as the most fundamental, illuminating, and potentially transformative sites of conflict.

With increasing boldness and cogency, women of letters have refused to remain "exculpate[d] and extricate[d] from history" ("Double Helix" 46), especially the history of war. More specifically, in the first half of this century British women's experience and understanding of the Great War acquired increasingly ominous dimensions with the spread of fascism. Their own vexed positions as women within a patriarchal, militarist culture externally threatened by an overtly fascist one seems to have catalyzed both an acute ambivalence and, perhaps consequently, a significant literary response. Their sometimes defiant and sometimes equivocal representations of women as full subjects in the cultural (re)production of war became at once a means of self-critique and a mode of self-defense.

Exposure of Britain's incipient fascism is conventionally attributed to Virginia Woolf, who in *Three Guineas* asked by what right the English "trumpet[ed] . . . ideals of freedom and justice" when, like any other dictator, the patriarchal state presumed "to dictate to other human beings how they shall live; what they shall do" (53). But conspicuously or in disguise, a good number of similar critiques surfaced in other women's war-related writing.[2] This phenomenon is not limited to the writers included here, of course, nor to British literature.[3] Nevertheless, the war narratives of Stevie Smith, Katharine Burdekin, Elizabeth Bowen, Virginia Woolf, and Doris Lessing share certain characteristics that invite their consideration as a group. Despite obvious national differences, as British civilians these women shared a history, a literary tradition, and a culturally specific perspective. More to the immediate point, each in her own way exposes and critiques the adversarial philosophical foundation shared by conventional gender systems and militarism—ways of seeing and being validated and reproduced by traditional representations of war. Accordingly, they all in some way radicalize the war story. The resulting narratives, however, consistently betray a characteristic ambivalence. Finally, although grounded in varied narrative modes—Parable Art, modernism, feminist polemic, realism, or speculative fiction—their war stories demonstrate with piercing clarity the enormous difficulty of finding a legible space outside the limits of known discourse and tenacious habits of mind.

This difficulty is more evident in Burdekin, Smith, and Bowen than in Woolf and Lessing, and the organization of the chapters that follow reflects this. To begin with Katharine Burdekin and Stevie Smith is also to emphasize the independence of their observations from those of Virginia Woolf. The fictions of Burdekin and Smith, although radically different, demonstrate early efforts to expose the story behind the densely interwoven stories of masculinism, nationalism, and war. Burdekin's futuristic dystopia *Swastika Night* (1937) powerfully condemns the Fatherland's fascism as an extreme but logical manifestation of the culturally hegemonic "cult of masculinity." Finally, however, her critique is somewhat compromised by her own indulgence in the patriotic discourse generated by her antipathy for Nazism. In her neglected war trilogy—*Novel on Yellow Paper* (1936), *Over the Frontier* (1938), and *The Holiday* (1949), Stevie Smith employs heterosexual romance and cross-dressing as tropes in order to expose the gender-inflected genesis of dominance and war. Caught in the crosscurrents of psycho-social and historical imperatives, her hapless protagonist ultimately becomes entangled in the ideology of conflict. Distressed by the seemingly inescapable division of human subjectivity into "masculine" and "feminine" modes, Smith's hero(ine) fails to negotiate this "difference" and can find no tenable state of being. Moreover, Smith finally backs away from the full implications of her intermittently oblique and cutting cultural critique.

Elizabeth Bowen's wartime writing—*The Heat of the Day* (1949), numerous short stories, and her family biography—is even more complexly double-edged. On the one hand, it subtly illuminates the gender-specific connections between storytelling and the two world wars. On the other, it reveals a submerged but intense struggle to negotiate Bowen's conflicting desires for both collaboration with and resistance to the overlapping registers of cultural masculinism. For this Anglo-Irish woman of the ruling class, collaboration wins the day. Still, the struggle is instructive, for it turns on the same ideological axis as the other, more openly oppositional texts.

Throughout her lifetime Virginia Woolf articulated prototypical theories of gender and war fundamental to the literature considered in this study, as the frequent allusions to her work attest. *A Room of One's Own* (1929) and *Three Guineas* (1938) are well known in this regard. War is a subject to which Woolf passionately, if indirectly, returned again and again in her fiction as well, culminating in *Between the Acts* (1941). However, readers tend to see in Woolf's final novel an acquiescence to history's immutable plot, a capitulation to despair. Inarguably, *Between the Acts* carries the weight of Woolf's war-induced doubts about the possibility of a different story for humankind. Nevertheless, for precisely that reason, it seems to me, in this wartime novel she intensifies her critique of the war/gender matrix. And she makes her most compelling effort to escape the conceptual and narrative constraints of the metaphysical paradigm she saw as fundamental to war in every sense.

Finally, in the encyclopedic *Children of Violence* series (1962-69) and in *The Golden Notebook* (1963)—a metafictional comment on and an integral part of *Children of Violence*—Doris Lessing elaborates on her predecessors' concerns. Against the ever-present backdrop of geopolitical conflict, Lessing insists on the basic similarity of the plots of war, romance, colonialism, and racial oppression. Even as she weaves together these various strands of history's "master" narrative, however, she unravels them, undermining their epistemological and narrative utility. Moving from the mundane to the mythopoeic, she seeks to transform consciousness by revising the war/romance plot in some of its multiple manifestations—the realist novel, history, and myth. She thus continues an imaginative project sustained throughout this "Century of Destruction."

Like the disenchanted soldier-writers of World War I, these women of letters consider themselves veterans of unnecessary and fruitless wars. Thus, like Siegfried Sassoon, they attempt (in Hynes's words) to "warn men against war, by telling them the truth about it" (23).[4] But their truth tells an "other" story—not the story of disillusioned and betrayed male combatants told by Sassoon and his fellow poets, nor the androcentric tale of *Men without Women* suggested by Hemingway's title for his collected stories. Rather, British women writing the Second World War excavate the metonymic aptness of romance as a trope for war to its deepest roots. And they warn not only men, but women and men together, for the truth that they tell is that we will continue to "make" war until we question and revise the larger ideological structures of which gender conflict and war are twin manifestations.

The familiar stories of World War II continue to horrify, fascinate, comfort, and compel: the Nazis with their swastikas, stiff-armed salutes, Panzer divisions, and Hitler Youth; the Holocaust with its death camps, crematoria, and ghostly survivors; Pearl Harbor and the *Arizona,* a battleship turned coffin; the "alien" Japanese and their fanatical kamikazes; the

Battle of Britain, Bataan, and D-Day; and the eerie, awesome mushroom clouds blossoming over Nagasaki and Hiroshima. These words and images are irrevocably inscribed in our collective Western consciousness. And we compulsively reiterate their accompanying stories, which achieved mythic status even as they first "made sense" of the (almost) inconceivable. In the midst of the revisionary postmortem of Vietnam and in the wake of the Cold War, our need to reinscribe the "Good War" has surged.[5] Our long-term, unabated love affair with the war story—and war—clearly compels consideration of the fundamentally inter-formative significance of the love story for war and the war story for love. The fiftieth anniversary of World War II and our obsession with the continued mythologization of that war make a resisting re-reading of the Second World War and its stories especially timely.

1

Discerning the Plots

[T]his, no less than any other war, is not a moral war. Greek against Greek . . . Roman against the world, cowboys against Indians, Catholics against Protestants, black men against white—this is merely the current phase of an historical story.
> —Neil McCallum, British officer, World War II

It's still the same old story,
A fight for love and glory,
A case of do or die.
The fundamental things apply,
As time goes by.
> —Herman Hupfield, "As Time Goes By," 1931

As if in response to these two overlapping and complementary assessments of war as never-ending story, contemporary peace activist Dorothee Sölle plaintively asks of "the storyteller and those who have passed the tale down . . . and believed it" a crucial question: "Is that all? . . . Do I have to be Abel if I don't want to be Cain? Is there no other way?" (quoted in Reardon, *Sexism* epigraph). Catalyzed by the psychological and cultural ramifications of the Great War, the experience of the Second World War, and the enormous cache of war narrative, Burdekin, Smith, Bowen, Woolf, and Lessing elaborated on these very questions in precisely the terms suggested by these three dialogic comments on war. Like McCallum, the embittered British officer quoted above, these writers recognized in World War II yet another act of an apparently ageless drama from which, as in Sartre's existential hell, there was no exit. Like him, they too read this ongoing story as a historical master narrative whose plot variations—whether inscribing conflicts of a geopolitical, expansionist, religious, or racial nature—all constitute and record essentially the same universal paradigm of adversity: the quest for dominance of an/other and for institutionalized, unimpeachable power.

The theme song from the classic World War II film *Casablanca,* while similarly identifying war as "the same old story," fills a notable void in McCallum's pointedly androcentric catalogue of typical adversity. Like the film itself, "As Time Goes By" testifies that the war story and the equally ancient and ubiquitous love story constitute integral, inseparable, and interactive plots within the grand narrative of human conflict, miscalled "the fight for love and glory." Of course, neither the film nor the song was intended as any sort of freshly illuminating juxtaposition of love and war, which have served as reciprocal metaphors so long as to have become a cliché. Many British women of letters, however, unearthed a less hackneyed and superficial significance in the perennial imbrication of the plots of war and romance. This significance is at once suppressed and underscored by the plot of *Casablanca,* in which both love and a tearful Ilsa ultimately capitulate to the male-defined necessities of war, thus enabling the heroic international solidarity of its behind-the-scenes—and exclusively male—combatants. Having been assigned to her hero-husband, Ilsa flies out of the picture, and the film closes with the image of Rick and Louis shoulder to shoulder in their stand against fascist tyranny.

As the war rages off camera, in good-womanly fashion Ilsa abdicates all decision-making and authority, sacrifices her happiness, stands by her man, and frees Rick and Louis (who have betrayed their countries through cynicism or cowardice) to salvage their tarnished self-respect. The point is not whether Ilsa did the right thing, but that she faithfully played her assigned part: in this war-engendered domestic drama, the woman, embodying emotion and desire, consents to function purely in support of men—the ostensibly real actors or agents. Accordingly, by denying her and what she represents, and by themselves signifying reason and the greater good, the men can use her to re-establish their heroic manly virtue. The film is thus a quintessential love/war story, for it confirms not only the privileged status of men, revalidated by the war, but the implicitly hierarchical dualisms (reason/emotion, strong/weak, denial/desire) embodied in essentialist notions of masculine and feminine, likewise reaffirmed by war in the abstract, if not always in actuality.

Accordingly, in the "battle of the sexes" many British women perceived not an empty cliché, but a meaning-laden trope of great explanatory power. In the illuminating backflash of world war, they espied what seemed the very core of the ideology of conflict that pervasively informs the history of humankind and the meaning-making stories with which we construct, interpret, and preserve that history. For (to borrow from the ur-narratives of the Judeo-Christian tradition) Cain and Abel represent but one strand in the larger historical/mythical narrative of human conflict.[1]

Enacting explicitly fraternal animosity, their relationship establishes one specific model of dominance and submission: the violent struggle for power of one man over another, a struggle in which the dual alternatives—executioner or victim, as Camus put it—are continually contested from potentially reversible (interchangeable) subject positions (see Camus, *Neither Victims Nor Executioners*).

As British women writing World War II understood, however, another paradigmatic myth resonates synchronously and reciprocally with that of Cain and Abel—that of Adam and Eve. But in this narrative, the rules are purposefully rigged. Potential contestation to the contrary, as conceived and written their story can ultimately have but one outcome, thus inscribing the multiply determined notion that "an attribution of gender difference marks a structure of permanent inequality" (Sedgwick 178).[2] Created in the image of a transcendent God, Adam figures as the prototypical whole human being, of which Eve, an afterthought, in turn figures as a secondary part, an extension. Adam consequently also enjoys a monopoly on the power of naming—the transcendent creator's prerogative to assign meaning and value, to manipulate whole systems of signification. Adam and Eve thus codify quite a different model of dominance and submission—one with which the notion of an unassailable hierarchical order based on a priori assertions of radical difference, separate spheres of activity, and contrasting access to power and knowledge has been historically, linguistically, and narratively inscribed as endemic to the human condition. What Burdekin, Smith, Bowen, Woolf, and Lessing variously recognized was that the stable and effectively naturalized condition of given dominance and subordination defined by Adam and Eve—the prototype of heterosexual romance—is precisely the model that Cain and Abel's heirs constantly strive to reproduce. Figuratively speaking, men vying to vanquish other men, whether in the name of national, racial, economic, ideological, or religious privilege, *seek to be Adam to the other's Eve*. In this way, the sex-gender system, codified in the plot of heterosexual romance, inflects and reinforces the ideology of conflict in its broadest sense. As we shall see, each of these writers perceived and explored this root connection—a connection that has become increasingly evident in the explicitly sexual rhetoric of war and conquest.

In *The Great War and Modern Memory*, Paul Fussell notes the "curious intercourse between [war and love/sex]. The language of military attack—*assault . . . thrust, penetration*—has always overlapped with that of sexual importunity" (270). What strikes me as curious, however, is that he finds this "intercourse" odd rather than definitive. In his meditations on the "association between war and sex," Fussell quotes from James Jones's World War II novel, *The Thin Red Line* (1962), in which a soldier hits on a measure of truth when he asks, "Could it be that *all* war was basically sexual?" (quoted in *GWMM* 271). A female character in Henry Green's wartime novel *Caught* (1943) makes the same observation: "War, she thought, was sex" (119). In the specific sense that this is so, war has become more openly and violently sexual with each skirmish since the Great War, as Fussell and others make clear. Susan Gubar, for example, has demonstrated that the images of reified femininity popular during World War II were blatantly and sometimes violently "eroticized" (231)—as in the case of pinup girls or the sexually alluring (and often promiscuous) women adorning propaganda posters (see Gubar, "This Is My Rifle").

On a somewhat different note, Fussell reports that during the war the word "fuck" became the "indispensable" cornerstone of the military's idiom of contempt, an "express[ion]" of resentment for both sides [officers and enlisted men], the one resenting the constant frustration of its *authority,* the other resenting its constant *victimhood*" (*Wartime* 95, emphasis added). Here we have another instance of the interpenetration of the basic war/romance plots, each group of men linguistically asserting their superior position as Adam to the other's Eve. In the case of the coerced, bullied, and symbolically feminized enlisted men, such rhetoric registers resistance to their humiliating predicament, their angry insistence that they are still men. Historians have similarly learned to characterize nations at war in terms of dueling male sexuality. In *The Causes of War,* for example, Michael Howard asserts that the British went to war in 1914 and 1939 "not over any specific issue . . . but to maintain their power; and to do so . . . before they found themselves . . . so impotent, that they had . . . to accept a subordinate position within an international system dominated by their adversaries" (16). As Theodore Roszak has argued, since the mid-nineteenth century the specifically "bully boy" nature of political and military rhetoric, marked by "compulsive masculinity," indicates that when countries go to war, their "virility"—their symbolic manhood—is at stake ("The Hard and the Soft" 92).[3]

Although sexual assault has long been associated with conquering armies, rape first became widely accepted as a metaphor for military aggression after the German invasion of Belgium in 1914, according to Susan Brownmiller. And although for some groups actual rape was the exception rather than the rule, World War II seems to have marked an exponential increase in the use of "fuck" to mean both sexual intercourse and "exploitation [or] assault" (Kokopeli and Lakey 233). The linguistic move toward violent male sexuality as a weapon of war thus coincided with the excrescence of fascist politics in Europe and the similarly figured military imperialism in the East. The "Rape of the Hun" and, later, the Japanese "Rape of Nanking" came to signify "criminal violation of innocent" countries and civilian populations (Brownmiller 44). Under Hitler, Brownmiller adds, "the ideology of rape burst into perfect flower" (49). "Patterns of German and Japanese aggression," she continues, "clearly in-cluded overt expressions of contempt for women as part of an overall philosophy of the master race" (64).

Brownmiller more generally argues that militarism by its very nature as a masculinist and mostly homosocial institution necessarily imbues its members with a "sense of . . . male mastery" and phallic power that even in the Allied armies could manifest itself as rape, if not regularly in prac-tice, then as a salient symbolic concept. In his discussion of the linguistic legacy of the war, Paul Fussell reports a corroborating instance of acro-nym manipulation: RAPWI—Rehabilitation of Allied Prisoners of War and Internees—became Rape All Pretty Women in Indonesia (*Wartime* 259). In this neat and compensatory reversal, by simple linguistic fiat the British transformed the letters from a sign of defeat and surrender into one of sexual mastery/violation of the colonized female Other.[4]

Imbrication and even conflation of the plots of romance and war obviously did not originate with World War II. In *Don Quixote* (1605), for example, Cervantes wrote, "Love and War are the same thing, the strata-gems and policy are as allowable in the one as in the other" (quoted in Wilden 169). Similarly, the women whose war writing we will examine were not the first to draw parallels between the sex-gender system and militarism/war. As scholars have amply documented, earlier wars sparked recognition of this historical and ideological connection among proto-feminists, such as Mary Astell and Mary Wollstonecraft, as well as any number of World War I era suffragists and/or pacifists.[5] At the turn of the century, Olive Schreiner, for example, linked femaleness to a capacity, even a propensity, for pacifism. Catherine Marshall and like-minded pacifists in the National Union of Women's Suffrage Societies (NUWSS) argued that "militarism by its nature implied the subservience of women." More spe-cifically, they reasoned that World War I was "what happened in a world where women were excluded from decision-making and female skills and characteristics were undervalued" (Kamester and Vellacott 15, 12).[6] Simi-larly, in "Militarism versus Feminism: An Enquiry and a Policy Demon-strating that Militarism Involves the Subjection of Women" (1915), C.K. Ogden and Mary Sargant Florence condemned the widespread war mind-set, which they believed had inevitably resulted not only in an androcentric society and the "perpetual subjection" of women, but in imperialism, racism, and religious intolerance as well (Kamester and Vellacott 57).[7]

Like Schreiner's tendency toward gender essentialism, verbal con-structions such as "militarism versus feminism" reveal, however, that the gender-centered critiques of militarism and war inspired by World War I usually did not themselves escape the oppositional logic that saturates, and on which is predicated, the ideology of conflict. At times neither did the writers of the next war. Still, testing their own theories of the psychology of gender, Burdekin, Smith, and the others tended to question and even refute earlier, reductive notions of direct causation—theories in which woman qua woman represented solutions to male-engendered problems such as sexism and war.[8] In fact, it was precisely this sort of over-determined representation of gender as binary difference—duly under-scored and reconstituted by war and its stories—that these writers variously mapped, interrogated, and in some cases, attempted to deconstruct.

Because most of these writers were explicitly concerned with notions of the gendered "self," it is useful to acknowledge their assumptions about what constitutes a self. Except perhaps for Bowen, who works hard to re-press her gender anxieties, all seem to believe that gender (or psychosexual identity) is more or less culturally constructed, even that one's "subjectivity," as it were, is largely determined by ideological mechanisms—by "social formations, language, political apparatuses," and so forth (P. Smith xxxiv).[9] Still, although they tended to see the "individual" as conflicted because of a disparity between her sense of "self" and society's script for her, this is not to say that they conceived of the subject as unavoidably inhabiting a series of contradictory "subject-positions." Indeed, to varying degrees, they all assume that human beings are potentially whole "individuals." They often speak of, or imply, the "whole" (Lessing) or "androgynous" (Woolf) or "unified" (Smith) self as an ideal. In modified Jungian fashion, Burdekin and Smith write of the "divided consciousness," "repression of the feminine," or an excess of "masculinity." Their notions of the "feminine" and "masculine" generally seem to be an amalgam of an unknown quantity of predisposition and a liberal dose of ideologically interested socialization—the familiar nature/nurture question. Woolf and Lessing are harder to pin down. Although sometimes Woolf similarly speaks of "uniting" the masculine and feminine, she also insists on the need to deconstruct this opposition, which for her begins as a metaphysical duality. Lessing's idea of the self, influenced by Laingian psychology and Eastern philosophy, is perhaps the most complex. It implicitly admits (in contemporary parlance) the existence of multiple subjectivities, a result of the subjecting effects of the symbolic order, beginning with language. But she also proposes the colligation of these "selves" into a psychic "whole," achieved by tapping into a presumably extra-symbolic oceanic consciousness. As Lessing's example demonstrates, despite the writers' assumptions of an ideal unified self, their meditations on the "sexed subject" sometimes loosely prefigure poststructuralist theories of the self. Still, they never abandon the humanist ideal.

The writers' understanding of contemporary psychological theory was, of course, only one determinant influencing their considerations of the sex-gender-war matrix. Their task was infinitely complicated by a whole constellation of pressures—historical, cultural, psychological, and narrative forces—that shaped their epistemological frameworks and ontological statuses, and, therefore, their literary responses. These forces cannot really be isolated, for they all at various points overlap and merge, as becomes immediately apparent when one considers the pressures exerted by the culturally disruptive phenomenon of war in general, by the afterwash of the Great War, and, of course, by World War II itself.

As Higonnet and Higonnet have observed, "War has acted as a clarifying moment, one that has revealed systems of gender in flux and thus highlighted their workings" (5). That is, while the world wars (but especially the Second World War) represented an intensification of the war/ romance plot as it had always been written, they at the same time foregrounded the inimical and arbitrary nature of war's culturally sanctioned script. Furthermore, the wars cumulatively illuminated a reciprocal connection between that script and the making—the ceaseless reproduction— of war as an inescapable human activity. Scrutinizing the foundations of war through the lens of its gendered plots thus brought to light both the absolute necessity and the very possibility of revising the modern, technologically apocalyptic tales of Cain and Abel/Adam and Eve. This developing awareness is directly linked to the sequential gender-specific implications of the two world wars.

Cultural historians and literary theorists such as Theodore Roszak, Paul Fussell, Eric Leed, Susan Gubar, Sandra Gilbert, Klaus Theweleit, and Elaine Showalter, among others, have shown from diverse perspectives that, in the cultural history of the West, World War I marked and intensified a cumulative disruption of the sex-gender system, often characterized as a "crisis of masculinity" (*BL* 3). As the religious, philosophical, artistic, and social verities of the previous era continued to erode, the first great war of the machine age "utterly changed the terms of war experience" (Leed 20). Its prolonged, dehumanizing, and previously inconceivable mass butchery transformed war in the modern imagination from a potentially glorious and heroic enterprise into a dreadful, ignominious, and generally debilitating ordeal—in Storm Jameson's words, "slaughter by numbers" (N.P. Macdonald 125). Lest anyone think her assessment singularly female, Jameson quotes Major-General Fuller of the British army: "There is no chivalry in modern war, there is little heroism, there is no pity. . . . This is not war, this is massacre, the ritual of the slaughter-house . . . this foul contest of machines" (125-26).[10]

Memoirs of the Great War (such as Siegfried Sassoon's *Sherston's Progress*) and the war's (then) shockingly cynical literature give proof to what Elaine Showalter has called the "inscription of male gender anxieties" crystallized by this "unmanly" sort of war ("Rivers and Sassoon" 61). Gilbert and Gubar have marshalled compelling evidence of the pervasiveness of these male anxieties and, moreover, profound resentment escalating into a widespread and multiform misogynist backlash after the war (see *Sexchanges*). Because the Great War jarred many into a sudden awareness of sexual discontinuities and discontent, it came to represent the "calamity that initiated the war between women and men" (Longenbach 104). To dispel the consequent "illusion" of the prewar period as a "sexual golden age" (Longenbach 105), however, James Longenbach points to Ford Maddox Ford's Christopher Tietjens (*Parade's End*) who, while sitting in the trenches, identifies his longstanding and "insoluble" problem as "the whole problem of the relations of the sexes" (Ford 491). For Ford (and innumerable others), Longenbach concludes, "the direct experience of the war made the already complicated issue of sexual difference intractable" (117)—as a plethora of World War I era literature volubly testifies.[11]

The "whole problem of the sexes" seems to have steadily gained momentum between the world wars, taking almost every conceivable shape. While one must avoid any reductive or totalizing explanation for the historical phenomenon of fascism, it is reasonable to speculate that the rise of fascism and the concurrent, widespread adherence to quasi-fascist beliefs signified in part a desperately insistent re-evocation of the "same old story," the war/romance plot perceived as jeopardized by radical instability within the sociopolitical framework, most disturbingly, within the sex-gender system itself. Hitler and other founding fascists constantly espoused the reciprocal notions that tyranny and war defined the essence of maleness, while democracy and peace signaled the degenerative influence of the "improving" status of women. Leila Rupp reports that, according to Nazi philosopher Alfred Rosenberg, the "female influence on the state meant the beginning of decline. 'Emancipated' women . . . were symbols of cultural malaise" (Rupp 16). The proto-fascist German League for the Prevention of the Emancipation of Women (founded in 1912), like Hitler, irrationally linked the women's movement to the mythical "international Jewish conspiracy to subvert the German family and thus to destroy the German race" (Evans 160). National Socialism set out to restore the "natural order" by restricting women to "*Kinder, Küche, Kirche.*" For fascists, "feminine doctrines" such as "pacifism and democracy" subverted the masculine "virtues" of "'hardness,' aggressiveness, and ruthlessness"—the virtues of war, on which, both Hitler and Mussolini argued, survival of healthy, virile nations depended (Evans 159).

As Richard Evans points out, proto-fascist Otto Weininger had already "erected this masculine/feminine, strong/weak dichotomy into a cosmic principle" (159)—a principle that expressed nothing new, but was merely an exaggeration of extant patterns of thought. Significantly, fascist thinkers extended this gender-inflected paradigm from Adam and Eve, as it were, to Cain and Abel. Jews and other non-Aryans, Hitler declared in *Mein Kampf,* like women, were weak and "necessarily . . . inferior" (quoted in Evans 158). Moreover, he characterized even his ardent followers in terms of feminine passivity and emotion. Hitler's leadership style, Evans notes, was predicated on the model of Hitler as "dominant male" and the so-called masses as "submissive female partner" (164). Albert Speer commented that Hitler's "aggressiveness and charisma elicited an almost masochistic surrender and submission in his audience—a form of psychic rape" (quoted in Brownmiller 49). "The people," Hitler wrote, "in their overwhelming majority are so feminine by nature and attitude that sober reasoning determines their thoughts and actions far less than emotion and feelings" (*Mein Kampf,* quoted in Evans 163). Thus, he rationalizes the domination of any and all others in stereotypic terms of heterosexual romance. With characteristic megalomania, Hitler would be Adam to everyone else's Eve (or Eva).

No hindsight was necessary to recognize in fascism an aggressively defensive response to multiple disruptions of Western culture's sex-gender system. In *Women and a Changing Civilization* (1934), Winifred Holtby quotes an unnamed friend: "There had been a rise of feminism; there is now a reaction against it. The pendulum is swinging backwards, not only against feminism, but against democracy, liberty, and reason." Holtby cites Nazi Germany as "the most conspicuous, the most deliberate and the most characteristic example" (151-52). Similarly, in *The Psychology of Fascism* (1943), while rightly conceding that the "economic, historical-traditional and political" causes of fascism are multiple and complex (56), psychiatrist Peter Nathan describes fascism as "an attempt to make a man's world," an attempt to "cover up . . . fear of being weak, unmanly, impotent," "a struggle against women" directly linked to the sexual and general "emancipation of women" (52, 53, 57). He goes on to note that fascists project their own perceived weaknesses onto women and then "make war on them and the symbol of them," while identifying themselves with the "opposite desired characteristics. The fascist forces women to be the things which he wants them to be. . . . Woman becomes his feelings of inferiority, the part of himself he despises and hates, the part he is frightened of. When he has projected his own softness he can become the masculine hero which he feels he needs to be . . . . This projection is no new thing, but we have it now in a particularly acute form" (57).

Nathan's analysis of fascism, though lacking subtlety, prefigures a recent, more theoretically informed anatomization of the psychology of fascism. In *Male Fantasies,* a disturbing analysis of the proto-fascist Freikorps, which evolved out of the disastrous settlement of World War I and formed the kernel of the developing Nazi party, Klaus Theweleit explores the fascist warrior's "desires and anxieties" (Rabinbach and Benjamin ix). He locates these unconscious feelings in deep-seated fear and consequent loathing of the feminine—within and without—and all that the subsequently projected, reified feminine has come to represent. For the fascist even more than for others, Theweleit argues, women embody male fears of contamination by or mergence with the "Other," perceived as dissolution and death. In its "extreme . . . political polarization of gender" (xix), fascism combats the breakdown of boundaries, most particularly between male and female (or Self and Other) and between the bourgeois individual and the (socialist) masses, also figured as female. According to Theweleit, in the fascist psyche female sexuality carries the threat of male castration. The "erotic male-female relationship" thus perversely signifies a grotesque embrace of disfigurement and death; "love and destruction" are intimately linked (1:83). In this psychic milieu, militarism and war, in which masculinity is broadly conceived in terms of "hardness"—a sort of "sustained erection of [the warrior's] whole body" (1:244)—become an offensive mode of defense, a psychic armor against both castration and/or mergence or dissolution. The "hard" male body (aggressive, ruthless, erect) has unassailable boundaries; hence the emphatic insistence on boundaries in fascist theory and practice (1:418).

The relationship of the proto-fascist soldiers to women, Theweleit continues, is not an aberration. On the contrary, it "represents a segment within the continuum of bourgeois patriarchy—and . . . within the genesis of fascism" (1:362). The most radical aspect of Theweleit's argument, then, is that fascism is not merely a "form of government or . . . a system in any sense" but, infinitely worse, a "*mode of producing reality . . .* that is constantly present and possible" (1:220-21, emphasis added). Under certain "determinate conditions," he concludes, fascism becomes the dominant mode of reality production. Not just the masculine mode of European fascism before and during the Second World War, but our mode of reality production, part of a general conceptual framework. Theweleit identifies "male-female relations" as a fundamental example of this process. Following Theweleit's analysis, then, proto-fascist texts and other cultural artifacts of prewar Germany yield up precisely the same insight as many of the woman-authored texts of World War II. Indeed, the British women's texts seem like photographic negatives of Theweleit's materials, telling fundamentally the same story, but one in which the polarity (or the relation of foreground to background) has been reversed.

In a study entitled *Revolutions of Our Time: Fascism* (1973), Otto-Ernst Schüddekopf fails, interestingly, even to consider anything explicitly related to gender as one of the "driving forces of fascism." He does, however, accurately point out that fascism was not "an isolated phenomenon but . . . an integral part of the history of political ideas in Europe" (86). That fascist ideology permeated political thought well beyond the borders of western Europe and found articulate adherents in Britain before the war has been well documented. Winifred Holtby offers up the obvious example of Oswald Mosely, leader of England's Union of British Fascists, which Angus Calder estimates boasted over thirty thousand adherents at its peak in 1934. According to Holtby, Mosely once declared, "We want men who are men and women who are women" (161); no doubt everyone understood exactly what he meant. But Holtby also cites Sir Herbert Austin, a British industrialist, who in 1933 quoted Hitler to support Austin's unoriginal argument that all women workers should be replaced with men and made to go home and stay there. Holtby does not have to strain for examples. More recently, John Harrison's *The Reactionaries* (1967) probes the fascist leanings of modern British men of letters, including Yeats, Lawrence, Eliot, and Pound. Similarly, in a study of D.H. Lawrence's "turn against women," Cornelia Nixon discusses the quasi-fascism of, among others, Yeats and Wyndham Lewis, the latter of whom "identif[ied] decadence as 'the feminization of culture'" and at one point "hail[ed] Hitler as a force for racial, economic, and social regeneration" (6).

Such instances may seem uncharacteristically extreme, but as Europe edged its way toward the abyss of total war, in Britain the notion of war as an ideal opportunity for the separatist forging of true manhood, and feelings of ambivalence, distrust, and even hostility toward women were far from unusual. As J.B. Priestley admitted, "the call [to enlist in World War I] was really little to do with 'King and Country' and flag-waving and hip-hip-hurrah. It was a challenge to what we felt was our untested manhood" (quoted in Bailey 194). Even though the eventual sexual trauma of that war dispelled this myth for many, it failed to lay this longstanding notion completely to rest. Or, perhaps precisely because of the ongoing destabilization of the sex-gender system for which the First World War had become a symbol, many men stubbornly seized upon the Second World War as a man's essential testing ground.

In *Unconditional Surrender* (the final novel of his wartime trilogy), Evelyn Waugh wrote that "even good men thought their private honour would be satisfied by war. They could assert their manhood by killing and being killed" (300). For actual combatants, however, the test seems to have been more complex than Waugh's character suggests. In his war memoir *Alamein to Zem Zem*, Keith Douglas (killed three days into the Normandy invasion) wrote that during the several years he waited to see action, he "never lost the certainty that the experience of battle was something I must have" (15). When that action finally commenced (in North Africa), he thought of it as "an important test, which I was interested in passing." He continues, "It is exciting . . . to see thousands of men . . . living in an unnatural, dangerous, but not wholly terrible world, having to kill and to be killed, and yet at intervals moved by a feeling of comradeship with the men who kill them and whom they kill, because they are enduring and experiencing the same things" (16). Alun Lewis, a one-time pacifist and another poet killed in the war, chose to experience combat not "for the thrill of it nor the horror . . . though both these attract," but for the "authority" of experience war would confer on him, and "to share the comradeship of war, and of death" (quoted in Hewison, *Under Seige* 129).

The intensity of combat clearly holds its own attractions, but Douglas and Lewis are representative in the importance they attach to the male camaraderie afforded by war. "The enduring emotion of war," William Broyles reports, "is comradeship"—trusting another man "with your life" (58). War, Broyles seems to say, creates the necessity, and thus the opportunity, of bonding with another human being with an intensity and an urgency that no other situation allows—not even marriage, he explicitly stipulates. But this human connection is rendered all the more satisfying, Douglas and Lewis imply, because it consists of men passing muster together, so that each can witness, encourage, and approve the worthiness (manliness) of the other. Comradeship, with its mutual validation, provides perhaps the most deeply satisfying aspect of combat in part because, as Walter Ong has argued, "masculinity is never fully achieved but must be continually earned" (quoted in Hartsock, "MHW" 138). In this sense, masculinity always dwells in a potential state of crisis and must be, therefore, not only relished, but jealously guarded in both its individual and collective states.

In World War II this proved an especially difficult task, for the culturally sanctioned definitions of gender continuously threatened to implode as the necessities and cruel mechanisms of war revealed radical disjunctions between the discourse of gender and actual experience. This created a space for shifting perceptions and a new cognizance of gender (and its stories) as social constructs. For many combatants, World War II, like its predecessor, revealed an enormous and ironic contradiction between the perversely persistent ideal of war as a manly (and man-making) enterprise and their military experience. As Don Jaffe and other critics have argued, much of the male-authored literature of World War II sought to convey that "war stripped man of his manhood, reflected his absurdity and capacity for evil" (36). Paul Fussell documents this demeaning process in *Wartime,* in which his descriptions of military life—with its call for unquestioned obedience, its strict hierarchy, "petty authoritarianism," oppressive restrictions, and inevitable dehumanization—mimic women's lives in the extreme. Ironically, then, the war as thus perceived forced men into a feminized subject position in which they became anonymous and interchangeable, were made to endure tedious boredom, and were treated like unthinking children. Waugh's *Sword of Honor,* Mailer's *The Naked and the Dead,* and Heller's *Catch-22,* among other war fictions, variously depict the military as a "quasi-fascistic institution" (*Wartime* 83). As one British soldier complained, "I joined the army to fight fascism . . . only to find the army full of fascists" (quoted in *Wartime* 179). John Keegan (*The Face of Battle,* 1977) argues that the impersonalization, deliberate cruelty, and coercion of modern war reduce the role of soldier to that of inconsequential "victim" and make war "increasingly . . . intolerable" (322, 317). In its own way, then, World War II continued rather then assuaged the "crisis of masculinity" in which the Great War had played such a climactic part.

This crisis has another aspect, of course, for even more than the First World War, the Second brought about radical changes in women's lives: in particular, huge numbers of women moved into traditionally male activities, many of them contributing directly to the war effort. Priestley's *British Women Go to War* includes color photos of women manufacturing torpedoes and cannons, handling barrage balloons, servicing anti-aircraft guns, loading shells, and working as Air Raid Precaution wardens, in addition to more traditional activities, such as nursing. Other wartime histories, Cassin-Scott's *Women at War 1939-45,* for example, take "warrior women" (3) as their sole subject (ironically, this text, published in 1980, is part of a "Men-at-Arms" series). To be sure, these wartime transformations of women's lives did not necessarily effect a radical, longterm elevation of women's status. Indeed, while women in "men's jobs" were for the most part ultimately accepted as necessary, they were subject to derision and ridicule and were paid less than men for the same work. As Angus Calder observes in *The People's War,* "Men were notoriously more equal than women" (400). Nevertheless, he judges that even though World War II brought about nothing as dramatic as the women's vote, it had perhaps even "more significant" effects on women's attitudes than had the previous war. Although many continued to accept without question their subordination to men, a "new type" of woman emerged from the war, one with considerable "spirit of independence," one who shunned conventions and traditional morality (400). Sexual liberation exacted its price of course. In *Bombers and Mash: The Domestic Front 1939-45,* Raynes Minns relates evidence that the sexual double standard became quite literally more visible than ever: women with venereal disease were sometimes covertly marked by their examining physicians with purple dye as a warning sign to any potential sexual partners, thus giving new meaning to the term "marked woman." According to Minns, condoms were distributed "not to prevent women's pregnancies, but to protect men from venereal disease" (180). While women were condemned, ostracized, and even fired from their jobs for unsanctioned sexual activity, Calder reports that men in the armed forces were at times encouraged to be promiscuous, such as when an American sergeant stationed in England told his men to "do something about" the contraceptives awaiting their use (313).[12]

To counterbalance emergent narratives—stories about impugned masculinity and selectively discarded femininity—that uncovered and even threatened to disassemble the sex-gender system, it seems that traditional plots had constantly to be reinscribed, especially the story of "men who were men and women who were women." In their study of the literature of the two world wars, Cadogan and Craig note that romance and formula writers pushed the notion that British women were "deeply feminine" and would be glad to give up their wartime freedom and responsibility (195).[13] Typically conflicting narratives emerge from *They Made Invasion Possible* (ca. 1944), an encomium to those "Women in Slacks" who were so successfully doing "a Man's job"; Peggy Scott introduces her material by assuring readers that "the majority of girls [*sic*] are looking forward to running homes of their own, not to running a man's job for him" (7, 8). Ironically, even as J.B. Priestley optimistically seized on the war as having compelled welcome changes in "our habits of thought" (*PS* 38), it seems never to have occurred to him that essentialist claims about men, women, and war constitute one of our more dangerous habits. In *British Women Go to War*, for example, while praising women's war efforts, he vaunts "woman" as "the natural conservor of life" for whom "the tasks of war . . . have no special appeal . . . as they often have to the other and more destructive sex" (59).

In a BBC "Postscript" (August 4, 1940) in which he describes a visit to two factories, Priestley provides a revealing example of how his own story of gender representation undergoes automatic adjustment to compensate for war-induced changes in reality. The first factory, he reports, employed mostly women, "young and feminine, and very natty in their coloured overalls" (*PS* 49). Their workplace was a "rather neat, ladylike affair." We learn nothing of what they actually do. In contrast, he describes the other factory, which seems to have no female employees, as "grimmer and more masculine"; it "vibrated with power." Clearly impressed by the rather menacing nature of their work—"men shot-blasting," the "sinister hum," the "unearthly demon light," the "terrifying crack and flash of seven hundred and fifty thousand volts"(50)—Priestly seems to cast the male worker in the role of Thor or Hades. Now that women have entered the factories, it is apparently no longer enough for men to be mere mortals; they must be gods.

When women weren't being represented as brave girls struggling to do "men's work" and to preserve their femininity, they were more familiarly depicted as objects of male desire—or, in Arthur Marwick's words, as "sex symbols and morale boosters for the troops" (*Home Front* 139). The wholesome, keep-the-home-fires-burning ideal found expression in Vera Lynn, the "Forces' Sweetheart," who sang sentimental ballads such as "We'll Meet Again" and acted as liaison between men of the armed forces and their families. Two quite different instances of London's wartime popular culture exemplify the more blatantly sexual codification of women—the Windmill Theatre and Jane, a cartoon character featured in the *Daily Mirror*. E.R. Chamberlin (*Life in Wartime Britain*, 1972) reports that the Windmill, known for its nude "girlie" shows, "courageously" remained open throughout even the Blitz: "night after night . . . the Revue made its gaudy, fragile, indestructible gesture of defiance" (114). Defiance of more than German bombs, I would add. Chamberlin points to this tenacity as "a legendary example of the human capacity to maintain routine under the most violent conditions of abnormality" (114). Exactly so, but the routine stubbornly maintained here is adherence to the seemingly "indestructible" sexual symbolic order that throughout the war (and outside the theatre) was continuously being thrown into question. Similarly, Jane, the "nubile, scantily clad but virtuous" cartoon heroine, who had been dubbed "Britain's Secret Weapon" and was "much relished by the troops," finally completely disrobed on V-E Day (Cadogan and Craig 173, Calder 288, P. Fussell, *Wartime* 105). In this context, Jane's long-awaited total nudity, her stripped and nakedly commodified body, functions both as reward for and symbolic marker of British victory, signalling not only an end to war on the western front but a victorious conclusion to the sex war on the home front. As if to flaunt the decisiveness of that victory, after the war the Windmill Theatre proudly boasted, "We never closed" (Marwick 139).

Once again Priestley seems representative when he articulates what he identifies as the typical male attitude toward the "mysterious opposite sex" (*PS* 76). In a "Postscript" broadcast devoted to "women and the war" (22 September 1940), he describes his feelings as "an uneasy mixture . . . of fine dashing male contempt and half-secret respect, and even fear." Those men who do not share his ambivalence, he adds, mistakenly feel "all contempt or all fear." The wartime strain on "normal" gender relations—the result of long separations, familial dislocations, unusual sexual activity, marital infidelity, intense male bonding, psychological assaults on the soldiers' masculinity, battle fatigue, disabling injuries, women's increased independence and responsibility, and so on—only made this ambivalence more intense. And the forced realization that, given half a chance, women in many ways exceeded the too obviously artificial boundaries of conventional femininity often evoked more fear, resentment, and in some cases even contempt than it did respect. Despite the absolute necessity of womanpower in the war effort, resistance (male and female) to the redefinition of women's roles remained strong.

Significantly, the strongest resistance—and the most obvious repugnance—was directed toward women in uniform. The Home Guard refused to admit women at all, and female conscription met with vigorous objections from (among others) those who fearfully predicted the emergence of "Amazon armies" (Chamberlin 124). Calder reports that, for some, uniforms on women "at once suggested immorality" (335), as if merely donning the masculine costume was the same as taking on male sexual practice—but without its sanctioning privilege. Cadogan and Craig note that the *Daily Mail* readers specified uniformed women as the most "annoying aspect" of the war (195). As bizarre as this seems (more annoying than the blackout, evacuation, or rationing?), Calder himself makes a related but more disturbing observation that underscores just how vital and tenacious the old stories of men, women, and war were. In response to published photographs of liberated concentration camps, in which he must have viewed the skeletal bodies and vacant eyes of the survivors, if not the even more grotesque image of heaped corpses, Calder identifies a photo of "'Hitler's Beast Women,' the leering female wardens of Belsen" as "perhaps the most horrifying of all" (566). Here were women—not "real" women, of course, but animals, beasts—not only capable of discarding the costumes of feminine incapacity, but of stepping right into the "master's" role and playing it to its most brutal and tragic conclusion. The photos' evidence of (wo)man's inhumanity to man seems to have offended not only Calder's sense of human decency, but his sense of natural human order, his assumptions about human (or, more accurately, male and female) being. While the sexually disorienting implications of British women in uniform were "annoying," German women clad in Nazi uniforms, those profoundly unfeminine costumes of murderous depravity, apparently proved shocking, even "horrifying" enough to obscure the true subject of those pictures from view. Unlike Jane, when the war was over women could not and would not publicly disrobe, of course, but at least they would eventually strip off those grotesque military uniforms, signifiers of masculine authority and power that disfigure—or, more accurately, unacceptably reconfigure—the female body.[14]

For many British women, then, World War II proved the most ironic of wars. The Allied and Axis powers' fight for supremacy—the continuing saga of Cain and Abel—was not the whole story. The too-familiar rhetoric and policies of fascism—its chauvinistic nationalism, colonizing militarism, oppressive masculinism, in short, its phallocratic ideology—begged comparison with the incipient and even overt fascism in Britain's own patriarchal, militarist state, which in turn asserted and maintained sexual, racial, and territorial privilege by blatant and institutionalized disenfranchisement of those designated as Other. Because of the war's double threat to the stability and legitimacy of its own sex-gender system, Britain's patriarchal hegemony made every attempt to (re)assert its political and narrative authority over the feminine (feminized) Other. Thus, on both the home front and on the frontlines the war did indeed mark an "escalat[ion of] the war between the sexes" (Gubar, "This Is My Rifle" 240). In addition, while Britain legitimately opposed grievous wrongs committed by the Axis powers, in particular, Nazi Germany, at the same time it continued to justify its own unconscionable imperialism, its colonization of the racial Other. With alarming if disguised similarity to the fascists, then, Britain (and the Allies) had no quarrel with history's seemingly immutable "master" plot—a gendered drama of literal mastery; they simply wanted the authority to determine its outcome. With startling and illuminating clarity, World War II thus re-enacted the "same old story"—the "fight for love and glory"—on an epic scale: patriarchal nations quarreling about which is the better man, which can force the (feminizing) surrender of the other—Britain refusing to submit to Germany's strutting phallic aggression, to assume the female subject position;[15] the fascist powers obsessed with becoming Adam to the Allies' subjugated Eve. For Woolf, Lessing, and the others, however, the local and global "resurgence of patriarchal politics" was just the beginning of the Second World War's story and, what is more, the stepping-off place for their own (Gubar, "This Is My Rifle" 227).

However, even if all of the authors under discussion here had been equally inclined to charge England with casting out the mote in its own eye, such an enterprise would have been from the onset fraught with difficulties. And they were not equally inclined, for their material, political, and historical positions varied considerably. For example, while Burdekin, Smith, and Bowen were more or less contemporaries, Woolf (born in 1882) was the child of a tenacious Victorianism, and Lessing (born in 1919), of a post–World War I skepticism. While Bowen, an Anglo-Irish aristocrat, had politically conservative sympathies, Woolf, a Bloomsbury bourgeois, and Lessing, an anti-imperialist African colonial, were decidedly radical. They therefore all perceived the war and its stories from substantially different perspectives. Accordingly, they speak not with one voice; rather, their voices blend, sometimes in harmony, sometimes in counterpoint, and sometimes in fugal variation. Even individually, however, they never speak univocally, for each seems to be in dialogue with herself, struggling to reconcile conflicting impulses triggered by the often contradictory pressures of war. In their varied and acute ambivalence, these writers illustrate with unusual complexity Marianne Moore's observation in "In Distrust of Merits" that "[t]here never was a war that was not inward."

To begin, while the war renewed ironic contemplation of British-style fascism, it intensified dread and revulsion for the more virulent and life-threatening Continental strain, thus prompting identification with Britain's violent struggle for survival. Under threat of extinction, the British way of life cried out for preservation, warts and all. The all-too-obvious evil of fascist rule left little doubt that it had to be not merely withstood, but forcibly eradicated. Unlike World War I, this war was clearly necessary and justified. As Mrs. Temple, the heroine of Vita Sackville-West's wartime novel *The Grand Canyon*, declares, "We had to fight. . . . In order to overcome a thing [fascism] we hated even worse [than war]" (261).[16] Unlike Mrs. Temple, however, not everyone acknowledged the war's moral ambiguity. State-sponsored propaganda and popular media (mis)represented the war as an unequivocal "parable of good and evil" (*Wartime* 164). The night-and-day representation/perception of Russia before (archvillain) and after (stalwart friend of freedom) its invasion by Germany is a case in point. As Paul Fussell has pointed out, its participants cast into the roles of heroes and villains, World War II encouraged and validated the stark, seductively simple logic of dichotomous thought, for it followed that "the division between other dualisms had to be as total . . . without shading or complexity" (*Wartime* 165). This insidious effect of the war on consciousness was a major concern and sometimes a serious obstacle for writers attempting to foreground the war's broader psychosocial implications and/or to call into question the inevitability of humanity's neverending cycle of adversity.

Women's active support for and participation in the two world wars constituted another major source of ambivalence. Philip Larkin's poem "MCMXIV," which portrays the naïve complacence of Edwardian society and the eagerness with which men voluntarily enlisted for service in the Great War, ignores both the recruitment and voluntary enlistment of women in the war effort. Nonetheless, the poem's closing line, "Never such innocence again," could just as accurately allude to the increasingly unavoidable conclusion that women, in one sense or another, have always collaborated with the making of war. Ann Wiltsher (*Most Dangerous Women*) and others have documented the alacrity with which most women, including feminists such as Emmaline and Christabel Pankhurst, jumped on the jingoism bandwagon at the onset of World War I (see also Playne, *Society at War*). The Women's Social and Political Union (led by E. Pankhurst) demonstrated their shifting sympathies by changing the name of their newspaper from *The Suffragette* to *The Britannia* and dedicating it to "King and country." Making an abrupt about-face, Emmaline Pankhurst announced, "I who have been against the government am now for it. Our country's war shall be our war" (quoted in *WW* 112).[17] Many such women may have felt it necessary and wise to support the government in this time of crisis, especially if they ever hoped to win the vote. (And, of course, women's support of the war effort did work toward obtaining suffrage shortly after the war.) But political expedience, support of loved ones, or even concern for England's well-being do not adequately explain the infamous white feather phenomenon (women handing ununiformed men white feathers to flag their putative cowardice), which reinforced the sex-gender system's reciprocal relation to militarism: "The wearer of the uniform is the idol, the hero of the day; just as the laggard is frowningly regarded with chilling indifference, often mingled with disdain. English women and girls have developed into ebullient, 'boiling' patriots, whose value as recruiting agents cannot be overestimated" (quoted in *WW* 112-13).[18]

Women writers of the period often lent their voices to the chorus of militaristic nationalism: Mrs. Humphrey Ward, Cicely Hamilton, May Sinclair, and Rose Macaulay, to name but a few. Others commented more obliquely on the complex and varied roles women played in the making of the war. In *Return of the Soldier* (1918), for example, Rebecca West depicts the conspiratorial effort of three women to cure a soldier's shell shock, which has taken the form of a partial (and analgesic) amnesia. Whatever their differing motives for restoring "normalcy," the women return the hapless soldier to the exigencies of his day—to his loveless marriage (the home front) and to the frontlines, both of which, in an act of self-preservation, he had expunged from his memory, as if sensing their root connection. Vested interest in the system as it is and a selfless sense of duty ironically combine to salvage and reinforce the dysfunctional status quo, including not only the horrors of war, but the sex-gender system itself, with which war as we know it has become (and perhaps has always been) perversely interdependent.[19] Adumbrating many of the women's war stories of World War II, *Return of the Soldier* illustrates humanity's self-perpetuating *danse macabre,* the "same old story," which it seems most women had their reasons for maintaining during the Great War.

As Eve Sedgwick has pointed out, at certain moments in history it becomes particularly clear that "'patriarchy' is not a monolithic mechanism for subordinating 'the female' to 'the male,'" but "a web of valences and significations that . . . can . . . offer both material and ideological affordances to women as well as to men" (*Between Men* 141). Thus, as Mary R. Beard has argued, the "union [of war and state] has not been solely a masculine manifestation of power and values" (*Women as Force in History* 279). Be that as it may, many women writing about World War II were acutely conscious that the power and values which had manifested in yet another cataclysmic eruption of violence, though not essentially male, were nevertheless decidedly and injuriously masculinist. This state of affairs compelled exposure and, for those capable of imagining the necessary narrative and epistemic shifts, radical reformation.

In *On the Side of the Angels* (1945), Betty Miller pointedly uncovers the mutually constitutive relations between the politics of gender and militarism, evenhandedly depicting how the assumptions giving life to "the fight for love and glory" pervade the consciousness of both sexes to their mutual detriment. Straightforward and rather self-contained, Miller's novel introduces the fundamental premise shared by the more exploratory and/or potentially transformative texts discussed in the chapters to come. The plot concerns three couples: Honor Carmichael, a housewife and mother, and her husband Colin, a doctor conscripted into military service for the duration of the war; Honor's sister, Claudia, a teacher, and Andrew, her fiancé, "boarded out of the army" because of some minor heart ailment; and, finally, Claudia and Captain Neil Harriot, a Commando temporarily stationed with Colin. Each couple illustrates several of the overlapping psychosocial tangents of the sex-gender/militarism-war matrix. Colin and Honor embody the long list of abstract dualisms (mind/body, strong/weak, reason/passion, and so on) with which masculine and feminine are conventionally identified and which the ideology of war assumes and (re)constructs. Disturbed by the war, their marriage becomes a battlefield strewn with the psychic and cultural wreckage of irreconcilable difference.

Militarism affords Colin welcome release from the "rigid confines, the destroying intimacy, of private life" (124)—a release from (ironically named) Honor, who represents "fertile disorder" to the men (119). Excluded from Colin's "privileged . . . male world," which recognized no "loyalties outside the rigid artifact of military life," Honor knows that "the uniform . . . had changed him" (39, 104). She likewise senses her newly illuminated and specifically female inadequacy: "Honor understood . . . that she humiliated [Colin] by her presence . . . she became aware, in a moment of burning shame, of her own femininity: the fullness . . . all that was inchoate, ununiformed about her: of that which was capable of giving offence, of making her innately unacceptable to the men before her" (39). Miller thus seems to anticipate Klaus Theweleit's notion that the boundedness, the rigidity of homosocial military life protects the masculine and potentially fascist psyche from the inchoate formlessness, the "fertile disorder," and, paradoxically, the "destroying intimacy" of the feminine Other. This disassociation and denial, Miller makes clear, protects such men "both from disturbing elements within themselves and, equally treacherous, those at large in the undisciplined civilian world" (39). To allow Honor, a "Trojan horse" (224), to enter the sacred enclave of masculinity is in Colin's eyes a breach of defenses, a rupture of the walls that rightly exclude the perfidious enemy.

Significantly, war affords Colin not only freedom from domesticity and civilian responsibility, but the ultimate "freedom" from a meaningless mortality. "Death," Colin thinks, "in the dramatic form permitted by war, was . . . not unattractive: something positive: a culmination, not a mere dissolution" (127). As Nancy Hartsock observes in "Masculinity, Heroism, and the Making of War," death in battle can represent a self-defined victory over mortality, a victory denied women, whose soft and enveloping bodies signify the very dissolution such men fear. For men like Colin, to die the hard, masculine death of a soldier in battle is to master death by investing it with a predetermined significance.

The contrasting ways in which Colin, Honor, and Claudia relate to and perceive Colonel Mayne, Colin's commanding officer, betray the gender politics permeating the institution of militarism. Between Mayne and Claudia, who "was not married to one of his officers" and was thus not in competition with him, there exists a "state of armed neutrality" (40). Although she poses no direct threat to his authority, her femaleness requires him to "observe her [body] . . . very much as he might assess the nature and quality of an enemy's equipment" (41). While Claudia dispassionately defends herself against Mayne's machinations, Honor feels assaulted, is "deeply antagonized; repelled" by the power he represents (145). She recognizes the telling similarity between militarism's hierarchical pattern of command and an extreme form of heterosexual romance: Mayne's position, "the position of a man . . . in authority over others . . . was not unlike that of a sheik with a harem of competitive wives: an unprogressive state of affairs" (169). She perceives Mayne's unchallenged authority as not only antiwoman, but as inimical to life itself, "as if [Mayne's] presence . . . could blight the sweetness within her: as if, voluntarily sterile himself, he had the power to create sterility about him; a power that he chose in full consciousness to exercise; withdrawing from the confusion of natural life and accepting in place of it . . . a military order" (145). The unnatural order, the rigidity, the ever-so-masculine boundedness, and the mechanisms of power with which men like Colonel Mayne stave off and control the disorder of life (ultimately figured as feminine), is for Honor as sterile, as life-denying as the wars such men live to fight.

Despite Honor's apparent alignment of femaleness with fecundity and maleness with sterility and death, Miller avoids such Manichean codification by implying a more sophisticated awareness of war's role in the cultural construction of gender and, reciprocally, men's and women's consequent collaboration in the cultural reproduction of war. Claudia's triangular relationship with Andrew and Captain Herriot, one a failed soldier and the other a warrior-hero, leads her to comment, "Charity isn't the only thing that begins at home, apparently. So does world war" (202). At first dismayed by Andrew's defensive assertion that she agreed to marry him because she was seduced by his uniform, "the brass buttons . . . the revolver—the paraphernalia of power," Claudia resents his offer to release her from their engagement (30). "Women love war," Andrew declares, "It's a known fact. They esteem it very highly if a man kills himself for their sake. . . . In the same spirit, what could be more gratifying than a mass slaughter, a never-ending series of gallant suicides—?" While Andrew's sense of loss and emasculation prompt his bitter and resentful remarks, Claudia's intense attraction to Captain Herriot forces her to search for whatever truth lies behind Andrew's words.

Claudia agrees to the sexual encounter proposed by Herriot despite their mutual recognition of the "hidden nature of the association: not . . . spontaneous and creative, but on the contrary will-bound, mutually destructive" (212). Claudia's inevitable comparison of the two men in her life, especially how others perceive and respond to them, brings her to a disillusioning understanding of the gender-inflected psychology of war:

> Andrew in his civilian jacket, his civilian hat, ignored by the crowd, belittled by the glances of women: Andrew . . . branded by the violence not committed: by the brutality not perpetrated; the ignominious innocence of hands that have never shed blood. Different, indeed, the acclaim that greets the man who bears, in symbol, the mark of Cain. . . . [W]e are not outraged at the murder of Abel, she thought. On the contrary. We hate Abel, the guiltless man, the victim: it's Cain we love: Cain, the killer. And we permit war in order to justify that love in our hearts. [213-14]

Claudia has discerned the terrible truth behind Andrew's earlier observation that we all "like soldiers. Otherwise, there'd be no wars" (131). Willingly or not, consciously or not, we all have been seduced by the symbolic significance of the military uniform, by the masculine ideal that ultimately makes power, in Henry Kissinger's words, "the greatest aphrodisiac."

Miller usually tells her story from the female characters' points of view, but her omniscient narrator manages to convey that, as far as Andrew and Herriot are concerned, Claudia's insight into the heart of war's self-perpetuating story is (quite ironically) beside the point. Their phallic rivalry, a contest for possession of Claudia, becomes a localized expression of the greater conflict: "Andrew and Neil Herriot found themselves face to face across the narrow length of the table. Something passed between them, they looked at one another steadily without smiling, locked in some indefinable conflict . . . which because of its nature could find no overt expression, could only work itself out through the medium of a third, a separate personality" (135). Their rivalry exemplifies the asymmetrical erotic triangle persuasively analyzed by Eve Sedgwick in *Between Men*— a homosocial rivalry in which two men manipulate a woman "as a counter in an intimate struggle of male will that is irrelevant and inimical to her" (181). Like the fundamentally similar though somewhat differently nuanced threesome of Colin, Honor, and Colonel Mayne, this triangle manifests the "special relationship between male homosocial . . . desire and the structures for maintaining and transmitting patriarchal power" (Sedgwick 25).

Andrew eventually prevails, not because Claudia can extricate herself from a tangle of desire and perception she does not fully understand and cannot deny, but because Andrew ultimately proves the better man. For Herriot turns out to have been a fictional man, a simulacrum of heroic masculinity created out of reciprocal desires: his longing to prove himself a "real soldier" rather than the ordinary member of the Home Guard and the family man he is in truth; and everyone else's desire (especially keen in time of war) to make men more than human, to create larger-than-life heroes. As Andrew says, no one saw through the charade because no one wanted to: "We preferred the fairy-tale we ourselves had helped to create" (234). "Mutual failure" to dispel the fiction and to escape the larger story in which they remain disconsolate players remains Claudia and Andrew's only foundation for marriage. With ironic self-knowledge and resignation, they enter into a sterile "union of insomniacs" (236). For they have been awakened to the knowledge that they live out dramas of their own making, and they cannot dream. Paradoxically, as though caught, self-aware, in a waking nightmare, they cannot break the drama's momentum. They keep on running in place, never getting anywhere.

Conceptually mired in the interlocking narratives of war and romance, the best Claudia and Andrew can hope for is a sterile truce. Similarly bogged down in cultural and literary conventions and their epistemological foundations, the most Miller can achieve is a stalemate. Despite her insightful disclosures, at her story's end there is no escaping the fact that men, women, and war ineluctably constitute one another. In this way, Miller's novel can be seen as a transitional text. While her exploration of the mutually formative nature of the enculturation of gender and the ideology of war maps some of the same territory as do the texts we will study in more detail, her apparent failure to question the inevitability of both her characters' assumptions and of her own plot locates her novel on the margins of the traditional war story.

The majority of twentieth-century war literature enacts some form of antiwar protest, to be sure. The men (mostly) who fought in these wars, from World War I to Vietnam, passionately protest modern war's deliberate cruelty, dehumanization, mass destruction, erosion of humane values, moral ambiguity, and, quite simply, its stupidity. But even the most fierce and eloquent of these critiques, by virtue of their telling, their emplotment, tend to recreate and, ironically, to reinforce a fundamental ideology of conflict—particularly in terms of the sex-gender system. Thus, if one relied on conventional antiwar narratives to supply the rejoinder to Dorothee Sölle's plaintive call to storytellers—"Do I have to be Cain if I don't want to be Abel? Is there no other way?"—the answer would have to be: if not Abel, then Cain, for we simply cannot imagine a way out of our narrative impasse. For what is a story but conflict?

As Hayden White alerts us in "The Value of Narrativity in the Representation of Reality," narrative historically and conventionally consists in notions of conflict and authority—concepts quite specifically defined and structured, I should add. Historians—much like traditional storytellers—White continues, "have transformed narrativity from a manner of speaking into a paradigm of the form that reality itself displays to a 'realistic' consciousness." Ultimately, he argues, "[n]arrativizing discourse serves the purpose of moralizing judgments" (24). Thus, although situations and events may in and of themselves be value-neutral, in the very selection, articulation, and emplotment of a story's components storytellers tend both to reproduce models of reality as ordinarily perceived and to supply the appropriate moral. Or, as White similarly argues in "The Historical Text as Literary Artifact," narrators employ certain "story types" in order to endow their story's constituent parts with "culturally sanctioned meanings" (88).[20] This is not to say, of course, that narrative per se is inherently and hopelessly corrupt, but rather, that our consciousness, thoroughly informed by notions of hierarchy and brute conflict, limits our conceptual repertoire, essentially blinding us to the fact that stories of competition and mastery (as in the stories of biological and social evolution) represent a very specific and over-determined emplotment of humanity's historical trajectory.[21]

In a discussion of ancient tales of war (in *Myths to Live By*), for example, Joseph Campbell betrays his adherence to the notion that the "history of man" gives proof to Oswald Spengler's moralizing axiom that the "one who lacks courage to be a hammer comes off in the role of the anvil" (quoted in Campbell 170). Referring to the work of anthropologist L.S.B. Leakey, Campbell explains that we are all descended from *Homo habilis,* "a meat-eater, a killer, a maker of tools or weapons," and so named "able or capable man." In Leakey's tale of "man's" origin, "able man" overwhelms and ultimately destroys his less violent "competitor," who in this typically didactic narrative scheme was clearly disabled by not having been a killer. Spengler's conclusion that "man is a beast of prey"—not only stronger but more intelligent than his "vegetarian victims"—represents for Campbell "simply a fact of nature." This "fact" has been borne out, Campbell adds, by the primitive "mythologies of war and peace," in which war is most often "affirmed" as "not only inevitable and good but also the normal and most exhilarating mode of social action." Less frequently, ancient myths depict war as undesirable—a denial, however, that often requires that "life itself, *as we know it* . . . be negated" (198, emphasis added).[22] Although Campbell is not hawking war as preferable to peace, he clearly cannot conceive of life, duly confirmed by our earliest stories, except in terms of the hammer and the anvil, Cain and Abel. He fails to consider that "life . . . as we know it" could be different—that is, that modifying *how* we know would transform *what* we know and *how we tell it*. Thus has the story of humankind "as we know it"—and our notions about the form and content of narrative itself—been conceived, encoded, naturalized, sanctioned, and passed down.

Extrapolating on the "strong connection between narrativity and the idea of conflict" modeled by the historical compulsion to narrativize (and thereby to justify) war itself, Nancy Huston argues that "men . . . have made war into the paradigm of all narratives" ("Tales" 280). While Huston's account of war narrative takes into consideration that women have been a "captive . . . audience," have acted "supporting roles . . . essential to the . . . plot," and have even coveted men's leading roles in such stories, she challenges women, usually located on the actual and narrative margins of war, to "invent other paradigms" (274, 280). This sort of recognition that women may occupy a privileged imaginative space vis-à-vis war stories should not preclude the possibility that men too may invent new, non-adversarial narrative models.[23]

Historically, however, the link between life-threatening conflict as an epistemological/ontological model and narrativity—a union that gives rise to reality as it has been ordered, history as it has been "made," social systems as they have been constructed, and lives as they have been lived and inscribed—seems to have been the particular preoccupation of women writing World War II. In addition to exposing the "same old story," they often tried to revise it, that is, to reconceive and rewrite it. However, as Teresa de Lauretis has argued, even potentially subversive thinking can be "contained within the frame of conceptual opposition that is 'always already' inscribed in . . . 'the political unconscious' of dominant cultural discourses and their underlying 'master narratives'. . . and so will tend to reproduce itself, to retextualize itself . . . even in feminist rewritings of cultural narratives" (1-2). Accordingly, they experienced what, in a different context, Shoshana Felman has identified as the "difficulty of the woman's position in . . . critical discourse": "to speak not only against, but outside of the specular phallogocentric structure, to establish a discourse the status of which would no longer be defined by the phallacy of masculine meaning" (10). Although Smith, Burdekin, Bowen, Woolf, and Lessing all variously resist traditional representations of war, their resistance is complicated and sometimes even undermined not only by the pressures of their individual sociocultural positions and of the war itself, but by the insidious modes of perception their texts otherwise call into question. From the resultant clash of discourses there nonetheless emerges a persistent call for altered states: deconstruction of the state of mind that perceives and thereby prescribes reality in terms of perpetual hierarchy, opposition, and otherness; and, accordingly, transformation of contingent (individual and collective) states of being.

The state of literary discourse, the ideologically saturated means by which these writers chose to voice their dissent and their ambivalence, becomes both the subject and object of their transformative impulses. Although firmly grounded in one literary tradition or another, each of the war-evoked texts examined here embodies alternative narrative strategies that function in one of two ways: to model and enact precisely the revision or deconstructions the text invokes or, conversely, to undermine its own radical position. The latter instance all too clearly demonstrates these writers' inevitable vulnerability to the very consciousness and discourses they would disclose and disarm. Nevertheless, they all in some way employed "textual practice as . . . intervention *in/against* cultural hegemony" (emphasis added) and attempted "radical *rewriting,* as well as a rereading, of the dominant forms of Western culture"—in this case, those inscribed within the war/romance plot (de Lauretis x, xi). As if in anticipation of Dorothee Sölle's frustrated query about states of narrative and states of being, they all variously sought some rescription of, some alternative to, the same old story, so that the fundamental things would not apply as time goes by.

Claiming that "this was a war to which literature conscientiously objected," Paul Fussell notes that the "byproduct" of World War II (in contrast to World War I) was not a literary outpouring, but "something close to silence" (*Wartime* 133, 132). Had he read the war's women-authored texts with different eyes, he might not have concluded, "There was nothing to be said" that was not mere repetition (134).[24] Indeed, he might have recognized that it was precisely their conscientious objection to history's and narrative's senseless redundancy that motivated certain women of letters to articulate what had remained lethally silent for too long. Despite the strong tendency of narrative toward cultural reproduction, stories (fictional and otherwise) such as those whose discussions follow bear out Helene Cixous's conviction that "writing is precisely *the very possibility of change,* the space that can serve as a springboard for subversive thought, the precursory movement of a transformation of social and cultural structures" (879)—a space in which we can learn to achieve altered states by learning how to change our stories and our minds.

2

Inscribing An/Other Story

Katharine Burdekin, Stevie Smith,
and the Move toward Rebellion

I sometimes think . . . we're all prisoners of war.
—Betty Miller, *On the Side of the Angels* (1945)

As Samuel Hynes has demonstrated in *The Auden Generation*, the 1930s in England was a decade of economic, social, political, and literary crisis. Hynes identifies his principle subject as "the generation *entre deux guerres*," and the point of his inquiry as "how the war behind them and the war ahead entered into their work, and how the forms of imagination were altered by crisis" (9). Though he purports to be concerned with the "men and women" of this generation, in truth Hynes focuses on an exclusively male literary tradition.[1] His relative obliviousness to woman-authored literature and its significance both generates and is partially generated by his particular characterization of the literary consciousness of the 1930s: the consciousness of men whose feelings toward the Great War were "deeply ambivalent, a mixture of revulsion at the brutality and waste of it, guilt at not having fought in it, and envy of those who had" (21).

This envy, George Orwell explained in "My Country Right or Left," is for "the vastness of experience they had missed." This experience, he makes clear, has a specific and vital significance for men: "You felt yourself a little less than a man, because you had missed it" (141). Christopher Isherwood perceived this sentiment as widely shared:

> We young writers of the middle 'twenties were all suffering, more or less subconsciously, from a feeling of shame that we hadn't been old enough to take part in the European war. . . . Like most of my generation, I was obsessed by a complex of terrors and longings connected with the idea "War." "War," in this purely neurotic sense, meant The Test. The test of your courage, your maturity, of your sexual prowess: "Are you really a Man?" [*Lions and Shadows* 74-76]

Even if other members of this generation did not consciously share the perception of war as a crucible of manhood, Hynes assumes that they did.

He asserts that for "the 'thirties generation, that frontier between peace and war" must have meant more than transition from symbol to action, for "to enter the world of war was to take the Test that their fathers and brothers had passed in 1914-18" (244).

Central to Hynes's selection and interpretation of the literary tradition of the 1930s, then, is the highly problematic relation of war to masculinity, a relation that informs many of the literary forms, themes, and motifs he finds characteristic of the era. This specific formulation might seem necessarily to preclude women writers from consideration. Paradoxically, however, at another level it demands their inclusion, for the female contemporaries of the so-called Auden generation had their own responses to the coming war and, specifically, to the widely shared assumption of men's privileged and essential relation to war and war discourse. Two women in particular, Katharine Burdekin and Stevie Smith, fit within the tradition Hynes describes; but the fit is tellingly imperfect.

According to Hynes, the literature of this decade overwhelmingly inscribes an anxiety-fraught response to the contemporary sociopolitical crisis—a response that eventually became an obsession with what seemed impending apocalypse, the inevitable war against fascism. A brief look at some of the decade's most conspicuous literary conventions reveals the specific ways in which these women's novels share in the storytelling tradition Hynes describes. To express their sense of personal anxiety and cultural catastrophe, writers of the 1930s often combined two usually discrete literary modes: fact-based "documentary" and fictional "fable" or "parable" (*Auden Generation* 228). The resulting literary hybrid, designed "not to describe the world, but to change it," tended to collapse the distinction between the real and the imagined, the literal and the symbolic, and the personal and the political (208). This "Parable Art" often took the shape of fictionalized autobiography—a myth of the self that, typically, assumed much broader significance. And the journey, especially forms in which passages and the crossing of frontiers represented "interior journeys and parables of their times," became "the most insistent of 'thirties metaphors" (228, 229).

Smith's war novels, an extended roman à clef, consistently employ variations of this journey motif, most notably in *Over the Frontier* (1938), to produce very much the sort of "autobiographical-historical-parable" Hynes describes (322).[2] Moreover, for her description of the landscape of war over the frontier of female consciousness, Smith turned to surrealism, the method Hynes identifies as perfectly suited for representing the era's increasingly grotesque material realities and the nightmarish psychic disequilibrium they evoked. Burdekin similarly ventures into the surreal in *Swastika Night* (1937), a pure example of another form of Parable Art:

the "prophetic, admonitory, apocalyptic" novel, which expressed fear of the aftermath of war more than war itself (232). *Nineteen Eighty-Four,* the best known "nightmare parable" of the World War II era, actually follows a long line of predecessors, of which Andy Croft judges *Swastika Night* the "most sophisticated and original" (209).[3]

Clearly Burdekin's and Smith's novels share in the dominant literary tradition of the 1930s. At the same time, however, as women they had different stories to tell; indeed, their fictions variously resist the hegemonic readings and renderings of men, women, and war. Precisely this resistance together with the resulting discursive tensions and discontinuities transform their texts into potentially revolutionary revisions of the traditional (male) literature of war. *Swastika Night,* an obscure work by a forgotten writer who in the 1930s seemingly took refuge behind a male pseudonym, is a "speculative fiction"; its third-person narrative, impersonal in the extreme, achieves a cautious distance from its aggressive and explicitly feminist analysis of fascism. In contrast, the *Over the Frontier* trilogy, an ignored series of novels by a writer known almost exclusively for her poetry, is an introspective "fiction" whose first-person female narrator, almost inseparable from the author, refuses or is unable to distance herself from her ultimately disjunctive meditations on gender and war.

Although the narrative strategies of these two writers differ radically, Burdekin and Smith provide an appropriate introduction to this re-exploration of the fictional landscape of World War II for a number of reasons. Most fundamentally, they characteristically locate their analyses of political tyranny and armed coercion within the framework of war's reciprocal relation with the systematic construction of gender, thus repudiating the so-called difference between the personal and political. Furthermore, they typify the related ways in which the writers included here were directed and constrained by the forces of history in general and the pressure of the war with fascism in particular—a war that generated an unresolvable tension between a fear of aggressively militaristic fascism abroad and a reluctant complicity with militarism and masculinism much closer to home.

In addition, Burdekin and Smith explore war as a dangerously seductive manifestation of age-old myths and mechanisms of power, which together form a self-recreating cultural matrix grounded in a masculinization of being and a pervasive ideology of adversity. Such metaphysical and material processes, they conclude, insure perpetual war. Finally, their interrogation casts these two writers into a perilous "no woman's land" at the edge of possible discourse. In their dissimilar endeavors to inscribe the mutually formative stories of gender politics and war, Burdekin and Smith demonstrate the unequivocal need to reconfigure conventional plots and discursive modes. Their rebellious reworkings of war stories reveal that ready-made tales, told in recognizable, reassuring ways, ultimately work to contain, undermine, disable, or even silence dissenting and, especially, re-conceptualizing "other" stories. Paradoxically, however, their efforts also demonstrate that attempts to articulate such subversive stories continu-ously modify the shape-shifting character of our meaning-making fictions.

SWASTIKA NIGHT

I have always been scared of you
With your Luftwaffe, your gobbledygoo.
And your neat mustache
And your Aryan eye, bright blue.
Panzer-man, panzer-man, O You—
Not God but a swastika
So black no sky could squeak through.
Every woman adores a Fascist,
The boot in the face, the brute
Brute heart of a brute like you.
—Sylvia Plath, "Daddy" (1962)

Like Sylvia Plath, Katharine Burdekin in *Swastika Night* turns to the un-relenting, homicidal totalitarianism of Hitler's fascism as a powerful trope for the institutionalized psychosocial tyranny of men over women. But Burdekin's narrative, a political dystopia, fashions a broader indictment than Plath's. Although Burdekin focuses on gender, specifically the "cult of masculinity" she identifies as fascism's root and branch, her trenchant analysis maps widespread connections between the personal tyranny of men over women and political tyranny in the broadest sense. Indeed, Burdekin's text inscribes an ever-widening circle of relations within which individual instances of anguish are merely the innermost ripple of distur-bance, the center of a seeming infinity of ever-larger circumscriptions, end-lessly connected. The private/personal remains, but with boundaries dis-solved; it thus becomes inseparable if not indistinguishable from the public/political. In this way Burdekin typifies the writers I discuss, for whom World War II provided an unparalleled opportunity to explore the disturbing congruencies between patriarchy's masculinism and the Fatherland's fascism and to argue, more broadly, that personal and political tyranny is the death-dealing, closeted progeny of masculinist culture.

Burdekin explores the ramifications of the widespread entrenchment of fascism by setting her novel seven hundred years after a projected Axis victory. Germany and Japan have divided the conquered nations and have subjected their citizens to similar forms of militaristic totalitarian rule and indoctrination. The plot centers on an old Nazi knight named von Hess, whose family has preserved Hitlerdom's only extant records of the twentieth century, and on Alfred, a rebellious English subject whom von Hess enlists to pass on this secret knowledge. Alfred, who hopes to live up to his historic name by uniting the subjugated peoples and freeing them from Nazi domination, categorically rejects most of the tenets of Hitlerism and plans nonviolent insurrection. He proves an astute analyst whose radical insights surpass those of his teacher.

Throughout the novel, Burdekin employs expository dialogue to voice her analysis. Although the novel's plot is minimal—indeed, the fictional frame obviously functions as a vehicle for didactic exposition—its premise is daringly insightful and vividly drawn. Burdekin's portrait of a fascist future consequently haunts the imagination; and her analysis seems startlingly contemporary. Like all futuristic dystopias, *Swastika Night* extrapolates from a present reality, proposing not to predict the future but to critique the present and to speculate about possibilities. In order to project a logical and persuasive exaggeration of current trends, she unravels the ideological threads of the fabric of her culture—its conceptual paradigms, social institutions, social systems, and contemporary political events—and reweaves them. Following the convention of "cognitive estrangement," Burdekin displaces her projection in time and creates an alternative reality, thus rendering the analysis less threatening and, ideally, more accessible.[4]

What is more, Burdekin mediates her message through a doubly male voice. First, she wrote under the pseudonym Murray Constantine.[5] Considering the generally unpalatable substance of her political analysis, Burdekin's position was quite sensitive. As England pondered its options in dealing with fascist aggression, Burdekin, like Woolf, mounted a written assault on masculinist ideology—especially militarism—in which not only the Germans but also the British were deeply implicated. A male pseudonym at once authorized and defused the audacity of her choice of subject and the analysis that followed. In addition, the only agents in her novel, including the characters through whom she speaks, are also men—one a guardian of the purloined past, the other a would-be savior of the threatened future. Unlike the other works we will examine, *Swastika Night* focuses on, even privileges, male consciousness. Because the women of this future are too oppressed to act or even to think, speaking through male protagonists is a plot necessity, but one that has meaningful implications. Like Woolf, who in *Three Guineas* addresses a man representative of all men who yearn to "prevent war," Burdekin insists that men and women together must take on their common "enemy." She emphasizes that each sex must free itself of internalized ways of seeing and being that reproduce the dominance/submission paradigm at war's—and tyranny's—dark core. Thus a man recognizes the centrality of gender to the ideology of dominance, a narrative tactic that emphasizes that Burdekin did not wish to vilify men but to condemn the system that produces masculinism. Accordingly, she depicts the central male characters' struggles to transcend their own conviction of masculine superiority and the efficacy of violence. *Swastika Night* thus relates no simple wartime parable of the victimization of women by men. Indeed, within its frame men and women alike are victims of the ultimately self-destructive "cult of masculinity," a tragic situation which, Burdekin insists, too closely resembles that of her own historical moment.

In *Swastika Night* Nazism has been elevated to a militaristic religion predicated on the glorification of male tyranny and the absolute diminution of women—a stark projection of patriarchal culture's gender polarization. "I believe in pride, in courage, in violence, in brutality, in bloodshed, in ruthlessness, and all other soldierly and heroic virtues" reads the Creed of Hitlerism. The Hitlerian code of ethics thus reduces manliness to a rabid state of hypertrophied "masculinity" and valorizes aggressive combat and brutal oppression (6). At the head of an "immutable" hierarchy of being, God the Thunderer and his Son, the Holy Adolf Hitler, "not born of woman, but Exploded!" comprise a dual deity (7, 5). The lowest orders include women, who "have no souls and therefore are not human," worms, and finally Christians, despised for their "effeminate" ethic of mercy and nonviolence (9). Burdekin's depiction of Hitlerism thus dramatically illustrates certain gender-based arguments put forth by World War I–era peace activists and refined in more recent analyses. In a 1986 report from an international peace conference, for example, Betty Reardon articulates the consensus conclusion: Militarization results from the privileging of "negative masculine values, specifically those . . . which encourage and reward aggressive behavior and equate power with the capacity to coerce, to impose one's will and pursue one's own interest at the expense of others" ("Militarism and Sexism" 190).

The women in *Swastika Night,* heads shaven and subsisting on minimal nourishment, are routinely indoctrinated with the notion of their natural inferiority and total lack of will: "[B]e submissive and humble and rejoice to do man's will, for whatever you may think . . . it is *always* your will too" (13). The birth of a female child is a "disgraceful event," but the women learn to be "passionately proud of a male child," whose loss they soon and forever grieve, for male children are removed from the mother's contaminating influence at the age of eighteen months (14). Every woman is the property of the state and of any man who claims her. Except in the case of young girls, who may be damaged or produce sickly offspring, rape as violation is inconceivable because no woman has the right of refusal: "as rape implies will and choice and a spirit of rejection on the part of women, there could be no such crime" (13). Notwithstanding their procreative duties, which they consider unpleasant, the men of Hitlerdom live in a world apart, completely free from the taint of femininity. Thus, as Patai explains, "phallic pride has become the organising principle of society," a social order in which "men forever affirm . . . their masculinity and women, reduced to female animals, ever embody . . . a reassuring contrast" (Intro., *SN* ix). The principle of separate spheres, as Virginia Woolf sardonically affirms in *Three Guineas,* had the militant support of not only "Herr Hitler and Signor Mussolini," but British cultural institutions, including the church (180). "The emphasis which both priests and dictators place upon the necessity for two worlds is enough to prove that it is essential to their domination," explains Woolf, adding, "[T]here can be no doubt that we owe to this segregation the immense elaboration of modern instruments and methods of war" (181).

Swastika Night's homosexual culture seems to fly in the face of those theories of patriarchy that, as Eve Sedgwick reminds us, "suggest that 'obligatory heterosexuality' is built into male-dominated kinship systems" (3). As Sedgwick points out, however, and as the "counter-example of classical Greece" demonstrates, patriarchy does not "structurally *require* homophobia" (4). In her depiction of a militarist/masculinist culture *in extremis,* Burdekin actualizes what Sedgwick identifies as the "potential unbrokenness of a continuum between homosocial and homosexual" (1). In *Swastika Night* the radical devaluation of women/femininity and the congruently profound differentiation of male and female have closed the discontinuity in the homosocial trajectory. While in our culture this trajectory dichotomizes homosocial "as against homosexual" (3), in Burdekin's novel it telescopes to the point that homosexuality becomes the normalized expression of male homosocial bonding, and heterosexuality a distastefully deviant form of desire.

An ancient document that unlawfully records pre-Hitlerian history establishes a gender-encoded link between the past and this projected future. The heretical text explains that in Germany a post World War II "fear of Memory"—fear of the knowledge that Germany lost the First World War, that all empires eventually crumble, and that women once were strong, intelligent and desirable—grew into "hysteria" (79), a suggestively ironic lexical choice. A physically weak but bloodthirsty knight named von Wied (modeled, Patai suggests, on Otto Weininger) captured the prevailing hysterical mood in a tome that not only elevated Hitler to the status of God, but offered the total erasure of history and any sort of uncongenial knowledge as a remedy to Germany's fear of psychic and political emasculation.[6] In a move that neatly theorizes Germany's response to that loss as Burdekin imagines it, Walter Benjamin attributes double meaning to Germany's having "lost" the Great War. In the first and obvious sense, Germany suffered military defeat. In an even more psychologically devastating sense, "The victor appropriates war, and makes it his own; . . . the vanquished loses possession of war and is forced to live without it. . . . And we have lost," Benjamin continues, "one of the greatest wars in world history, a war intertwined with the whole material and spiritual substance of our people. The significance of that loss is immeasurable" (quoted in Theweleit, vol. 2, 356-57). Apropos of *Swastika Night,* Theweleit concludes that "the German psyche . . . is imprinted with the loss of war—the First World War in particular. The Great War touched the masculinity of several German male generations in its most sensitive area; in the conviction that German men were born to be warriors and victors. It deprived them of the victory they considered their 'birthright' and subjected them . . . to a narcissistic wound of the first order" (357).

As if to support Burdekin's insights once again, however, Theweleit ultimately argues that the fascist "psychic economy[,] which place[d] sexuality in the service of destruction," originated in a deepseated "fear and hatred of the feminine," which in Germany's case was exacerbated by loss of the war (Rabinbach and Benjamin 2:xiii, xii). As von Hess explains, von Wied's book "exactly caught the feeling of the nation at the time," not only *because* German men longed to erase any memory of defeat, but most particularly "because of the part about the women" (*SN* 80). Thus, Burdekin has transcribed a glaring example of male gender anxieties rooted in feelings of powerlessness and the psychosexual wounding that Elaine Showalter and Sandra Gilbert, for example, have argued followed the Great War, even for those who "won" it. How much greater this anxiety must have been for those who lost the war. Having once suffered severe humiliation and emasculation, the Nazis urgently needed to eradicate this psychic trauma from memory and, at the same time, to insure it would never recur. In *Swastika Night* winning World War II provides just that possibility. Swollen with vanity in their soldierly dominance of half the world, von Hess explains, German men came to feel it beneath their dignity "to risk rejection by a mere woman. . . . They wanted *all* women to be at their will *like the women of a conquered nation.* So in reality the Reduction of Women was not started by von Wied. It had already begun" (emphasis added, 81). In her depiction of the reactionary establishment of "German Manhood" and its necessary complement, the "Reduction of Women," Burdekin lays bare the causal link between the stories of Cain and Abel/Adam and Eve, and strips the male dominant/female submissive relationship of its chivalric, paternalistic overlay.

Since the war and outside the context of fascism per se, a host of feminist thinkers have articulated theoretical principles that apply to Burdekin's multifaceted analysis of male fear and resentment, and women's consequent subordination: splitting off and reification of the "feminine," man as the measure and signifier of humanity, anatomy as destiny, woman as constructed reflection of male ego, woman as commodity, the trivialization of rape, fear of feminization, the devaluation of female infants, the simultaneous deprecation and exploitation of women's bodies, and so on. The list promises to proliferate endlessly.

Swastika Night enacts all of these aspects of men's dominion over women and, with characteristic literalness, still another: the eradication of women from history. The Society of Hitler teaches that Hitler, not born of woman, never had to endure a woman's defiling presence. History has been (re)written to conform to ideological requirements, but (typically) is widely read as objective and irrefutable fact. When Alfred, who suspects much of the past has been obscured, studies a photograph that clearly shows the real Adolf Hitler standing next to a beautiful, healthy woman, years of conditioning blind him to this woman's true nature. He observes not a young woman, but a beautiful boy, thus dramatizing feminist historians' contention that history, written from a male-dominant perspective, has effectively rendered women qua women invisible. Moreover, history and other cultural texts have so thoroughly shaped our perceptions that we literally see what we expect to see.

Burdekin, then, encourages recognition that history is a narrative process of selection and interpretation determined by ideology in the broadest sense, or, in Hayden White's words, by the "stories" that "we conventionally use to endow the events of our lives with culturally sanctioned meaning" ("Historical Text" 88). As White has argued, historical narratives are actually "verbal fictions . . . as much invented as found" (82). Events do not constitute a story, but must be "emplotted," that is, "*configure[d]* . . . according to the imperatives of one plot structure or mythos rather than another" (84). By highlighting the fictive quality of historical representation, Burdekin opens history to scrutiny, re-evaluation, and revision.

And by positioning her critique in characters who insist on interrogating their past, she encourages a second look at her own historical present. Despite some modification, the reader easily recognizes the social institutions of the fascist future as those which constitute the infrastructure of Western culture. The Society of Hitler combines the state, the military, and the church into an oligarchical ruling structure with many characteristics of medieval feudalism. The basic combination of church and militaristic state is nothing new in either fact or fiction; indeed, it has become a convention in postwar speculative fiction.[7] Nevertheless, Hitlerism's grounding in pre-existing structures merits some attention. As Louis

Althusser has shown, the complex ideological nature and function of social institutions (or "apparatuses") usually remain self-disguising. To counter this tendency, Burdekin conspicuously calls attention to the ways in which Hitlerism as a militant religion and as a political ideology are mutually sustaining.

As profoundly patriarchal as Christianity had always been, it proved inadequate for the nascent state of Hitlerdom for three reasons: it represented women, albeit as vessel, as a blessed and worshipped instrument of God; Jesus, the Son of God, preached mercy, forgiveness, compassion and nonviolence; and, finally, Christianity's basic tenet of salvation through faith available to all implied a fundamental equality. The supposedly "effeminate" and democratic nature of Christian dogma became theoretically untenable when the ideology of virile masculinism evolved to its brutal extreme. Selectively borrowing from various Western myths, including Christianity, the Germans fashioned their own self-justifying religion. Hitler's tenets of racial purity, masculine supremacy, intolerance, hatred, and war in this future come to reside in God *and* the state, enjoining religious and nationalistic fervor. The logical ease with which the church and state merge with militarism (as they have so often in the past) in both form and function suggests that the Judeo-Christian mythos is metaphysically compatible with other masculinist institutions. In *Swastika Night* the church could easily move into the unequivocal position of the militaristic state because the "feminine" side of the dualistic paradigm was totally removed from the public domain and relocated in the utterly powerless and dehumanized female body.

Clearly, despite the Nazi's disdainful eschewal of Christianity, Burdekin recognized its phallocentrism and foresaw its willing acquiescence to the "Reduction of Women . . . because there always had been in the heart of the religion a hatred of the beauty of women and a horror of the sexual power . . . [that] women with the right of choice and rejection have over men" (73). In this Burdekin once again prefigures Woolf, who in *Three Guineas* quotes Saint Paul as representative of the Christian church: "For the man is not of the woman; but the woman of the man; for neither was the man created for the woman; but the woman for the man. . . . Let the women keep silence . . . let them be in subjection" (166-67). This spokesman, Woolf decides, "was of the virile or dominant type, so familiar at present in Germany, for whose gratification a subject race or sex is essential."

In *Swastika Night*'s fascist evolution of religion, the notions of woman as mere vessel and the male seed as the source of all life validate the phallic legacy of the actual past/present—a legacy enacted in various Christian stories, including that of Christ's "immaculate conception," and reproduced by our immasculated language (in the word "seminal," for example).[8] Echoing the early "scientist" who claimed to see under the microscope tiny, fully formed infants within sperm, Alfred's Christian friend Joseph explains, "The whole child, whether male or female, is complete in the seed of man. The woman merely nurtures it in her body" (183).[9] In an effort to squelch potentially subversive knowledge, the Nazis encourage ignorance of biology throughout Hitlerdom; "they were afraid the biologists might prove . . . that it is the male who determines the sex of the child, and then no one [could] ever blame a woman for not having sons" (104). Thus, Burdekin locates women's devaluation and subjugation not only in women's potential power to direct or reject male sexuality, but also (as Patai rightly points out) in men's "fundamental fear and jealousy of women's procreative powers" (Intro., *SN* ix).

As Andy Croft explains in his study of *Nineteen Eighty-Four*'s antecedents, Burdekin identifies the resulting "sexual hysteria" not only as the cause of gender inequality, but as integrally related to fascism's extreme "racial theories" (209). Although Croft does not trace this root connection between sexism and racism/nationalism, his observation is accurate, for Burdekin's text explicitly inscribes consonance between these forms of dominance. The premises of the Hitler Creed, with its equation of masculinity and the "soldierly virtues" of brutality and bloodshed, have made the "Germans . . . [the] greatest exponents of violence the world has ever seen" and the conquerors of half the world (25). The "subject races," like the women, are considered inherently—biologically—inferior. Hitler's pseudo-genetic theory of Aryan superiority in *Swastika Night* has been further spiritualized into the Mystery of the Holy Blood, the "divine doctrine of race and class superiority," by virtue of which German men are fated to rule all others (21). Like similar stories of women's anatomical "destiny," fictions of genetic racial inferiority constitute a potent cultural fable that posits the notion of racial Otherness while stigmatizing such subjects and rationalizing their "natural" subordination.

Furthermore, as von Hess's summary of the methods states have used to socialize conquered peoples makes clear, the patriarchal state uses identical techniques to subject the "second sex." One method is "to make the foreign subjects feel that they are better off inside the Empire than out of it, to make them proud of it . . . and to allow them to attain full citizenship by good behaviour" (134). Such co-opted subjects then "proudly and gladly called themselves Roman [or English or whatever] . . . and shared in the privilege of the ruling race." Another method is to "make the subject races think themselves fundamentally inferior, believing that they are being ruled by a sacred race . . . and to deny them equal citizenship for ever" (134). As feminist theorists since de Beauvoir have demonstrated, patriarchal socialization, with all its subtle complexity, combines these methods with reliable results. Despite enfranchisement and other legal niceties, in 1939 Virginia Woolf had no difficulty substantiating her double-edged claim that "the law of England denies [women] . . . the full stigma of nationality" (*TG* 82).[10] The continued privileging of "masculine" values, even more prevalent in time of war, ensures that women unconsciously retain their feelings of inadequacy and even abnormalcy. Women are thus psychologically and socially manipulated into "good behaviour" and complicity with the very system that denies them equality, but within the confines of which they often nonetheless identify themselves as proud citizens. Such compromised citizenship ironically often results in the kind of uncritical nationalism that contributed to the white feather ritual in England during World War I and, later, to some Axis women's enthusiastic support of Fascism.[11] This analysis, now a mainstay of feminist theory, was quite provocative when Burdekin incorporated it into her fiction.

Burdekin also calls attention to the ideological role of language. Like the women, non-German males in Hitlerdom have no surnames, a variation on the tradition of a woman taking first the name of her father and then of her husband as she moves from the symbolic stewardship of one male to another. On a similar note, the Germans allow the subject nations to retain their own language, thereby keeping German—supposedly a masculine language—"sacred." Subject peoples learn German only for their masters' "convenience." This privileging of the father tongue presumes the same value structure and function as does our society's privileging of not only the conqueror's native language but, more generally, various forms of "masculine" discourse. Such discourse may be considered masculine by virtue of its cognitive shape (e.g., "rational"), or its discipline (e.g., "scientific"), or its origin in male experience (e.g., combat). In its twice-over male-voiced exposition, Burdekin's narrative lays claim to these supposed virtues. For *Swastika Night* this strategy must have seemed efficacious not only because it deflected *ad feminine* criticism, or brought credibility to the novel's ostensibly fantastic premise, but for the equally compelling reason that it lent "permission to narrate" the story at all.

But Burdekin convincingly belies women's exclusion from war's discursive terrain by pointing up female complicity with the cultural reproduction of war, which she traces back to the culturally determined positioning of the "other" within hierarchical thinking. In this way Burdekin establishes yet another link between subject races and women, finding them both guilty of a "crime against life"—"acceptance . . . of fundamental inferiority" (107, 106). Her analysis accounts for the self-perpetuating dynamic of dominant-submissive human relations: "while consciously urging them to accept their inferiority," men at the same time "unconsciously despise" women and others for doing so. But here the comparison falters, for while in *Swastika Night* the nations under German rule, especially England, have at other times themselves been conquerors convinced of their own worthiness, most women have always accepted, even if only unconsciously, the lie of their subordinate status. This difference underscores the notion that, unlike other cultural markers, gender signals (presumably) permanent inequality.

Condemning feminine compliancy, Burdekin once more indicates that her critique targets an ideological system that implicates and victimizes both sexes. When von Hess is asked what the women did when von Wied's theories gained acceptance, his reply is brutally revealing:

> What they always do. Once they were convinced that men really wanted them to be animals and ugly and completely submissive . . . they threw themselves into the new pattern with a conscious enthusiasm that knew no bounds. They shaved their heads until they bled, they rejoiced in their hideous uniforms . . . they pulled out their front teeth . . . and they gave up their baby sons with the same heroism with which they had been used to give their grown sons to war. [82]

Once again Burdekin's text alludes to the historical realities of women's lives, and here the point of women's sacrifice of their sons is particularly germane. In World War I the role of mothers became the subject of both state propaganda, which endeavored to exploit it, and antiwar poetry, which disdainfully condemned it. The propagandistic "Little Mother" letter, as Paul Fussell tells us, "reprehend[ed] any thought of a negotiated peace and celebrat[ed] the sacrifice of British mothers who [had] 'given' their sons" (*GWMM* 216). In *Goodbye to All That* Robert Graves sardonically records that this bogus letter elicited real ones, including one from a mother who claimed, "I would now gladly give my sons twice over" (quoted in *GWMM* 216). Sassoon's "The Hero," inveighing bitterly against this ethic of motherly "sacrifice," depicts a mother's reaction to her son's gallant death; the report—ironically, a lie—does more than assuage her grief: "her weak eyes / Had shown with gentle triumph, brimmed with joy, / Because he'd been so brave, her glorious boy" (quoted in *GWMM* 7).

Burdekin's assessment of the female citizen's potential for violence reveals a whole range of involvement, from passive sanction and vicarious triumph to active participation. She thus includes women among those culpable for this new Dark Age of Fascism. Von Hess's forbidden book relates a relevant and grotesque story of male-centered enmity between women. Unable to accept the necessity of women making themselves ugly, one young woman scoffed at a group of the self-mutilating "von Wied women," who then punished her for noncompliance by murdering her and mutilating her body, tearing out her eyes and hair and cutting off her nipples. The law of the fathers is here enforced with a vengeance by those women who repudiate their own vision, their own "I," and their own sex.

In Burdekin's analysis of women's role in their own subjugation and the reproduction of institutionalized violence, then, women have been collaborators, as their shaved heads testify. Nevertheless, with equal severity Burdekin explores militarism's ideology of brute force and its manipulation of gender identity. Even von Hess, who embraces treason and heresy rather than suppress what he knows of truth, assumes that women can never be equal to men because "they can not be soldiers. . . . There must always be force of some kind, to uphold any kind of law" (107-8). In this way Burdekin demonstrates the truth-value of Alfred's ostensibly absurd claim that the "human values of this world are masculine. There are no feminine values," he explains, "because there are no women. Nobody could tell what we should admire . . . or how we should behave if there were" (108). And there are no women because they have always accepted their inferiority and "an imposed masculine pattern" (109). This crime, in turn, resulted in their loss of "sexual invulnerability and . . . pride in their sex," a loss that prevents development of "their little remaining spark of self-hood and life" (108).[12] In language that prefigures the closing scene in Woolf's *Between the Acts*, Burdekin vaguely traces this hierarchy of gender, rooted in a presumption both of woman as "Other" and the necessity of force, back to the "tribal darkness before history began" (107).

The contemporary relevance of Burdekin's critique further emerges from her re-reading of world history, which locates all empire building on the same plane as that of Nazi Germany. According to the von Hess family history, however, England holds a special position in the chain of old empires, each casting its shadow on the next, for a "tremendous bitter black jealousy" of the vast and powerful "British Empire was one of the motive forces of German imperialism" (78). Such knowledge is clearly heretical for both its imaginary and actual audience (78). Von Hess, whose rhetoric once more points up the ineluctable conceptual link between masculine sexual prowess and the conquest of nations, explains that "[u]nshakable, impregnable Empire has always been the dream of *virile* nations" (78, emphasis added). Weak nations, like women, such rhetoric implies, can be forcibly penetrated by the potent war machine of the manly nation, which itself remains inviolate. Ironically, this sort of sexually charged war discourse effaces the distinction between the personal and the political on which masculinism depends and that its proponents invariably take such pains to maintain.

Burdekin's extrapolation of fascist society as the ultimate phallic fantasy dramatized masculinism's fatal flaw—its inherent self-destructiveness, born of the isolation and castigation of the "feminine." In the totalitarian society of *Swastika Night*, as in *Nineteen Eighty-Four,* creativity is unknown and change undesirable, thus affirming a premise common to political dystopias: "the ultimate natural decay of authoritarian government . . . is complete stagnation" (*SN* 147). Stasis and sterility are the inevitable by-products of oppression and repression, the regulating social and psychological mechanisms of culture having become so rigid that everything within suffers paralysis and eventual dissolution.[13] Moreover, controlling the present by obliterating the past, the Nazis have "cut all culture off at the root," resulting in a cultural vacuum: "We can create nothing . . . invent nothing. . . . We are perfect, and we are dead" (120, 121).

Von Hess's claim for the perfection of his manly culture can only be read as doubly ironic, for although he foresees Hitlerism's demise, his causal analysis stops short. While he judges totalitarianism a dead end, like Winston Smith he does not question the gender paradigm integral to his authoritarian value system.[14] Only Alfred, whose colonized subject status allows him to perceive the parallels between women and "subject races," questions the hegemonic definition of masculinity. This leads him to decide, with yet another ironic turn, that Nazis are not men at all, but only boys who "hide behind" biological determinism and "think that violence and brutality and physical courage make the whole of a man" (28, 29). Incapable of independent thought, reliant on an a priori assignation of manliness, and repelled by the "feminine" qualities of "gentleness and mercy and love and all those foul things," Nazis have had no chance of becoming men with souls, that is, human beings. Their obsession with masculinity has transformed them into a sad and grotesque race of strutting un-men. Burdekin's stinging indictment assumes even more force when she proposes that men unknowingly contribute to a self-perpetuating cycle of their own emasculation: "You hide behind the Blood because you don't really like yourselves, and you don't like yourselves because you can't be men" (28).

Burdekin's depiction of the ambiguous female response, which further dramatizes the sterility of authoritarianism, proves more ironic still. Apparently too convinced of their own unworthiness to resist, the women have so thoroughly absorbed masculinist ideology that their self-effacement becomes deadly and complete: they gradually stop bearing girl children, thus ensuring human extinction. This can be interpreted as the women's final and complete acquiescence to misogyny—a self-annihilation born of literal selflessness—or as their unconscious rebellion, a literal end to the reproduction of masculinist culture. As the text clearly indicates, however,

Burdekin knew that it is the male who determines the sex of a child. The decline in female births, then, from another perspective signifies the realization of a misogyny and/or a death wish so profound that it has become imprinted on male chromosomes. Either way, isolation and subjugation of the "feminine" ultimately translate into death of the human. This plot development unequivocally repudiates historical fascism's claim that its designation of motherhood as women's *raison d'etre* would "reawaken the desire for children" and thus reverse Europe's Depression-induced decline in the birth rate (Rupp 34). In any case, the "tragedy of the human race" is not, as von Hess declares, simply "women's blind submission" (*SN* 70). Like a coin, this fatal flaw has two sides: "We have made ourselves too strong . . . and we're dying . . . of our own strength," von Hess admits (76-77). The complement to women's submission is men's dominance, the necessary partner in the "*danse macabre*" that threatens to carry us, Burdekin stresses, not simply to war, but to oblivion (70).[15]

Burdekin deflects the communal struggle to reconceive human being onto Alfred, who strives to unlearn hierarchical thinking, phallocentrism, and the efficacy of violence. All prove more or less beyond his means, a fact that points to the extraordinary difficulty of breaking free of conceptual paradigms and modes of action. Alfred's flawed method for discounting his own colonized subject status and reversing the "reduction" of women is to reject the idea of innate inferiority by embracing the untenable paradox of separate but equal superiority. "To feel . . . superior" to all "different" forms of life—as women are different from men, he assumes—is a "condition of healthy life" and the prerequisite to equality (*SN* 112). Women, then, must learn to feel superior to men if they are ever to throw off the "imposed masculine pattern" that has always prevented them from becoming true women, whatever that may be (109). Ironically, his solution is to impose the "highest possible masculine pattern of living on women," the very cause, Alfred has already admitted, of women's "inferiority" in the first place. He further suggests explaining to women their "crime" against themselves and humanity—their pliancy and self-effacement—and simply telling them they must consider themselves superior. If women had as much respect for themselves as men, Alfred reasons, the use of force against women in any capacity would become "unthinkable" (108). Sensing the inadequacy of his plan, he must concede that "it would take a very long course of impersonal and objective thinking before any German could realize that he *could* still feel superior without making anybody else . . . feel inferior" (110-11).

Clearly Alfred—and, it would seem, Burdekin—is struggling to negotiate the unknown quantity of sex difference and the notion of equality despite that difference.[16] He cannot, however, envision male and female except in terms of mutual Otherness. This ontological divide is made even less negotiable by his thwarted effort to posit "superior" as a concept that holds meaning without reference to "inferior," an insupportable lexical legerdemain. Moreover, although Alfred recognizes profound flaws in the concept of male as conceived by his culture, out of apparent necessity he turns to men's lives as models and to men as teachers meant to raise female consciousness. He expects, in short, to create self-respect in women by masculine fiat, an indication that he is far from abandoning his male-centered perspective. When he exhorts (threatens, actually) Ethel, "his woman," to take good care of his new infant daughter, Ethel can grasp this unprecedented idea only in terms of caring for the child "as if she were . . . a boy" (164). With this plan Alfred is—must be—satisfied.

Burdekin's depiction of Alfred's emerging revolutionary consciousness raises several questions with which feminist thinkers continue to engage: How can we come to any real understanding of gender as long as the male remains our standard of measure? Or while socialization plays an indeterminately large role in our becoming? Is women's oppression rooted in biology and/or culture? How can we express concepts for which we have no language? Or conceive of ideas we cannot express? How can there even be a female "subject" (and women who speak as female subjects) under the "purview of masculinist discourse" (P. Smith 144)? How can women have a sexual identity that is not constituted by phallo-logic? Finally, how can we effect social change without a(n) r/evolution of consciousness and, conversely, how can we achieve the latter without social change?

This final two-sided question resides at the heart of Alfred's goals and Burdekin's dilemma. The most immediate difficulty is how to spread the gospel of nonviolence within a culture locked into the notion of conflict as both natural and necessary. Although Alfred dislikes violence, he cannot escape a lifetime of conditioning. Fatally wounded, he must pass on his dream of spiritual revolution to his son, whom he enjoins, "Be—less stupid and less—violent" (195), advice undoubtedly meant for Burdekin's readers. Clearly, *Swastika Night* passionately warns against the valorization of war and masculinism, with all this implies. Von Hess, having traced Germany's "madness" to "militarism and conquest," urges Alfred to warn his corevolutionaries against "accepting violence as a noble, manly thing," and flatly declares that "conscious rejection of war must come" if humanity is to survive (114, 131, 150).

Despite her astute analysis of the dangers of militarism, however—her respect for the moral courage of pacifists not withstanding—Burdekin's text does not call for pacifism, at least not in her own historical moment. On this point—the necessity of unlearning violence—Burdekin seems clearly aligned with her conflicted English protagonist. Nazi fascism constituted too great a threat to turn away from, as her novel so dramatically insists and as she herself concedes. The publisher's note in the 1940 Left Book Club edition of *Swastika Night* assures readers that the "picture painted must be considered symbolic of what would happen to the world if Hitler were to impose his will (as he must not). . . . While the author has not in the least changed his [*sic*] opinion that the Nazi idea is evil, and that we must fight the Nazis on land, at sea, in the air, and in ourselves, he has changed his mind about the Nazi *power* to make the *world* evil" (quoted in Croft 198). Writing before the war, Burdekin imagined a hellish future that could only convince the British of the frank necessity of not merely resisting, but utterly defeating Nazi Germany. During the bleak early years of the war, apparently sensitive to the danger of defeatism, she disclaimed her prior estimation of fascism's power. The reality of the war only strengthened her already firm conviction that to fight was morally imperative. In *Swastika Night* peaceful resistance, though touted as an ideal, is deferred to some indefinite future. Burdekin's horrific projection of Germany's completed genocide of the Jews and life under the jackboot's heel amply justifies England's role in the coming war. For most English citizens, World War II was (and remains) a just war. This disjunction characterizes much of the World War II literature in which a critique of war is central: condemnation of social structures and systems that perpetuate war, especially militarism, juxtaposed against the clear necessity of stopping Hitler no matter the cost.

As susceptible as anyone else to anxieties evoked by this war and to the epistemological confinement of historical reality, master narratives, authorized discourse, and language itself, Burdekin at times becomes enmeshed in contradiction. Indeed, in some ways she writes herself into a discursive corner. The difficulty Burdekin evinces in imagining revolutionary means to actualize her truly (for its day) revolutionary analysis cannot be located solely in narrative conventions such as plot, character, and point of view, however. One must also consider the related difficulty of breaking away from historically and experientially ingrained modes of thought and behavior, a task as difficult for women as for men, even if women have more to gain.

At one point in the narrative, for example, Burdekin interrupts her critique with a thinly veiled address to her English contemporaries, an exposition on democracy and moral courage situated in dialogue between her two rebellious male characters. As they debate the weakness and strength of democracy, Burdekin's clear hierarchy of discourse privileges democracy over authoritarianism as the superior, though more fragile, system. Democracy tends to deconstruct itself into chaos, von Hess proposes, because of an inherent contradiction: the supposed equality of individuals is continuously undermined by the contrary assumption that some few individuals have "strong characters" and are thus competent leaders, while the greater number are "weaker" and "cannot be trusted to live rightly without laws" (146). Thus, even democracy does not escape the divisive effects of the hierarchical, adversarial habit of mind that has been the focus of Burdekin's critique all along. Alfred's response lacks his usual acuity, however, as if Burdekin's voice on this point fails her. He can only speciously suggest that people ought not to abandon democracy "just because it's *difficult*. . . . They ought to be so certain it's right that they can face any difficulties" (147). Thus, rather than undermine her support for democracy by examining its contradictions, Burdekin elides the radical implications of her political analysis. Accordingly, her narrative quickly returns to the subject of war, which at once evoked her interrogation of democracy and silenced it. She seems to have understood that war threatened to destabilize England's parliamentarian government, to restrict individual freedom, and to redefine the limits of power and locate it centrally. Democracy has never had a fair chance, we are told, "because of the menace of war. Soldiers cannot be democrats, and armies, even armies of democratic countries, were always authoritarian" (147).[17] Within the shadow of war, then, Burdekin must negotiate conflicting antipathies and competing discourses. Although the state is endangered from within, in 1937 the danger from without was perceived as far greater. In even the most iconoclastic women writers, the terrors of fascism could impose a censoring silence.

On occasion, in fact, Burdekin slips off the margin and steps squarely into the discursive realm of uncritical nationalism. While she conscientiously includes the British in her critique of imperialism, she does not resist an encomium to the redemptive English character, whose "toughness of moral fibre" makes even the "ordinary" Englander "hard to move to dubiously moral courses by spiritual pressure" (114). Still, her praise is by no means a mere exercise in self-congratulation. Instead, her rhetoric serves to encourage tolerance for those who stand by their principles despite great pressure to abandon them, in particular the Society of Friends and other pacifists.[18] Burdekin does succumb, however, to a crude comparison of the English and the Germans, stating baldly that Germans lack this moral rectitude and, further, that if Britains can resist the "germanisation of their character, and somehow, in the face of all the deception they will suffer, remain themselves, there will be soul-power in Europe after the passing of this dark evil time" (115). Here Burdekin seems to be alluding to Mosely and his Union of British Fascists and to anticipated excesses of wartime propaganda, which would condemn pacifists as traitors and whip up fear and racial hatred.[19] Her uncharacteristic burst of unabashed national pride thus serves propagandistic purposes of her own—purposes engendered, however, not only by her fear of fascism and of the corrupting power of even a just war, but by her own war-intensified vulnerability to nationalistic and racial prejudices.

Finally, one must consider to what degree Burdekin's variously motivated narrative strategies, in particular her "male impersonation," compromise her critique and her ability to envision truly fundamental change. The universalized male point of view is distressingly familiar. The two central characters spend a great deal of time authoritatively discussing women, especially their propensity for submission, identified as the "tragedy of the human race" (70). In contrast, women in this novel are essentially voiceless; they are, in fact, cowering, subhuman creatures fit only for breeding—and, more important, are so because they actively *choose* to be. The fate of humanity, as usual, lies in the hands of wise men who understand women far better than women themselves do. All in all, then, like so many war stories, her narrative, emplotted according to a requisite representation of the reality she opposes and would subvert, cannot exceed its hermetic limitations. The boundaries of Alfred's rebellion mimic those of his creator's.

Ironically, in her seer-like role as interpreter and critic, while Burdekin attempted to adopt the authoritative voice of a modern Tiresias, she was ultimately relegated to the thankless and frustrating role of a Cassandra. Burdekin's critique of masculinism, though multiply mediated through a male pseudonym, male characters, and a harsh condemnation of Nazism, apparently generated enough antipathy and/or apathy to merit expulsion from literary history. Now that it has been readmitted, we find that, much like her characters and, indeed, several of the other writers to be discussed, Burdekin stands in what Terry Eagleton calls a "dissentient conflictual position" (*Criticism and Ideology* 181)—on the unstable fissure between the dominant ideology and one struggling to take shape against it. *Swastika Night* enacts not merely an ambivalence, but a disjunction or discontinuity. In her attempt to mediate between contemporary actuality and future possibility, between the cultural stories she knows and a barely conceivable story of nonviolence and sexual equality, Burdekin must negotiate the indeterminate gap between patriarchal discourse and an/other story. Her text is finally deflected away from a realization of fundamentally altered modes of seeing and being. The resulting discontinuity, however, does not mute her rebellion; rather, it bespeaks the courage and radicalism of her endeavor.

In the year following the publication of *Swastika Night*, Stevie Smith published *Over the Frontier*, the chronological and thematic center of the only three novels she ever wrote. The first and best known, *Novel on Yellow Paper* (1936), introduces Pompey Casmilus, the protagonist of the first two novels, and presents seemingly disconnected episodes of her life, including her romantic entanglements and prewar travels to Germany. The last of the three novels, *The Holiday,* though written during the war, was not published until 1949; by that time Smith had revised it to focus on postwar chaos and malaise. Although perhaps she intended no such thing, these novels form a curious sort of wartime trilogy, which, like *Swastika Night,* does not depict the actual war at all. Quite unlike Burdekin, however, Smith inscribes the nexus of gender conflict and geopolitical war with deceptive obliquity.

THE *Over the Frontier* TRILOGY

Always we were split in two. . . . From this division . . . came the experience of one part of ourselves as strange, foreign and cut off from the other which we encountered as tongue-tied paralysis about our own identity. We were . . . always . . . immigrants into alien territory. We felt . . . ill at ease. The manner in which we knew ourselves was at variance with ourselves as an historical being-woman. Our immediate perceptions of ourselves were locked against our own social potential.
       —Sheila Rowbotham, *Woman's Consciousness, Man's World* (1973)

The method . . . is to bring the patient back to the idea which he [*sic*] is repressing; a long journey . . . without maps, catching a clue here and a clue there, until one has to face the general idea, the pain. . . . This is what you have feared . . . you can't avoid it . . . you can't turn your back . . . so you may as well take a long look.
       —Graham Greene, *Journey without Maps* (1936)

"To keep out of war or not to keep out of war, that was . . . the question," wrote Stevie Smith in 1938, the same year she published *Over the Frontier* (quoted in Barbera and McBrien 117). In the most obvious sense, Smith's Hamlet-like meditation refers to England's increasingly desperate efforts to avoid confrontation with Germany. In another, more provocative sense, however, it can be said to allude to Smith's unconventional choice to make war the center from which her novel, a roman à clef turned fantasy, spins out its exploration of female being and experience. Either way, the question is purely rhetorical, for as Pompey Casmilus, Smith's fictional alter ego, admits, "Oh war war is all my thought"—and inevitably so, for "we have in us the pulse of history and our times have been upon the rack of war. And are, and are" (*OF* 163, 94).

The "rack of war" to which Pompey refers comes to signify much more than geopolitical conflict, which ultimately becomes both catalyst and trope for the two other wars in which Pompey finds herself a combatant: the war of heterosexual romance and her inner struggle to come to terms with her conflicted psychosexual identity (or, to paraphrase Rowbotham, a "self" at odds with "historical being-woman"). War becomes a catalyst not only because it is "obsessively present," to use Hynes's phrase (194), but because it foregrounds gender assumptions, at once disrupting and reconstituting "normal" gender relations. And war becomes Smith's chosen vehicle because it so dramatically expresses the ideology of conflict she finds at the core of being and thus all human relations. Ultimately, the war provides for Smith a means to interrogate the reciprocal relation between, on the one hand, war as social institution and mode of discourse and, on the other, the cultural construction of gender. *Over the Frontier* is, then, explicitly a war narrative, but decidedly an unconventional one. For Smith appropriates the male genre of war narrative to articulate a *woman's* experiential truth. And in so doing, she explodes certain myths about women that once made war a manly prerogative and war literature an exclusively male "field of discourse" (Huston, "Tales" 274). Moreover, she exposes the deadly duality at the heart of masculinist modes of seeing and being, a duality that for Smith's protagonist becomes an ontological black hole from which nothing seems able to escape.

As Smith's readers have often noted, her novels are strongly autobiographical. Like her creator, Pompey Casmilus is an unmarried secretary in a publishing firm who lives with her aunt in a London suburb and travels to Germany in the years just before the war. As in some of her shorter fiction, most of the novels' characters are recognizable as Smith's family and acquaintances. Two of Smith's lovers, one without the disguise of a pseudonym, play central roles in Pompey's life. Not until the second half of *Over the Frontier* does the trilogy radically depart from Smith's actual experience. Even then, Pompey's experiment with militarism, in particular her appropriation of male power, can be interpreted as Smith's fanciful yet profoundly serious exploration of her conflicted consciousness and of an alternative to her own circumscribed life. As Jane Watts has said, Pompey is "unmistakably Stevie-centered" (5).

Smith's ambitions and deepest sense of self seem to have been rather tragically incongruent with her culturally mandated possibilities. Her biographers, Barbera and McBrien, record that friends recalled her frequent plaint, "I should have been a boy" (23).[20] This desire seems to have been rooted not in any conscious devaluation of her gender per se, but in regret and frustration for the restrictions it imposed. Small in stature and frequently characterized as childlike, Smith indicated how much she chafed at gender prescriptions with measured but spirited rebellions. Noted for her unfeminine riding style, Stevie, christened Florence Margaret and called Peggy, adopted the name of a popular jockey. Smith's dislike for her life-long work as a secretary ("an awful strain") must have been all the more bitter for its having been the only practical alternative she could see for herself (Barbera and McBrien 188).[21] And the prosaic nature of her job, which she considered a "punishment," must have proved all the more un-satisfactory given her earlier desire to be an explorer (103). Smith's long-ing for a romantic, adventurous—and to her mind more meaningful—life's work is eventually attributed to Celia, the protagonist in *The Holiday*, who says, "the reason I am often so sad" is that "I ought to be . . . a pirate" (37).

One usually male prerogative she did not deny herself, though she felt qualms about it, was the choice not to marry. In the early 1930s she wrote, "I thought [marrying] was the right thing to do, one ought to—that it was the natural thing to do . . . but I wasn't very keen on it" (quoted in Barbera and McBrien 58). Acknowledging that she was "too selfish and interested more in her own thoughts," Smith avoided marriage despite the "unnaturalness" of her desire and the complications it brought to her relations with men (65). Once again a fictional character, in this case Pompey, seems to speak for Smith, articulating her aversion to mar-riage, especially the cult of domesticity, which Pompey sardonically de-scribes as a "Fiction for the Married Woman" (*NYP* 169). Pompey much prefers "friendship," the intermittent "rhythm" and relative freedom of which is "antipathetic to marriage" (215).

Smith's art often gives voice to her ambivalence about marriage, and more often than not depicts unhappy and even bitter husband-wife rela-tions. Love is war, marriage protracted warfare, and the home a battle-ground. "Sunday at Home" (1949), originally entitled "Enemy Action," is the story of a married couple's quarrel set against the backdrop of fall-ing bombs. Ivor, "wounded in a bomb experiment" and feeling "a lost man," complains that Glory, his wife, fails in her role as social and domes-tic helpmeet (*MA* 44). Glory, whose "hopeless" gestures suggest "the classic Helen . . . above the . . . blood and stench of Scamander Plain," can only cry miserably at her estimation of this marriage, "[t]en years of futile war" (45). Ivor, who fearfully hides in a cupboard when the bombs fly, has been psychically unmanned during his own creation of deadly ar-maments. Ironically, the only Glory now his is a wife who, to his mind, fails to reconstitute his masculinity by embracing the feminine role of ideal wife. Instead, Glory feels a hostage to love—and burns lunch.[22]

Even more so than in this brief tale, Smith's first two novels conflate war and heterosexual romance, making each a gloss on the other. Pompey's antagonistic relationship with Karl (*NYP*), for example, coincides with her increasing hostility and revulsion for fascist Germany. And her bittersweet, ultimately doomed relationship with Freddy (*OF*) eventually leads her over the frontier of war to a greater understanding of the psychology of power. War is finally an appropriate frame for personal and international relations because the same fundamental struggle for dominance poisons them both.

A friend of Smith's suggested that the affection Stevie shared with Karl Eckinger, her "Nazi boyfriend," "foundered finally on politics—'a kind of ethnic intellectual antipathy'" (quoted in Barbera and McBrien 56, 55). Smith's depiction of the Pompey-Karl romance certainly supports this conclusion. Karl's Romantic and uncritical love for all things German, along with his reciprocal disdain for anything English—except Pompey, whom he judges "not so much so English"—enrages her (*NYP* 42). For Pompey is as unashamedly English as Karl is German. In fact, this couple, in their "winter campaign of love and strife," comes to signify the worsening relations between England and Germany in the 1930s:[23] "blacker and blacker grew the storms and the whole of our sky was overcast" (56). Finally, Pompey sadly reports, "an icy crackling wrath . . . lies in rimy ridges on us both" (57).

Fascism ruined Germany for Smith, who once loved to travel there but came to hate it. Similarly, in *Novel on Yellow Paper* the blood lust and cruelty Pompey sees infecting Germany leave her despondent and desperate to get out: "now look how it [Germany] runs with uniform and swastikas. And how many uniforms, how many swastikas, how many deaths and maimings, and hateful dark cellars and lavatories. Ah how decadent, how evil is Germany to-day" (119). Pompey thus condemns Germany for its aggression and cruelty and even advocates British martial intervention: "I think they . . . should be prevented. . . . God send the British Admiralty and the War Office don't go shuffling on . . . too long-o" (119, 117). Pompey is no pacifist and neither was Smith. In her review of Vera Brittain's pacifist testimonial, *Testament of Experience,* she finds many of Brittain's suggestions "silly" and her principles ironic; for Smith, the pacifist is "the peculiar fruit of our successful fighting history, for . . . no country that was not a successful fighting country could afford" to tolerate its pacifists (*MA* 194).[24] In "Mosaic," an essay published in March 1939, Smith wrote, "If there is no possibility of two opposed ideologies existing side by side, then the choice must be made, even the choice of war" (*MA* 107). Peace Pledges turn to ash in the uncompromising flames of war, for "when war has broken out there is no existence of a private peace, you fight for your country or, refusing to fight, you yet fight, and directly for the enemy. That is the . . . most horrible demand of war; the State must have your conscience." Smith was clearly not immune to the either/or habit of mind expressed in the nationalist/militarist discourse she uses here, albeit not without regret.

Nevertheless, she was more aware than most that cruelty and even tyranny are not national characteristics, that the abuse of power and privilege recognizes no state boundaries, and that wartime atrocities occur bilaterally. In *Over the Frontier* Pompey visits an old friend, Ian Crawford, the "kindest and most . . . honourable of men" (63), who had been a British officer in the Battle of the Somme and, later, in Russia.[25] Ian's World War I narrative, typically ironic, reflects "the way the Great War establishes the prototype for modern insensate organized violence" (*GWMM* 227). Ian reports that the Russians exiled men to frozen death in order to save bullets. But he also recounts that British and Australian troops killed recaptured Russian deserters by "rip[ping] their stomachs up with bayonets" (64-65). For Pompey his confession that "We would have murdered our own grandmothers" calls into question the axiom that "British do not maim or mutilate" (65). Now she is haunted by "[u]neasy ghosts stirring through the pages of our history." The ugly truth of Ian's timely narrative of the past not only demonstrates war's power to transform the best of men; it also recalls other subversive texts, such as those of Wilfred Owen and Siegfried Sassoon, that continue to demand revision of British history and cast cold illumination on Smith's historical present.

If the men who fought for their countries have more in common than Pompey knew, then what of the countries themselves? Is the story of England's virtue a convenient but misleading fiction? Is, perhaps, England's imperialism more nearly comparable to Germany's expansionism than it is comfortable to acknowledge? Pompey, never reluctant to share even her most unpopular opinions, dislikes the "hypocrisy" of those who make "excuses" for "war conquest" and who won't admit that "our hands have not been clean" (*OF* 97, 98). "I understand the motives of my country," Pompey declares, when it turns a blind eye to Belgium's colonization of Africa but becomes morally outraged in response to the story "of la petite Belgique . . . debauched by the advancing Pruss" (99). Incited by England's highly selective historical script, British "men spring to arms" to avenge the ravished honor of "poor little Belgium" (100)—in this familiarly gender-encoded storyline, a damsel in distress requiring manly and chivalrous rescue. England's carefully scripted propaganda consistently justifies its own (and the Allies's) territorial aggression even while reprehending it in others.

Pompey does not find the British as guilty of power lust and the cruelty it begets as the Germans of 1937, a "whole race . . . gone . . . mad," but locates the difference in style rather than in motivation (*NYP* 117-18). Britain's working assumption, she reasons, is that "[n]o empire has long survived a too savage oppression of subject peoples" (*OF* 101).

Pompey finds a great deal of truth in the observation that English politicians and diplomats "heal the wounds which the British sword has dealt"
with assertions of a national moral imperative to procure "the happiness
and the rights of other people" (103, 104). In this way, "England weak-
ens the world's moral power of resistance to her deeds of violence by
making it possible for the world to say that England's victims will in the
end become reconciled to the English sway and even happy under it"
(103). Described in these terms, England's methods assume an alarming
resemblance to one of the two methods of subjugation identified in
Swastika Night. An honest assessment of the situation forces Pompey to
concede that the quest for power, with its consequent violence and oppression, directs the lion's paw as well as the jackboot.

Just as she must come to terms with the fictitious nature of culturally
sanctioned stories that make claims for England's moral superiority, she
must acknowledge that essentialist tales of female difference likewise fail to
hold up well under scrutiny. While Karl represents the aggression and even
violent cruelty with which Pompey once identified only Germany, in her
romance with Freddy she becomes the aggressor. Like England, though,
she eventually manages to justify the fatal wounds she inflicts with protestations of self-defense. All such rationalization aside, Pompey knows she
makes "a most perilous attack" on Freddy's "essential dignity and . . . humanity" (*OF* 41). On embarking for Europe, she mercilessly marks him as
her prey: "I will hunt you to earth in some green forest of Deutschland,
be sure that you will not escape me" (114-15).

And he does not escape, for Pompey, during her brief but violent
military career, kills his double, a "rat-faced" enemy in whose face she
espies the "cruelty, hostility, obstruction" she has always deplored (*OF*
249). In this same face she glimpses Freddy, who had tried to entrap her
within the killing confines of domesticity. "Married to Freddy," Pompey
once despaired, "I should be dead" (*NYP* 235, 236). The superimposi-
tion of these two images becomes the personification of the "smug insuf-
ferable conviction" of hegemonic authority she despises. Prompted, she
says, by "liberalistic world-conscience," Pompey shoots her two indistin-
guishable enemies (*OF* 250). Nevertheless, her self-righteousness is belied
by her earlier admission that "if one is weak and one is strong, the strong
will overbear the weak" (29)—a starkly succinct statement of the ideology
of conflict, to which Pompey increasingly realizes she is as susceptible as
Karl and Freddy.

This knowledge is, in fact, the bitter reward that awaits her "over the
frontier" and the thematic knot that finally ties together all the seemingly
disparate threads of Pompey's narrative. To appreciate the sophistication
of Smith's intricate design, one must see the congruent war/romance

plots within the larger context of the novel's underlying pattern—an ongoing search for a tenable psychosexual identity. Pompey, a woman entangled in a male-dominated culture, refuses to don the costume of femininity and play her assigned part: she rides "like a man," makes her own living, writes what she likes, travels freely, speaks her mind, and, above all, refuses to marry and celebrates her sexuality. Feeling the tiger within her, "that mighty and unhappy creature, captured in what jungle darkness for what dishonourable destiny," she struggles to escape the cage of gender and the stories that erect it (*NYP* 270-71). Thus, she experiments with the most male-identified of roles, the soldier, offered up by the unusual circumstance of war. But escape is not nearly so straightforward as this scenario implies, for she fears that identification with this wartime alternative may lead to an equally dishonorable—and equally unacceptable—destiny, a danger already recognized by Virginia Woolf: "how unpleasant it is to be locked out; and I thought how it is worse perhaps to be locked in" (*Room* 24). Pompey is at war with herself on two fronts.

Smith's assertion of the discrepancy between Pompey's sense of self and her culture's definition of women is immediately apparent in the startling and decisive act of naming her protagonist, one of Smith's many instances of myth revision. Pompey Casmilus is a composite of names borrowed from two male figures, one historical, the other mythic. Pompey refers to the Roman general and Casmilus, more obscurely, to Hermes or Mercury. The name Casmilus thus invests Stevie/Pompey with the Olympian power of the unpopular messenger of the gods who guides the dead to the nether world. Smith pays tribute to Casmilus in a riddle poem in which he is called "The Ambassador," an ironic yet appropriately politic role for the conveyer of her unwelcome message. As this ambassador "rides . . . through hell looking two ways," Smith borrows from yet another mythical figure, Janus, Roman god of gates and doorways, thus twice-over affording Pompey access to forbidden territories (*Selection* 114). The Janus-like characteristic of seeing both sides likewise endows Pompey with extraordinary vision. Finally, "Hermes-Cas," as Pompey playfully calls her namesake, is also a "Master Thief," the "shrewdest and most cunning of gods" (Hamilton 33). In "The Ambassador" he has stolen "the trident, the girdle, / The sword [and] the sceptre," all signifiers of power and privilege.

Pompey's adoption of these multiple male identities provides Smith with a useful avenue into the war narrative and empowers her to juggle various roles within that frame. Pompey's full name not only renders her identity sexually ambiguous but enjoins mortal and god, warrior and ambassador, messenger and thief. Her self-definition is a step toward calling into question the paradigm of gender as a closed system of essential and discrete opposites and its corollary concept of separate spheres. This naming is actually a multiple renaming for, like "Stevie," "Pompey" is an acquired name she finds more fitting than her given one, Patience, whose Latin root means "to suffer." While Pompey undoubtedly suffers, she is neither patient nor passive, but rebellious. Pompey thus refuses to assume the role of Eve, claiming instead the symbolic prerogative of Adam.

Still, the legacy of power Pompey at first happily claims as her own proves as two-sided as the Janus, a fact Pompey recognizes even before she sets out on her mysterious journey "over the frontier." A self-directed caveat identifies Casmilus as the "shiftiest of namesakes, most treacherous . . . and delinquent of Olympians" (*OF* 87). Pompey recognizes Casmilus as "a great devil" comparable even to Satan, especially as depicted by Milton (30). She identifies Milton's Satan as a literary archetype for the seductive beauty of evil that, with infinite pride and ambition, seeks apotheosis through power and willingly courts damnation as the price of failure. After all, though in Hell, Satan becomes his own god. Fearful of becoming trapped in "the house of Hades," Pompey warns herself that too complete an adoption of her male persona—especially as drawn in her culture's aesthetically compelling literary "masterpieces"—jeopardizes her soul (86).

Milton's poetic rendition of Satan's fall, a "sweet abomination" (32), epitomizes the cultural and literary traditions with which Pompey/Smith must contend: "in the beginning" opposing forces vied for domination, thus establishing an ontological and narrative model. As "the Word of God" and Milton tell it, then, paradise has always been lost. Pompey warns that storytellers who presume and beguilingly reinscribe a struggle for dominance as the origin and very meaning of human existence are themselves "great devils" (32). Ultimately, though, Pompey's observation becomes profoundly ironic. Although she avoids becoming one of the devils she fears, she cannot ultimately escape the adversarial duality that posits an intractable opposition between masculine and feminine, self and other.

Pompey's name, then, signifies not only a woman's appropriation of male authority (social and literary), but the danger such action entails. The seemingly insouciant secretary, caught up in plots of heterosexual romance and appalled by the prospect of marriage, longs to cross over into the forbidden territory of male being and privilege, but fears the power of that experience to lure her over its darkest edge. Pompey often speaks of her ongoing struggle with a darker self, a "hateful demon" whose "predatory" thoughts threaten to "open a door that never never will . . . be shut again" (28, 44). And Smith conspicuously claims the discourse of war as the metaphorical vehicle for Pompey's inward "battle." Dancing to music only she can hear, Pompey feels "an exhilaration of the spirit" but at its "centre" she finds "a heart of darkness," for "within the music there is . . . a clashing of steel on steel. It is very menacing, very military, this rapidly increasing . . . thrusting, driving, marching" (49, 50). Saddened and frightened by the "compelling" insistence of these "unruly" thoughts, Pompey suffers "waves of conflict."

This conflict is intensified by the equally strong anxiety and guilt Pompey experiences in response to laying claim to conventionally masculine forms of self-assertion, such as the power of naming and self-definition. Pompey's determined rebellion, dating back to her childhood, earns her own disapproval. Remembering how she asserted her independence as a girl in school, Pompey is self-censuring: "I was more than cross, I out-Heroded them all" with "this hateful non-cooperative feeling" (*OF* 83). As a literary allusion, "out-heroding Herod" implies a self-deprecating critique of her youthful nonconformity, figuratively dismissed as somewhat histrionic overacting. As an historical allusion, however, it recalls Herod's obsequious betrayal of his own oppressed people in exchange for power and identification with the conquering enemy. Pompey's trope therefore also suggests a fundamental treachery: to refuse her disabling femininity and to identify with the "enemy" is to betray her sex twice over.[26] With yet another turn, however, the sardonic tone of the passage attenuates her self-criticism, once again revealing acute ambivalence: Pompey may regret her rebellion but she also relishes it. In circumstances that adumbrate her ride "over the frontier" into militarism, she finds exhilarating liberation in horseback riding, her "gallop that goes headlong over rough country and *takes a girl out of herself*" (84, emphasis added).

The tearing conflict Pompey has always experienced escalates into crisis on the eve of World War II precisely because of her vague awareness of some deep link between war and emerging gender consciousness. Like many others, Pompey identifies World War I as a watershed for relations between the sexes and somewhat wistfully looks back to "1910 and la vie heureuse before the war came to put another thought into the feminine head, that only before then had to think of love. . . . But now it is all very different . . . and there is a great burden of stress and strain" (*OF* 22).[27] Typically ambivalent, Pompey later thinks that "nostalgie [*sic*] for the past" is "perhaps not so aktuell [*sic*] as [some] imagine" and that intelligent people no longer conform to "exclusively masculine and exclusively feminine types . . . but always there will be much of one in the other" (150, 149).

The stress and strain Pompey notes, which seriously affect her own well-being, seem to arise from two related sources. First, intelligent women must "contrive to make the best of both worlds, concealing a masculine intention in a feminine phrase" (150). Second, too many people attempt to deny the coexistence of "masculinity" and "femininity" in each individual. While Pompey thus posits the existence of conventional "masculine" and "feminine" qualities, she refuses the Jungian notion that they are innately sex-specific, one set dominating in men and another in women. Her complaint is that psychosexual development is culturally coerced. Due to society's valorization of the "masculine," females and males alike repress their "feminine" qualities. Pompey labels these the "flag-wavers of both sexes," thus positing an explicit causal link between, on the one hand, the identification of "feminine" traits with weakness and, on the other, national assertions of strength and superiority (152). In perverse symbiosis, such notions help to create the institutions of imperialism and war. Furthermore, such "men will pretend to be so masculine it would surprise you . . . and talk a lot about Jews and women for *a dirge and a disturbance of all peace*" (151, emphasis added). Thus, male fear and loathing of weakness, epitomized by and isolated in the "feminine," likewise erupt into personal oppression and hostility toward all and any "others."

Significantly, though, Pompey's scorn falls most heavily on her own sex, specifically on women who try to recreate themselves as men, who attempt "by their clothes . . . to approximate . . . the masculine physique" and indulge in "pseudo-feminist talk" (151). Pompey expresses the violent hope that their own "Chimera" (her ironic nickname for Freddy) will "turn and rend them . . . tear them to pieces . . . until there is nothing left of their little feminine bones that have been protesting a great deal too much" (152). Apparently without irony, she advises such women, "remember to be feminine . . . but once out of bed, pursue your own way, but do not make such a fuss up, it is for *a dirge and disturbance of all peace*" (emphasis added). Pompey's repetition of this last phrase (which earlier alludes to the hyper-masculine flag-wavers), added to the vehemence of her supremely ironic anger toward women who dress in masculine clothing and espouse feminism, strongly suggests that it is *Pompey* who protests too much. Moreover, her wish for murderous violence against too-masculine women at the hands of Freddy-like men indicates profound guilt and even self-hatred.

The obvious conflict and guilt Pompey feels because she prefers male power to female powerlessness surface in a recurring dream, which enacts a symbolic wish-fulfillment. In her dream, she sits at a desk, as she would when performing her secretarial tasks, except she is "in uniform," an aberration that alarms and confuses her: "it must not for a moment appear that I am in uniform . . . to me something that is not perfectly assimilated" (135). When Freddy enters the dream and confronts her, demanding to know "From whom is your commission?" Pompey becomes defensive and denies her military attire: "[S]urely you could not . . . think that I am sitting here under orders from an authority I do not know I do not recognize to exist? I hold no commission. By God I swear it." Pompey can lie to Freddy but not to herself, for "the stars on [her] collar are . . . burning, piercing, tearing," and she knows the "dream-reality" has raised "questions that must be answered" (136, 137). Nevertheless, she chooses to dismiss the dream's most conspicuous and incongruous element, "the war motive." She still cannot acknowledge the heavily determined symbolic attraction of this male costume.

As Virginia Woolf observed in the same year *Over the Frontier* was published, the primary function of the "symbolic splendour" of various male costumes is "to advertise the social, professional, or intellectual standing of the wearer" (*TG* 20). Moreover, Woolf adds, "the connection between dress and war is not far to seek; [men's] finest clothes are those that [they] wear as soldiers" (21). Thus, an officer's uniform is a sign of the highest rank in society's hierarchy of being, connoting privilege, power, and virility—the potency equated with male sexuality and maleness itself. Although dreaming of clothing herself in richly symbolic male attire, however, the still recognizable Pompey does not wish to *become* a man; rather, as a woman warrior, she aspires to the privileged status and power of men.

Women warriors are of course fairly well represented in literature. Barbera and McBrien, in fact, write that "Stevie cast Pompey as something of an insouciant and *stürmish* Maid of Orleans," thus reviving an old literary tradition (117). Pompey has little in common, however, with traditional women warriors. As Nancy Huston has observed, Athena, Artemis, the Amazons, the Valkyries, and Joan of Arc, virgins all, were denied sexuality and motherhood, attributes supposedly antithetical to their status as hunters or warriors (see "The Matrix of War"). In contrast, Pompey is a fully sexual being. Struggling with an ambivalence unbecoming the woman warrior tradition, she fights for her personal freedom and nothing less than her ontological integrity.

Unlike some female modernists, Smith did not herself adopt a male costume, seeking what Susan Gubar has called "blessings in disguise."[28] She seems, however, clearly to appreciate clothing's "crucial symbolic role" in women's "confinement within patriarchal structures"; Pompey, her surrogate, "escape[s] the strictures of societally-defined femininity by appropriating the costume" she at this historical moment most identifies with the freedom she is denied ("Blessings" 478). Like Virginia Woolf, however, she discovers that costumes (like the stories they embody) have a magical power to "mould our hearts, our brains, our tongues to their liking" (*Orlando* 188). Thus, she shares with her female contemporaries the tendency Sandra Gilbert has observed "to imagine costumes of the mind with . . . irony and ambiguity" ("Costumes" 393).

Although Pompey must be cajoled into assuming masculine authority, she realizes, "I am a very willing captive . . . it is a relief to me . . . a direct orientation of my thought" (*OF* 167). Her uniform becomes "an outward visible sign . . . of pride and ambition" (220). Pompey feels "great joy" and liberation from the normal restrictions of her life, which she unhappily "must seem not only to endure but to approve" (221). As she crosses the frontier of male prerogative, however, she complains that her "hateful uniform is already putting such unfemale thoughts into my head" (228). She fears that she and her male companion will "outdo each other in cruelty" because of the "utterly detestable" thoughts compatible with the uniform. Her fears are well founded, for a moment later her pained horror at the thought of human suffering turns to indifference, and she "thank[s] the God of War to be rid of tea-cups and tattle and the boring old do-all-nothings of a finished existence" (229). The uniform, that quintessential symbol of power, adventure, and masculinity, despite its equally strong association with institutionalized oppression, violence, and death, paradoxically becomes a welcome passport to freedom from her stifling "life-in-death existence" (221). Pompey's feelings of relief and exhilaration bespeak her (misplaced) anticipation that joining in the conventionally male enterprise of war would "facilitate not just a liberation from the constricting trivia of parlors and petticoats but an unprecedented transcendence of the profounder constraints imposed by traditional sex roles" (Gilbert and Gubar, *Sexchanges* 299).

As Pompey becomes accustomed to her masculine costume and the military way of life, despite her gender she earns the respect of her "superiors" and deference from her "subordinates," the men whom she has come to see as "ours . . . to command and to visit with rewards and penalties" (*OF* 334). Having broken the code of female behavior, Pompey might well have earned only opprobrium and ridicule, but she clothes herself in her male identity so successfully that she also adopts its code of masculinity. Living with men, acting a male role, Pompey consumes a steady diet of military phallocentrism, a world view, as Elshtain says, "shot through with relations of domination and subordination, force and violence" ("Women as Mirror" 30).

To be sure, at first Pompey cannot tolerate the "food we must eat on this side of the frontier." In contrast, the "hardening process of . . . Tom's [her companion's] upbringing" enables him to consume it apparently without even noting its "evil . . . essence, so . . . unprincipled, uninformed by the merest whisper of a mere question of humanity" (240-41). Male socialization has made Tom what he is, and complete immersion in male experience promises to make the worst sort of man of Pompey.[29] Having "become almost too successful," Pompey asks, "what am I now? . . . I, [once] so apt for human comfort and the happiness and a shared experience . . . am shut in upon myself, have no tears, no sadness and no joy" (245). Alienation, apathy, and emotional sterility are the unfortunate result of Pompey's adaptation to militarism, the most "masculine" of world views. The completion of her metamorphosis proves tragically ironic, for in killing her enemy (Freddy/rat-face), she assimilates him. In an act that once again points to a conceptual congruence between sexuality and the violence of war, Pompey pulls a revolver and places "the barrel between : . . [his] teeth, that open so invitingly upon slack lips" (250). She turns her borrowed weapon, a mechanized phallus, on her enemy in a defiant inversion of the heterosexual violence of war.

Like many of those who considered war evil but felt morally compelled to fight fascism, Pompey perceives her violence as necessary and justified. Still, although she attributes her success to her "white bright light of hatred for the evil of cruelty" and confidently proclaims "We are right," she eventually also recognizes the moral ambiguity and personal peril of her position (253-54, 255). In her participatory sanction of the war, she finds she has become infected with the "arrogance and weakness and cruelty" of the enemy, which has brought her to "a hatred that is not without guilt . . . is not a pure flame of altruism" (255-56). Pompey has nearly become trapped in the house of Hades she so dreaded.[30]

Her ability to escape entrapment is insured, however, by her realization that the ideology of conflict, which posits self and Other in ontological adversity, informs all forms of power within her experience, including her own. Meeting with the Generalissimo and the Archbishop, "violent . . . unscrupulous" men who accrue power and privilege through coercion, cruelty, oppression, and corruption, Pompey the warrior finally knows from whom she received her commission (261):

> [W]ithin my heart are thoughts that thought for thought meet theirs,
> to bridge and fuse into murderous intent.
> I am not less guilty than . . . Archbishop, not less guilty than . . .
> Generalissimo. [264]

In addition, Pompey accepts her own willing complicity: "[Y]ou see it is my fault. . . . I may say I was shanghaied into this adventure, forced into a uniform I intuitively hated. But if there had been nothing of me in it, nothing to be called awake by this wretched event," she would be "safely" and "sanely" ensconced in her other life (267). Meditating on her experience, she asks, "Are not all holders of privilege ruthless and cruel in their tenure[?]" and admits to power's insidious appeal: "I have allowed myself to be for a moment attracted, conceited to have the cloak of *their* privilege, for *their* purpose, thrown about my shoulders" (271). Deciding she has been politically naïve, she acknowledges that within the hegemonic world view, power is the last word, war its ultimate manifestation, and no one immune to its contagious perfidy.

As she sees it, then, during the war and its aftermath, Pompey is left with two equally untenable alternatives—the "death in life" that limits her to tea cups and the costume of femininity, or the equally deadly danger of loosing the demon who emerges from her "heart of darkness" when she dons the cloak of masculinism. These apparently opposed possibilities mimic the Cain and Abel model of being upon which the structure of militarism depends. Refusing to remain either predator or prey, Pompey finds herself in an historically ontological void, for war seems to preclude deconstruction of dichotomous opposition. In *The Holiday,* drafted during the war, originally entitled *Death and the Girl* and later revised, this schizophrenic dilemma is graphically expressed in the splitting of Pompey into two characters, both of whom suffer postwar depression and malaise.

Pompey Casmilus disappears, splitting off into a female identity, Celia, and a male identity, Celia's uniformed cousin Casmilus (Caz), who inherits Pompey's godlike name. Separately they personify the ambivalence, the double consciousness that tormented Pompey. Celia has none of Pompey's tigerish characteristics, but Caz has in his eyes the look of a panther who "turns to his kill . . . and will tear the heart out of it" (*H* 82). Celia "flee[s] the torturers" but Caz "pursue[s] to the death" (147, 148). While Celia asks, "Can resistance pass to government and not take to itself the violence of its oppressors?" Caz observes, "I do not know . . . that we can bear not to be at war" (10, 9). Barbera and McBrien perceptively read this doubling as "perhaps . . . Stevie's personal metaphor for the duality which makes her appear so paradoxical," an externalization of herself as the "classic androgyne, sundered and . . . separated from the 'other' without whom she can never be content" (168).

A life of fragmented being proves unbearable for Celia, clearly suffering more than Caz, who now holds the "commission," with its full legacy, that Pompey surrendered. Once Hamlet-like in her anguished meditation on being, Pompey/Celia becomes a tormented Ophelia, floating down an icy river of unbeing in search of a "fine long sleep and no dreams" until rescued by Pompey/Caz (*H* 93).[31] Desperate to escape her assigned role and to (re)join Caz, Celia drops her teacup (repeatedly a sign for devalued femininity) and "began to cry and scream, for there was such pain in my heart . . . that I was bent backwards as though it was an overdose of strychnine" (*H* 155). Separation from her "masculine self" is killing her, and she decides, "It was better . . . in the war. Now . . . the heart is gone out of it. . . . The victors, at war with the aftermath of war, grow tarnished. . . . The thoughts split up and the will slackens . . . [T]here is something devilish about war, devilish exciting I mean" (166). Ensnared in the "other" side of Pompey's trap, Celia ambiguously declares, "'For pleasure and profit together allow me the hunting of men.' It is exciting. . . . And it is masculine" (166). For Celia, who cannot live with Pompey's renunciation, even war is better than death in life. She thus desperately longs to join Caz, who will soon sleep in a bomb rack on a departing plane, thus literally replacing a bomb with his body.[32] He too wishes Celia could accompany him—not to attenuate his deadliness, but because "it would be just the life" for her, one she "would enjoy" (166). That Pompey could escape her double bind does not seem to be a conceivable possibility; the danger for Celia/Caz remains the same as it had been for Pompey. Her psychosexual rebellion has come to naught.

Smith's literary rebellion, in contrast, though convoluted and shot through with denial, never unconditionally surrenders to its own equivocation and anxiety. For although she does not (cannot?) imagine a story in which Pompey dissolves her dilemma, in both content and form Smith illuminates the frustrating misrepresentations and inadequacies of gender-inflected stories as they have repeatedly been told. The form of the novels as a whole provides one final example of Smith's habit of adopting a convention only to revise it. Although not a war memoir in the usual sense, Smith's trilogy bears a startling structural resemblance to the traditional war memoir as described by Paul Fussell. Like the romantic quest, it has three stages: "first, the sinister or absurd or even farcical preparation . . . second, the unmanning experience of battle ["characterized by disenchantment and loss of innocence"]; and third, the retirement from the line to a contrasting (usually pastoral) scene, where there is time for quiet consideration . . . and reconstruction" (*GWMM* 130). Thus, Fussell continues, "war experience and its recall take the form of the . . . most universal kind of allegory. Movement up the line, battle and recovery become emblems of quest, death, and rebirth" (131). Similarly, Pompey's "preparation" for battle is both sinister and absurd; her initiation, consisting of the archetypal "perilous journey" and "crucial struggle," results in profound disillusionment (130); and finally, (as Celia/Caz) she returns to a pastoral setting where she/they contemplate the shattering experience of war.

Not unexpectedly, however, Smith's fictional "memoir" starkly deviates from the male paradigm in two necessary and instructive ways. As a woman, Pompey cannot be "unmanned" in the conventional sense. In fact, she at first becomes more "manly." Deliberately eschewing those masculine qualities she finds corrupting, however, she consciously "unmans" herself—and thereby deepens her dilemma. As a result, Pompey's rebirth (as Celia/Caz) in the narrative's final stage is a grotesque travesty signifying not "reconstruction" but deliverance into an existence of psychic mutilation. In addition, Smith's atypical narrative is characterized by unexpected shifts from one literary mode to another, disorienting contrasts in mood and tone, and the seemingly chaotic expression of clashing discourses (Barbera and McBrien 112). The archetypal war "memoir," appropriate and useful in its own way, ultimately proved too unidimensional—too specifically male—for Smith and her tale of war. In order to tell an/other story, she was forced to modulate the existing symbolic order.

Smith's war trilogy, which enacts a struggle to come to terms with her psychosocial identity and her sense of that struggle's war-engendered crisis, thus represents a meaningful departure from literary tradition. She appropriates a male genre and a male-identified historical sequence in order to expose the fatally exclusive modes of seeing and being that war-as-story too often validates and reproduces. Her female warrior infiltrates the homosocial institution of militarism in ways that illuminate the more profoundly heterosexual ontology of war. Further, she suggests, as Betty Reardon and others have more recently argued, that the "hierarchical and oppressive structures which are characteristic of patriarchy . . . are the basic roots of militarism as well as . . . economic and political imperialism" ("Militarism" 185). Finally, in the telling of Pompey's unresolved story, Smith (like Burdekin) reveals that attempted escape from the conceptual prison of phallocentrism, even for those as wary and desperate as she, proves the most taxing struggle of all.

Smith was later to disavow *Over the Frontier,* saying, "It is horrible, I am so ashamed of it" (quoted in Barbera and McBrien 112). This is not surprising when one considers how objectionable and threatening she found her own literary and psychosexual rebellion, especially as enacted in her fantastical wartime adventures. As Smith's narrative draws to an end, Pompey reads from her journal—a self-castigating passage that can be construed as metafictional commentary: "[Y]ou say impudent things and are in continual alarm and apologizing for them. . . . You doubtless mean to say something, but hide your last word through fear, because you have not the resolution to utter it. . . . You boast of consciousness, but you are not sure of your ground, for . . . your heart is darkened and corrupt. . . . Lies, lies, lies" (*H* 174). Smith, who began by observing, "To keep out of war or not to keep out of war, that was . . . the question," is painfully conscious of her rejoining narrative's contradictions, silences, and gaps, out of which emerges her own tortured identity as an actor in search of a viable role—certainly not mad and powerless Ophelia, but not bloodstained Hamlet either. Moreover, in her ambivalence Pompey once again protests too much, for *Over the Frontier* ultimately tells not lies, but—as Smith may have understood only too well—a good deal of revelatory truth.

Despite their very different strategies, both Burdekin and Smith render versions of Parable Art that, like the male-authored texts of the decade, anxiously respond to the crisis of fascism and impending war. Similarly influenced by the ironic and disillusioned literary response to the Great War, women too wanted to "warn men against war, by telling them the truth about it." As Britons, Burdekin and Smith share many of the concerns of their male compatriots. As women, however, they uncover a truth with an altogether different dimension: historically and literarily, the codependent plots of heterosexual romance and war have together reproduced the "same old story" of loving arms to the mutual detriment of all. Finally, consciously or not, Burdekin and Smith inscribe war-exacerbated anxieties of authority and identity that render them vulnerable to the very consciousness and discourses they would expose and transform. Still, it is easier to appreciate the relative success of their endeavors when one compares their war stories with those of Elizabeth Bowen, who ultimately found the masterplots too compelling to resist.

3

Double-Voiced Discourse
Elizabeth Bowen's Collaboration and Resistance

For us, who by proxy inflicted gross oppression,
Among whom the humblest have some sins of omission,
War is not simple . . .
       —Anne Ridler, "Now as Then" (1943)

As if in response to Virginia Woolf's claim (in *Three Guineas*) that women have no country, in Elizabeth Bowen's novel *The Heat of the Day* (1949) Stella Rodney protests, "No, but you cannot say there is not a country!" (274). As a member of that hybrid class, the Anglo-Irish, with its "help-lessly conflicting loyalties" (Lee, *Estimation* 18), Bowen lacked the luxury of claiming any one nationality completely enough to take it for granted and thus either to embrace it unequivocally or to repudiate it on principle. In her preface to *Last September* (1929), set during Ireland's "Troubles," Bowen describes the

> position of . . . Anglo-Irish landowning families as . . . not only am-
> biguous but . . . more nearly heartbreaking than they cared to show.
> Inherited loyalty (or, at least, adherence) to Britain . . . in whose wars
> their sons had for generations fought, and to which they owed their
> "Ascendancy" lands and power . . . pulled them one way; their own
> temperamental Irishness, the other. [*SW&A* 202]

Living in England for much of her life, marrying an Englishman, and forming strong attachments in the overlapping circles of Oxford intellectuals and the English literati naturally strengthened Bowen's ties to England, making her divided allegiance even more pronounced.

    Bowen once observed that her youthful transplantation to England had created "a cleft between . . . heredity and . . . environment—the former remaining . . . the more powerful" (*P&C* 23). Thus, though she thought perhaps "England made [her] a novelist," she emphatically identified herself as Irish: "As long as I can remember I've been extremely conscious of being Irish. . . . [G]oing backwards and forwards between Ireland and England . . . has never robbed me of a strong feeling of nationality. I must say," she added, "it's a highly disturbing emotion" (quoted in Glendinning 189). More disturbing than ever at the time she made this admission, perhaps, for England was at war, while Ireland—in part to assert its sovereignty—maintained a conspicuous (and, to some, suspicious) neutrality.[1]

As Victoria Glendinning observed in her biography of Bowen, "the very strength of her identification with London at war heightened the tension always latent in the Irish/English duality" (189). Antoinette Quinn's diagnosis of "racial schizophrenia" seems, however, a more accurate assessment, for Bowen not only chose to live in London and work as an Air Raid Precaution warden during the war, but volunteered to write "secret reports" on Irish attitudes for Britain's Ministry of Information in the hope that she could do her part in "freedom's war" (Quinn 316; Fisk 248; Bowen, "Eire" 382). Irish historian Robert Fisk reports that she "did not try to hide her contempt for Irish men and women whose reactions to the war seemed either unheroic or ambivalent" (355). At the same time, however, Bowen bristled in response to England's accusatory "anti-Irish feeling": "The charge of 'disloyalty' against the Irish has always, given the plain facts of history, irritated me. I could wish that the English kept history in mind more, that the Irish kept it in mind less" (quoted in Fisk 356). England tended to forget that Irish blood was shed on Flander's Field, and Ireland could not forget that English soldiers had let Irish blood. While Bowen's decision to spy on the Irish may suggest that she found a pragmatic resolution to her conflicted loyalties, the resentful comments she clandestinely recorded must have pricked her conscience, making all too apparent the painful irony of her position: "What right have the British to keep denouncing the Nazis? Haven't they been Nazis to us for centuries?" (quoted in Fisk 356). With painstaking honesty Bowen noted that at the heart of the Anglo-Irish Ascendancy, of her family's "position and . . . power," lay a corrupting "inherent wrong"— a wrong embodied in the British Empire and personified by the Bowen family's predatory founder (a misanthropic colonel in Cromwell's military service). Generations later, her own tyrannical grandfather, a "dreaded . . . hard man" nicknamed "old Mussolini" more immediately incarnated the Anglo-Irish heart of darkness (*BC* 452, 292).[2] Bowen's awareness that Ireland had suffered under colonization by the British and the Anglo-Irish ruling class, dispassionately recorded in her family history, presumably lies behind her measured defense of Ireland, published in England in 1941: "While the rights of Eire's neutrality may be questioned, the conviction behind them must be believed" ("Eire" 383).

Other Bowen readers have noted that this intensified double bind heavily informs her wartime writing. Quinn, for example, pinpoints the war as the "event which provoked her most sustained imaginative response to the tensions of her Anglo-Irish heritage" (315). But the disjunctions that most animate and sustain her wartime writing are by no means limited to the relatively straightforward matter of conflicting national allegiance. Mary Cadogan and Patricia Craig, who find nothing subversive in *The Heat of the Day,* nevertheless keenly observe that in Bowen's wartime stories "the immediate, dislocating tension of war . . . has been suppressed or interrupted by another, more personal, obsessional stress or access of feeling" (201).[3] This unidentified "personal, obsessional stress" inheres in another, more insidious duality—that of being a woman variously divided against herself. This additional split necessarily complements and complicates her already vexed position as a "neutral" citizen at war. And rather than suppress the "dislocating tension of war," these converging fracture lines merge with and exacerbate it. As a woman with tenacious roots in both a colonized country and the colonizing power, as a female heir of the patrilineal and militarist Anglo-Irish tradition, as a woman at war with fascism, and as a woman writer compelled to transform her experience into art—in all these overlapping and inter-formative ways—Elizabeth Bowen was quietly, inevitably, and hopelessly at war with herself. Accordingly, in her wartime writing antipathetic notions of national identity and unavoidable betrayal repeatedly become entangled with similarly conflicting notions of gender ideology and literary form. The result is a dizzying oscillation of competing discourses.

In *Under Siege,* a literary history of wartime London, Robert Hewison cites *Bowen's Court* (1942), a highly personal recollection of her family's history, as an exemplary instance of a literary phenomenon specific to the war years: a "probing back into the past," an "outpouring of memory," which often constituted not merely a therapeutic return to a less stressful time or an exercise in nostalgia, but a "search of some explanation for the crisis of the time" (91, 90). Bowen offers a similar justification for her apparent indulgence in writing *Bowen's Court* as the world faltered on the edge of an abyss: "The past—private just as much as historic—seems to me now to matter more than ever. . . . Nothing that ever happened, nothing that was ever even willed, planned or envisaged remains irrelevant to to-day. *War is not an accident; it is an outcome.* One cannot look back too far to ask—of what?" (*BC* 453, emphasis added).

Here defining history and politics as an aggregate of private and public activity *and* human consciousness, Bowen alternately reconstructs her familial and national histories in search of the genesis of war and, in particular, of the crisscrossing paths that have led to the imminent nightmare of 1939. As we shall see, her journey back to the future thus constitutes a more personal—if less radical—variation on the historical pageant in *Between the Acts*. And, like Woolf's novel, Bowen's nonfictional enterprise emphatically brings home the notion that domestic dealings and social structures, private lives and state politics, individual psyches and cultural history comprise a mosaic of mutual determination. Individuals are "more than . . . time's products," she observes; they are likewise its "agents," making history even as "history" makes them (*BC* 452).

Bowen's structural interweaving of the two histories—her family's and Ireland's—underscores her assertion that the "pattern" generations of Bowens "unconsciously went to make . . . [had] its relation to the outside more definite pattern of history" (*BC* 451-52). And that pattern was disturbingly familiar to Bowen, who at the war's onset was struck by the salience of "subjection to fantasy and infatuation with the idea of power . . . [and] conflicting wishes for domination" in her family chronicle (454). This pattern, she claims, makes Bowen's Court "a fair microcosm, a representative if miniature theatre" in which personal and political antagonisms have played out their often violent dramas. Echoing Virginia Woolf in *Three Guineas*, Bowen declares, "the private cruelty and the world war both have their start in the heated brain."

Unlike Woolf, however, when Bowen turns (in *Bowen's Court*) toward the family to illuminate the kind of indivisible private and public tyranny that finds its more comprehensive expression in global warfare, she does not focus on issues of gender. Instead, with marked sympathy she implicates her family and, ultimately, herself in an ancient pattern of public dominance and submission in which she continues to play a dual and intrinsically contradictory role. For while she rather guiltily acknowledges the "inherent wrong" she traces back to her family's inception, Bowen also passionately shares their "great tie" to the land itself, their belief that the home is "society's strengthening complement," their attraction to the "virile set-up, the panache" of the British army, and their strong, consoling regard for the value of "lasting order"—for which Bowen's Court was source and symbol (*BC* 277, 156, 227, 125). "I am ruled by a continuity that I cannot see . . . the authority of . . . long tradition," she admits somewhat ruefully (449-50).

Toward the end of her account Bowen writes that her traditional values "have been accentuated rather than changed by war" (453). Accordingly, her fears that the war threatened cataclysmic change suddenly disrupt the otherwise placid surface of her text in a bitter denouncement of sociopolitical "progress." Her eighteenth-century ancestors, she concedes, undoubtedly

> lived in a Philistine, snobbish, limited and on the whole pretty graceless society. But [Henry Cole Bowen] got somewhere and lived to die

in his drawing room surrounded by hosts of children and the esteem of what looked like a *lasting order.* And to what did our fine feelings, our regard for the arts, our intimacies, our inspiring conversations, *our wish to be clear of any binds of sex and class and nationality, our wish to try to be fair to everyone bring us? To 1939.* [*BC* 125, emphasis added]

This rather shocking repudiation of democracy must be considered in the light of Bowen's conviction that the twentieth century's socially transformative upheavals had inevitably taken the shape of violent dispossession. Continuity and tradition for Bowen signified not simply the maintenance of a cherished (and ideally benevolent) order, but a means of restraining the dominant will both of individuals and of nations.[4] As Hermione Lee points out, along with everything else Bowen inherited the questionable notion of property as morally beneficial (27). As if to repudiate the violent revolutionary surge of socialist and democratic reform concurrent with World War I, Bowen writes that "while property lasted the dangerous power-idea stayed, like a sword in its scabbard, fairly safely at rest" (*BC* 455). Of course, this analysis more immediately refers to the decline of Anglo-Irish "landlordism," Catholic Ireland's struggle for Home Rule, and the resulting civil war. By World War II, disruption of the cherished and reassuring "lasting order" had for most Anglo-Irish become equated not with hope for a better future but with a new disorder defined by endless war.

In *Bowen's Court* World War I therefore assumes singular importance: Bowen chooses 1914 as the point at which to bid farewell to the stable quasi-feudal past and to greet, not without regret and trepidation, the advent of destabilizing democracy.[5] World War I begins "the chapter of different history" because "[a]fter 1918 came the war in Ireland with the burning down of many of the big houses. . . . [P]erhaps one does not say of Ireland that war began again, but that war resumed" (*BC* 436-37). And the same seems true of World War II, which not only intensified Ireland's ongoing quarrel with England, but seemed merely a resumption of the same old conflicts unresolved and even aggravated by the Great War, "that first phase of war" (436). In consciousness if not in history books, the wars one after the other nightmarishly coalesced into "War as we now know it . . . in its immense To-day" (437).[6]

In addition to pointing up the threat of socioeconomic instability, Bowen's bitter critique of democratic reform identifies gender equality as another clear threat to "lasting order." She just as unequivocally locates the continuation of this order in the family drawing room, filled with numerous progeny ready "to carry on the old tradition" (*HD* 72). Yet, if such enclosed scenes of male fecundity embodied for Bowen the tradition to which she eventually became the sole and first female heir, she must have found herself historically and biologically inadequate to "carry on" and thus doomed to failure and betrayal. Her habit (in *Bowen's Court*) of assigning roman numerals to the family's long line of Roberts and Henrys "as though they were kings" underscores the privileged status of aristocratic patrilineal continuity embedded in Bowen's worldview (*BC* 145). When she came into her inheritance, she regretfully lamented, "I had already changed my father's name for my husband's, and I have no children" (*BC* 448). The last of her line, yet stubbornly insisting on being addressed by her married name, Bowen knew she could not meet her ancestral commitment to tradition and continuity—that by virtue of being neither male nor mother, she was made to default. Her ambivalence at having been born female and thus betraying her legacy has unambiguous roots in her childhood. Noting that her parents had fully expected a male heir, to be named Robert in accordance with longstanding practice, Bowen assures us that "no one, from the moment the sex was announced, said a word against Elizabeth for not being Robert" (404). Perhaps not, but Bowen's sense of being the wrong gender surfaces once again in her seemingly casual confession that as a youngster she was "gratified by strangers calling [her] 'Sonny'" when she wore her "Robert-like . . . reefer coat" (406).

Thus, though effectively muted, the question of gender systematically interacts with that of cultural continuity throughout *Bowen's Court*. Moreover, occasional comments indicate how thoroughly Bowen had internalized her culture's masculinist bias. She finds, for example, the "wish to dominate" more "vulgar" in a woman (245); a "good woman" is "forebearing, understanding and mild" (250), which her examples lead one to understand means acquiescent and uncomplaining. Similar traits prove undesirable in men, one of whom earns Bowen's reproach for having been "a rather soft character . . . a little too womanish" (283). This traditional view seems especially incongruous when it emerges in her own experience, inevitably contrasting with her seemingly independent, self-assured, strong-willed approach to life. Once, for example, she wrote to a lover of the "subjection latent in every woman" and her desire for him to be "the traditional dominant male" (quoted in Glendinning 97).

Romantic passion is infamous for evoking egregious contradictions, however, and incidents such as this are suggestively at variance with other observations, which reveal that the masculine bias could also consciously chafe. Having observed in *Bowen's Court* that Colonel Bowen, the family "father," used capital letters when writing his sons' names but small letters for his daughters', Bowen (here, again, like Woolf) articulates her sensitivity to the predetermined lowly status, the indifferent fate, and the invisibility of most women in recorded histories, even her own: "And Mary and Hester—whose sex did not even allow them capital letters in their father's will? The fate of these two colourless girls is uncertain: they are said to have married" (77). Dispensed with in the customary fashion by both history and their father, Mary and Hester are here rescued from cultural disinheritance and historical oblivion by the last Bowen daughter. But little has changed, for as Bowen dryly adds toward the end of her family saga, "the past does certainly seem to belong to men" (380). And in 1941, as she completed her chronicle, she had no reason to believe that the future would be otherwise; nevertheless, she was contemplating the cost for women of their place in the patriarchal scheme.

Although she seems unaware of how completely her conflicting notions of gender intersect with and problematize her seemingly more immediate concerns with national allegiance and cultural continuity, Bowen does express her developing sense of the personal, social, and political as overlapping and indivisible. And she comes to see her own situation as paradigmatic. In addition, the war had foregrounded the notion of personal and political betrayal. If one teases out the submerged logic of *Bowen's Court,* then, one discovers a series of intricately tangled dilemmas: To side actively with England was to fight fascism but to betray Ireland. To betray Ireland was, paradoxically, to countenance tyranny and oppression. Further, to be female was to betray everything—the past and its traditions, the family, the Anglo-Irish legacy, and, it would seem, the future. To privilege maleness, however, was to betray herself and her sex. Finally, to contemplate a new order in which maleness was not privileged and in which women were not self-divided and self-effacing was to betray, once again, the tradition and continuity she had learned to believe vital to an orderly and meaningful civilization.

In short, for Bowen World War II seems to have fostered confrontation with sexual politics as nothing else ever had. But her problematic cultural identity, unique among the writers considered thus far, made her excursions into the disputed and largely unexplored territory of gender vis-à-vis war all the more personally compelling, threatening, and vexed. Unable to locate any unequivocal position in the (for her) overlapping areas of collaboration and resistance, Bowen continuously struggled to negotiate between them. In the preface to her wartime collection of short stories, *The Demon Lover* (1945), she wonders if "in a sense all wartime writing is not resistance writing?" (*CI* 50). For Bowen this is doubly true, for she resists both narrative collusion with the shape-shifting (patriarchal) enemy and, with equally anxious determination, her own traitorous resistance.

As Bowen explains in "The Roving Eye," a writer often sees what "he [*sic*] did not intend to see" (*SW&A* 60). For Bowen this was never more true than during the war, when "her uncanny intuitions, her flashes of insight" illuminated shadowy interiors usually obscured during times of (relative) peace (Ritchie 143). She cautiously admits that the war tapped into her unconscious, catalyzed "new bare alert senses," and released something straining to get out (*CI* 52, 47):

> Each time I sat down to write a story I opened a door; and the pressure against the other side of that door must, I found, have been very great, for things . . . came through with force and rapidity, sometimes violence. . . . The stories had their own momentum. . . . The acts in them had their own authority which I could not question . . . they were flying particles of something enormous and inchoate that had been going on. [CI 47]

Thus, similar to Stevie Smith—who renounced her psychic journey over the frontier of gender as "lies, all lies"—and Katharine Burdekin—who variously distanced herself from her oppositional discourse—Bowen adamantly denies the personal significance of her wartime stories. Although elsewhere she concedes that "any fiction . . . is bound to be transposed autobiography" (though so changed as to "defeat ordinary recognition" [*MT* 129]), in the preface to *The Demon Lover* she painstakingly depicts herself as a mere conduit for the collective "over-charged subconsciousness" (*CI* 48). "It is because the general subconsciousness saturates these stories," she adds, "that they have an authority *nothing to do with me*. . . . I cannot answer for much that is in these stories, except to say that I know they are all true" (*CI* 48, emphasis added; 52).

But Bowen tells more truth than she knows when she so astutely likens her tales to "snapshots . . . taken . . . in the middle of the *mêlée* of a battle" (*CI* 52). For as she strives to distill the essence of what she has felt "germinating" during the war, Bowen unavoidably inscribes the battle within, which, like *Bowen's Court*, doubles as a "representative if miniature theatre" of war: what Bowen felt "germinating"—and what emerges as a powerful undercurrent in her wartime fiction—is a high-stakes tug of war between a predominantly male resolve to restore or reinforce the patriarchal status quo and an overwhelmingly female, mostly inchoate impulse toward its subversion, a conflict she traces back to the complex ramifications of World War I. Held fast by the chains of her irresolvable ambivalence and alternately identifying with both sides of the struggle, Bowen must have often felt that "[t]here were too many theatres of war" (*HD* 308).

In an essay entitled "Elizabeth Bowen's Fiction" (1949), Elizabeth Hardwick accuses Bowen of being a "romantic feminist who serves up a perennial dish: the tragedy of the Fine Girl and the Impossible Man" (1114); in

Bowen's novels, she adds, men die to satisfy "woman's revenge" (1120). But this assessment does a grave injustice to Bowen's infinitely more complex and evenhanded depictions of women and men together. Hermione Lee more accurately points out that Bowen's work often illuminates both male and female "tyranny in a relationship" and, considered as a whole, usually balances her critiques of "parasitic" or overbearing women and insensitive, objectifying men (148, 147). An inevitably "immasculated" artist who also listens to her interior "resisting reader," Bowen consistently displays an aptitude for rendering male and female points of view with equal persuasion and acuity.[7]

In "The Cat Jumps" (1929), for example, everyone, even the children, suffers an "outburst of sex antagonism" evoked by the retelling of the true story of a man who murdered and then dismembered his wife (*CS* 365).[8] The grotesquely gender-definitive narrative awakens usually repressed resentment, fear, and mistrust between the men and women listening to the bloody tale: "voices came out from some dark interiority; in each . . . interchange a mutual vote of no confidence was implicit" (366). While the women dread physical violence, the men fear spiritual asphyxiation. Subterranean forces of "untold ages"—fed by the materiality of the word—wreak their damage uninvited. Fittingly, everyone ends up literally locked within their bedrooms—just as they are trapped within a register of mutual sex antagonism and irrationally compelled by the story that evoked it. The murderous husband may never have repented his crime, but it is a woman—significantly, the *storyteller*—who narratively and literally locks the doors, thus entrapping male and female alike and encouraging further violence. And they all perceive their actions in terms of preemptive self-defense. This tale of the embattled sexes illuminates the intrinsic role of narrative in not simply recording but invoking and justifying deep-seated and habitual patterns of perception and behavior. As a woman who tells stories, Bowen here suggests a self-reflexive awareness of her own ironic collaboration with the ongoing renewal of seemingly irrational hostilities between men and women.[9]

The tone of "The Cat Jumps," despite its macabre interior, is rather playful—apropos of "a baroque joke about the war between the sexes" (Lee 148). The mood turns quite somber, however, as Bowen explores permutations on this theme vis-à-vis World War II, which invariably deepens the divide between men and women. The very title of "A Love Story 1939," with its conspicuous date, suggests that the onset of the war engendered and required a love story of its own—one that would adequately limn war's insidious relation to romance and its emplotment. Even in neutral Ireland, the war defines and feeds the implicitly sexual animus between several couples, most obviously the Perry-Duntons. In their clash of wills,

Polly at first dominates, forcing herself on Clifford in decidedly masculine—and emasculating—terms that familiarly conflate violence and sexuality: "Her rape of Clifford . . . had been the climax" of her desire to possess him (*CS* 501). Though childlike and deferential to the point of servility, Polly has money, making Clifford a "bought" man and thus, it seems, no man at all. Soon after the war began, however, Polly noted a change in Clifford and the tenor of their marriage: "There had seemed no threat to Polly in Clifford's nature till the war began, with its masculine threat" (501). Sensing a definitive shift in authority and dependence, Polly slips into a deathlike "rigour" for which his pajamas serve as her shroud (507). Although nothing materially changes, the war seems to have rendered this impoverished relationship even more grotesque. Overshadowed by the distant war, their love story, like that of all the various couples in this tale, figures heterosexual romance as caught in war's crosscurrents and rotten at the core—dishonest, depleting, and even deadly.

Significantly, Bowen recalls that the Russo-Japanese War marked a crucial stage in her cognitive development, for it precipitated her first true awareness of a reality outside her own, a world in which "time held war" and "people grimaced with hate at each other and let off guns" (*SW&A* 26). Her consciousness of war as sexually divisive, however, dates to World War I. In *Bowen's Court* she notes that the Great War's advent was chiefly marked by the sudden absence of men—British officers and Anglo-Irish brothers and sons. She subsequently became cognizant of her role as the innocent, protected female. Jean Bethke Elshtain calls this familiar type the Beautiful Soul, who in complementary opposition to the Just Warrior embodies goodness and purity, and whose protection at once ostensibly motivates and justifies war.[10] Even as a teenager Bowen recognized that this role exacted guilt and onerous duty in return for male sacrifice: "The moral stress was appalling. We grew up under the intolerable obligation of being fought for, and could not fall short in character without recollecting that men were dying for us" (*MT* 16). Men and love were not often discussed, she recalls, "possibly [because] the whole sex had gloomy associations" (17). From her earliest awareness of war, then, it was already gender-encoded and fraught with paradoxical and unpropitious implications for romance.

These youthful perceptions were just as appropriate a war later, for the protected/protector paradigm seems rather paradoxically to have been strengthened in World War II despite (and because of) the conscription of women and the many civilian casualties on the home front(s).[11] In a June 1940 "Postscript" J.B. Priestley alludes to the assault on England in a panegyric to the "natural piety" of men who willingly fight to preserve their way of life, but the image he employs reveals that the rhetoric of the day refused to acknowledge the changing realities of total war and retained its dichotomous gender-encoding (10):

> [W]e watched the dusk deepen in the valleys below, where our women-folk listened to the news as they knitted by the hearth, and we remembered that these were our homes and that now at any time they might be blazing ruins, and that half-crazy German youths, in whose empty eyes the idea of honour and glory seems to include every form of beastliness, might soon be let loose down there. [11]

His closure with Hardy's "In Time of the Breaking of Nations" ("War's annals will fade into night / Ere their story die") simultaneously reinforces the notion that the story of the man and the maid is immutable, and denies the inter-dependence of gender systems and war that his own pre-industrial discourse recreates.

Even more revealing is the comment on patriotism attributed to "A Man in the Street" in the prewar anthology *What Is Patriotism?* (N.P. Macdonald 1935). The writer explains why the common man, who ordinarily has no wish to fight, does so in time of war: It is the "decent thing to do . . . when she [one's country] becomes involved in a struggle for her honour." "It is not without significance," he adds,

> that the Latin word for native country is feminine. One's country is a woman. And the tradition of masculine chivalry towards a woman lives on, though it is not the modern custom to prate of it in high-sounding phrases. . . .
> [The average man's] attitude towards her [one's country] is much the same as that of a lover towards his beloved. . . . [W]ithout thinking twice about it he would readily perform for her any service she might require of him. [304-05]

In this configuration war becomes both a mandatory act of dutiful sacrifice for which women are morally indebted and the requisite price men pay to earn the guilty gratitude of their kept women. During World War II female guilt and indebtedness became a recurring theme in women's verse. In "The Infinite Debt" (1947), for example, Rachel Bates ponders,

> A stranger died for me
> . . . .
> And how can I requite
> His wounds, his death who dies unknown
> And keeps my feeble flame alight
> With ransom of his own?
> All life, all love's his fee. [Reilly 11][12]

This paradoxical web of misdirected duty, guilt, loss, and mutual resentment will not release its mesmerized victims (of both sexes), who have been too long ensnared to see the trap for what it is but still suffer the sting of its debilitating consequences.

To be sure, the men/women/war design represents not a first cause but a reflection of the overall psychosocial matrix. As a character in *The Heat of the Day* remarks, "War . . . hasn't started anything that wasn't already there" (33). Nevertheless, for Bowen (as for Smith) the war serves as a metonymic trope of exceptional aptness and explanatory power—a figure for both her own multifaceted ambivalence and the larger historical/cultural disruptions of hegemonic continuity. If in *Bowen's Court* looking backward did not crystallize Bowen's tangled perceptions of war, cultural continuity, and gender, employing the same technique in her storytelling evidently did. For in *The Heat of the Day* and a number of short stories, Bowen looks to the Great War as a crucible of gender anxieties and animosity that continue to seethe and which find their most overt expression in the ideological and psychological violence of World War II. In her exploration of this etiology and its multiple manifestations, she suggests, among other things, that World War II figured a pitched battle between the sexes, in particular, a reactionary reassertion of male authority and dominion. In this way she continues the critical tradition of Burdekin and Woolf. Bowen's salient technique of recollecting and rescripting stories from the first war within the reformative context of the second further implies that on one level World War II signified a compensatory reenactment of that war, which had killed, mutilated, or traumatized an entire generation of men. Considered in tandem, "Songs My Father Sang Me" (1944) and "The Demon Lover" (1941), paradigmatic in this regard, also neatly capture the extremes of Bowen's shifting sympathies.

As the former story opens, a song from the "last war" plunges an unnamed woman into a reverie about her long-absent father, "one of the young men who were not killed in the last war" (*CS* 651). Her father's postwar dispossession draws a defining link between war and traditional manhood: "He was a man in the last war until that stopped; then I don't quite know what he was, and I don't think he ever quite knew either." Sadly, he does know: he has become merely an "ex-officer," a memory, an absence (653). The woman's mother, who before her wartime marriage had been a fun-loving flapper, also suffers a disheartening loss of freedom and identity: playing the role of proper wife, she "did not know what to look like now. . . . Mostly she looked like nothing" (654). Sociohistorical discontinuities have jolted them both, but neither recognizes the other's disorientation. Thus (bringing to mind the would-be fate of Brett Ashley and Jake Barnes) the war-born marriage self-destructs; the bored, dissatisfied, unfaithful wife becomes a nag, and the psychically wounded husband a vulnerable target. In an abortive effort to assert his diminished manhood, he adopts various "lordly way[s]" that only further provoke his wife's ire. Finally, he simply leaves, for he has not found peace at war's end, but a war of a different kind—a war that completes his emasculation and forces his desertion.

As Bowen's veteran bids his young daughter farewell, he obliquely refers to the complex relationship between the Great War, his loss of identity, and his failed marriage, a conjunction he senses but does not fully comprehend. Gazing at the peaceful English countryside, he tells his daughter, "I thought I'd like to see her again. . . . How I loved her." But then he adds, "I've lost her . . . or she's lost me; I don't quite know which; I don't understand what's happened" (657). The circumstances leading up to his wistful comments and his ambiguous use of the female pronoun result in the identification of England with his wife—both once loved, both irrevocably changed, both irretrievably lost—along with his manhood. For some men, then, the loss of personal potency and its consequences for male-female relationships becomes the loss of England, and conversely, England's loss.

At the end of the now adult daughter's story, the focus reverts to the wartime bar in which, like a battlefield, "smoke thicken[s]" and "khaki melt[s] into khaki gloom" (660). The setting could not be more appropriate, for a quiet but painful personal battle frames the daughter's story: before and after her tale the woman and her companion bicker, unconsciously echoing her parents, and wearily accuse one another of cruelty and lack of feeling. The woman is grateful her father is not there to hear the same old tune and same tired argument. The World War I song, resurrected in the next war, thus becomes a haunting wartime refrain, an objective correlative for both countries and couples at war. Moreover, the reciprocal connection between war and gender hostilities, explicit in the World War I story, spills over into World War II.

This motif also appears in "The Demon Lover." However, if in "Songs My Father Sang Me" the narrator's sympathies are clearly aligned with the pathetically undone father, in "Demon Lover" they unambiguously lie with the victimized woman. And the sexual antagonism, more violent and more sinister, originates in the masculine assertion of dominance and control of the (supposed) beloved. During World War I Kathleen had been engaged to a young man whom she remembered as somehow effecting the "complete suspension of *her* existence" (*CS* 665). "He was never kind to me," she recalls. "He was set on me. That was what it was—not love." In an act of death-defying self-assertion, before returning to no man's land the young soldier made an "unnatural promise": "I shall be with you . . . sooner or later. . . . You need do nothing but wait" (663). But when he was reported missing in action and presumed dead, Kathleen forgot their "sinister troth" and eventually married (664). Years later, during the next war, Mrs. Drover finds an enigmatic note which insists that "nothing has changed" and she is therefore expected to "keep [her] promise" to wait (662). Apparently asserting his adamantine will to possess her even from beyond the grave, the returning demon lover "without mercy" steals away the screaming and helpless woman in an ominously waiting taxi (666).

While the ex-officer in "Songs" feels disempowered by World War I and is helpless to recoup his losses, the transformed veteran in "The Demon Lover," resurrected in/by World War II, returns for restitution and revenge. More ambiguous than my reading suggests, this tale leaves room for the conclusion that Mrs. Drover's unstable, hypersensitive psyche cannot cope with war's unreality and she therefore conjures her own demon.[13] But whether she is the victim of a material act of violence or of her own fears does not change the fact that she unequivocally perceives World War II as diabolically revivifying a male aggression and will to power from which she thought the first war had unexpectedly brought final reprieve.

Thus, despite the very different circumstances of the two wars, in the second war one finds a resurgence of a familiar conflict that, as implied in *Swastika Night* and *Three Guineas,* conceivably arises from the resurfacing of the post–World War I male anxiety that women are responsible for breakdown of the social and political order. In their specific formulation of the argument that the historical and material circumstances of this war combined to precipitate an unprecedented crisis in gender relations, Gilbert and Gubar maintain that "the war that has traditionally been defined as an apocalypse of masculinism seems . . . to have led to an apotheosis of femaleness" (*Sexchanges* 262). Physically and psychologically wounded men returned from the Great War having to contend with, in addition to everything else, women's newfound financial independence and greater social and sexual freedom.[14] It is therefore not surprising that men felt profoundly threatened and sought to blame women for the supposed dissolution of the established (patriarchal) order, a breakdown culturally signified by the prewar emergence of the New Woman and later institutionalized by the newly won women's vote. But women's sense of liberation and empowerment, Gilbert and Gubar conclude, eventually faded into guilt, while male resentment surfaced in multiple forms of antifeminism.

The general and longterm effects of World War I on women's lives continue to be debated, but an imposing body of historical commentary supports the argument that, whether or not it significantly altered women's consciousness and/or direct political influence, the experience of the war and the consequent social changes did send shock waves through the sub-strata of gender relations.[15] In her history of women entitled *Lady into Woman* (1953), Vera Brittain, for example, observes that World War I transformed women's lives, increasing their level of responsibility and their financial independence, and thereby making them more confident and autonomous as well as less sexually inhibited (186). The upshot, she concludes, was that the "*practical revolution*" the war "created in the lives of once-sheltered women gave them a new awareness which enabled them to produce organic social changes by their votes" (194, emphasis added). Nevertheless, Brittain concedes, after the war most women "vanished into voluntary retirement" from the sphere of public influence, and "traditional influences resumed their sway" (187). Despite this concession, Brittain does not soften her assessment of the war as potentially transformative.

Ironically, the argument that women's supposedly natural pacifism and greater stake in securing the lives of their children would, after enfranchisement, lead to the abolition of war later came to be used to deflect culpability for World War II directly onto women, who (according to a vocal minority) apparently were too indifferent, lazy, frivolous, or simply ineffectual to effect any change. Renowned scientist and socialist J.B.S. Haldane, for example, denounced "'the women voters of England' whose interest in . . . the coronation or the latest murder had prejudiced the children's chance of survival" by diverting attention from preventing war (quoted in Cadogan and Craig 189). Professor C.E.M. Joad, a political and moral philosopher active in the government, sardonically remarked, "Before the war money poured into the coffers of the WSPU [Women's Social and Political Union] . . . in order that women might win the vote which, it was hoped, would enable them to make war a thing of the past. The vote is won, but war is very far from being a thing of the past" (189).[16]

Whatever the many reasons some men may have found for directing responsibility for the war away from themselves, Bowen makes this assignation of blame especially resonant in "An Unwelcome Idea" (1940). This story's title explicitly refers to the war's disruption of life's normal routine but seems also to express Bowen's attitude toward the surprising notion exposed in the text's only moment of ideological dissonance. As Mrs. Kearny and Miss Kevin discuss the effect of the war on their lives, the latter explains that her father immediately becomes truculent when she or her mother tries to discuss the war with him. "You'd think," she adds, "that the two of us originated the war to spite him; he doesn't seem to blame Hitler at all" (*CS* 576). While the bizarre notion that malicious women, and not Hitler, were responsible for the war seems indicative of a profound paranoia on the part of Miss Kevin and/or her father, it also reflects the war's psychosocial and historical undercurrent of sexual discord and mutual recrimination.

In a retrospective meditation on her wartime novel, Bowen comments that certain "stories were unconscious sketches for *The Heat of the Day*" ("On Writing" 11). "Songs My Father Sang Me," "The Demon Lover," and "An Unwelcome Idea" were undoubtedly among these, for the novel takes up their thematic threads and weaves them into a rich and infinitely more complex narrative tapestry. Unlike these three stories, *The Heat of the Day* captures the full range of Bowen's warring impulses. While she elaborates on connections between the two world wars and the war between the sexes, she also reproduces the multifaceted ambivalence her ambiguous position made inescapable. Thus, in this novel in particular Bowen seems, as Hardwick has somewhat unfairly complained, "often very far from being entirely of her own opinion" (1119).

Understandably, then, Bowen found *The Heat of the Day* "far the most difficult of all" her novels to write. "It presents every possible problem in the world," she explained (quoted in Glendinning 171). Noting the novel's consequent sense of "strain" and "struggle," Lee calls attention to its "unusually evasive surface," "over-use[d] double negatives," and "syntactical mannerisms," which she believes "express the oddness and dislocation of the war-time experience" and "establish . . . a very peculiar . . . frame of mind" (164, 165, 166). More specifically, the novel's opaqueness and stylistic convolutions seem outward signs of Bowen's inward wars—textual debris left in the wake of equivocation and denial. Responding to the charge of evasiveness, Bowen characteristically denied the discontinuities of her text. She described *The Heat of the Day* as "straightforward," somewhat disingenuously adding, "Nothing about it really needs to be explained" (quoted in Craig 116). Nothing, of course, could be further from the truth.

In *The Heat of the Day* one finds that Miss Kevin's father is not the only Bowen character to look to women rather than to Hitler as responsible for the war and its destruction. Robert Kelway, soldier turned spy, blames the emasculating power of women and England's consequent lack of virility for his psychological and physical wounds, as well as for his personal betrayal of England, a country that he claims had "sold itself out already" (268). Like the "ex-officer" in "Songs My Father Sang Me" (and like Bowen) Robert looks to the past for an understanding of the present. He is haunted by the memory of his father, in Robert's eyes an unman, whose "sex had . . . lost caste" and whose "fiction of dominance" and multitude of "[u]nstated indignities . . . burned deeply into the son's mind" (257, 258). Robert decides that the immediate cause of his father's humiliating failure is his domineering mother and the "man-eating house" she has made for the family (257). Castigating his mother and sister, he bitterly complains, "It never suited them that I should be a man" (278). Despite this assertion of manhood, he believes himself unmanned, like his father before him, and despairs, "I was born wounded; my father's son" (272). Thus effected by the dominating mother, impotence is passed from father to son.

Robert does not consciously trace the root of modern man's emasculation to World War I until he is wounded at Dunkirk and acquires a limp that tellingly varies from mild to severe depending on "whether he did or did not, that day, feel like a wounded man" (*HD* 90). The personal and strategic catastrophe at Dunkirk provokes Robert's bitter realization that the "illusion" of honor, manhood itself, died in the trenches. For him, consequently, the "world . . . is as dead as the moon" (276). Moreover, he sees himself as representative of the whole of English men: "Dunkirk was waiting there in us—what a race! . . . a race without a country. Unwhole" (272).[17] Robert's lover, Stella Rodney, whose female experience has shaped her perceptions quite differently, cannot empathize and decides, "This is some malady of yours" (275).

Robert's quarrel with England derives from his conviction that since World War I the so-called free countries, unlike the Axis powers, had lost their virility, a deterioration his personal experience has made unbearably acute. He feels he must attempt to reestablish what to his mind is the proper hierarchical order by recovering male dominance in a different context—that of fascism, in particular Nazi Germany. As he tries to justify his actions to Stella, his contempt for the general attenuation of male authority, his association of this loss with women, and his obsession with regaining power at any cost become clear. "Freedom," he declares, is a "racket." "Tell a man he's free and what does that do to him but send him trying to dive back into the womb? . . . [W]ho could want to be free when he could be strong?" he asks (268, 69). Paraphrasing Mussolini, Robert adds, "We must have law—if necessary let it break us. . . . To feel control is enough. It's a very much bigger thing to be under orders [than to give them]" (269, 273).[18] Betrayal of England and his family, Robert explains, "utterly undid fear. It bred my father out of me, gave me a new heredity" (273). Thus rejecting his "impotent" father, he turns to the potent Führer and the irresistible, uncompromising power of fascism.

Many of Bowen's contemporaries and even some of her more recent critics have found fault with Robert's characterization as a fascist traitor, citing inadequate and unconvincing motivation. Interestingly, a few of her male friends objected to Robert as "a woman's idea of a man," taking exception, perhaps, to his obvious psychosexual anxiety (Glendinning 173). Bowen's friend Rosamond Lehmann thought Robert a perfectly "solid" bit of characterization but was puzzled that Bowen had made him a fascist rather than a communist, a more common and (many thought) credible phenomenon. Patricia Craig, one of Bowen's biographers, similarly claims that Bowen "fails to be altogether convincing about how this ideology grew on him" (117). And Hardwick found Robert's betrayal contemptibly "incomprehensible" (1117). Nevertheless, Bowen's depiction of Robert, whom she identified as the "touchstone of the book" (quoted in Glendinning 173), is firmly supported by psychological and sociohistorical theory.

Theodor Adorno and Max Horkheimer, for example, explained fascism in terms of Freudian theory, specifically the father-son dyad of the family romance, and related aspects of group psychology. They observe that the fascist psyche may be rooted in "rage at the father" for what the son perceives as weak or "missing paternal authority" (quoted in Theweleit, vol. 2 xx). They elsewhere postulate that Hitler represented the "primal father," a "paramount and dangerous personality" to whom the group subject responded with compliancy and "surrender," an "extreme passion for authority . . . a thirst for obedience" (Adorno 124). Through the processes of identification and idealization, the leader-father figure additionally "serves as a substitute for some unattained ego ideal" (125). Accordingly, for Robert, Hitler seems to have gratified a "twofold wish to submit to authority and to be the authority himself" (127). This Freudian explanation is complementarily augmented by other theories more sensitive to both gender politics and a wider historical context. As we have seen, a diverse group of cultural theorists have explored the inter-relations between psychological process (particularly the male unconscious), gynophobia, misogyny, militarism, and historical fascism. As for the ex-soldier in "Songs My Father Sang Me" and numerous similar literary characters of the period (e.g., Somers in Lawrence's *Kangaroo*), for Robert Kelway 1916-1919 were the "awful years . . . the world lost its real manhood" (Lawrence 217). For some, only fascism could reinstate that manhood.[19]

Unlike Robert, Stella's son Roderick is just coming of age and is therefore working to establish his manhood for the first time. His response to the war consequently takes a different shape; yet he too seeks to guarantee continuance of patriarchal order and to fill the void left by "missing paternal authority." Like Robert, Roderick, whose father died of complications from wounds suffered in World War I, longs for a substitute father. He thus imagines he feels a "confluence" in himself of the three men he adopts as father figures: his biological father Victor Rodney, Robert

Kelway, and Cousin Francis—a recently deceased distant relative who has left Roderick the ancestral estate in Ireland. Roderick feels the need for fathering so deeply that he easily identifies with strangers, for he does not remember his real father at all, has developed no relationship to speak of with Kelway, and never meets Cousin Francis, who, it should be noted, has chosen Roderick as his heir and proxy son "in the hope that he may care in his own way to carry on the old tradition" (*HD* 87). Roderick, though to a lesser degree, also shares Robert's obsessive need for authoritative law. Indeed, this concern seems the rule rather than the exception for young Englishmen: "his . . . friends were all for the authoritarianism of home life; the last thing they wished was Liberty Hall" (52). Both Robert and Roderick, then, prefer authoritarian law and order to freedom, which compromises control and promotes disorder.

Although in the army, Roderick is indifferent toward it and, in contrast to Robert, seemingly indifferent toward even the war itself. Not unexpectedly, the two men's dissimilar ages, experiences, and circumstances lead them to view male hegemony from quite different perspectives. While Robert perceives it as lost, Roderick sees it as a long established and exclusive institution, membership in which would imbue his life with substance and direction. Thus, while Robert turns to fascism, Roderick looks to the traditional past. His cousin Francis's exhortation "to carry on the old tradition" provides Roderick with precisely the opportunity he seeks. When he inherits Mount Morris, a relic of the quasi-feudal past that offers him "a historic future," he has not yet "engaged" with the world (50, 49). But his new position as head of the estate makes all the difference. When visiting Mount Morris for the first time and ensconced in the "master's bedroom," Roderick experiences an awakening and finally discovers an identity with which he can engage: lord and master of his own changeless world. He thus feels truly alive for the first time and immediately "consider[s] the idea of succession" (312). The past and the order it promotes give this father-hungry man a meaningful future.

The most unsympathetic male character in *The Heat of the Day* also shares Robert and Roderick's war-strengthened preoccupation with order and control. Robert Harrison, an English spy, seems compelled to control the situation in general and Stella Rodney in particular. Rather like the calculating demon lover, but all too corporeal, Harrison asserts sheer will to power to establish himself as the dominant male. After discovering Robert's covert Nazi activities and developing a loveless obsession with Stella, Harrison confronts her, threatening to expose Robert unless she becomes his lover and breaks with Robert. Despite Harrison's vocation as government agent, coercing Stella to submit to his will is his only true concern—not Robert's wrongdoing, England's welfare, or even Stella's love. He begins and continues their relationship "on his own terms," his tone is that of "the person in power," and the "exaggerated quietness of his voice hint[s] at some undefined threat" (22-23). While the Germans daily bombard London, Stella thinks of Harrison—her countryman—as "an enemy," "like the Gestapo" (23, 33). No fool, she suspects Harrison's true motivation, which gives rise to what Eve Sedgwick calls an "eros of domination" (188): "The fascination for him in this thing with me could have been so much less me than himself[,] his all-powerfulness" (284).

Harrison similarly epitomizes the kind of misbegotten citizen Nancy Hartsock describes as the product of the Western political community, in which all learn to split off and reject the "feminine," and "*eros* takes negative . . . forms which point toward death rather than life" ("Prologue" 147). Such citizens, she argues, "are not simply strangers to each other but enemies who compete for dominance. . . . The search for reciprocal fusion with another takes the essential form of the search for the conquest of the other's will"—especially in time of war. Harrison and his story about Robert clarify for Stella the true nature of this war: "the grind and scream of battles, mechanized advances excoriating flesh and country, tearing through nerves and tearing up trees, were indoor-plotted; this was a war of dry cerebration inside windowless walls. . . . [F]rom the point of view of . . . the heart any action was enemy action now" (142).

These three men—Robert Kelway, Roderick Rodney, and Robert Harrison—despite circumstantial differences, are clearly linked, thereby strongly unifying the novel's theme of male desire for absolute authority, which intensifies to the point of obsession during the war. The two who are most alike share the same name, a fact rather pointedly revealed late in the novel. Albeit reluctantly, Stella earlier recognizes them as doubles: "It seemed to her it was Robert who had been the Harrison" (275). And an outside observer finds Robert's "behaviour . . . to have been that of Harrison exactly" (305). Robert is likewise identified with Roderick; among other things, they share a dressing gown that makes Roderick "look more like [him]self" (47). Appropriately, Bowen expresses their likeness metonymically and in terms of potential rather than realization, for Roderick is just coming into his male inheritance and has not yet experienced the war directly.[20] That all three of the novel's central male characters share essentially the same concern—uncompromised male dominion—and, even more significantly, are in a sense versions of the same man, attests to Bowen's conviction that their behavior is representative of a systematic male response to the war.[21]

Nevertheless, together these three men also partially delineate Bowen's pattern of collaboration and resistance, into which she draws the reader. Roderick, the most benevolent and likable, rescues the family estate from abandonment and ruin—from the "bitter necessity" that Bowen so dreaded for Bowen's Court and that for the Anglo-Irish had become a way of life (*BC* 16).[22] As the male heir Bowen never was, Roderick represents compensation for Bowen's failure and loss. Her sympathetic portrayal of both his metamorphosis from an awkward and fatherless youth to a masterful, landholding lord, and his rescue of the endangered ancestral past betray Bowen's complicitous admiration for the decidedly masculinist, aristocratic, colonizing Anglo-Irish tradition. What is more, her uncritical depiction tends to lull her readers into a similar collaboration. Harrison, however, unequivocally evokes one's condemnation and, thus, resistance to the unsavory side of a variation of the very tradition Bowen tends to idealize and defend against extinction. Men like Harrison, fascists in their atrophied hearts, breed and illuminate qualities in men that the women who love them would rather not see, after which strife becomes inevitable and trust impossible. As Stella says to Harrison, "You succeed in making a spy of me" (138). "To be in his embrace," she realizes, "would be to accept, for ever, that strength was left in nothing but obsession" (142).

Roderick would seem simply to represent the masculinist tradition at its benevolent best, and Harrison its unnatural perversion, if not for Bowen's co-identification of the three male characters and her highly ambivalent treatment of Robert, the one who links the two extremes. Although Robert's betrayals of both Stella and the democratic ideal tend to evoke the reader's anger and perhaps abhorrence, in his own way he is as much a victim as Stella. The most complex and pathetic of the three men, Robert signifies Bowen's apparent sympathies, in particular her pity and guilt: pity for men casually emasculated by cultural givens that promote psychic and physical violence, and guilt for her collusion with the system. Bowen's portrait of the "wicked" Mrs. Kelway and her "man-eating house" with its "swastika-arms of passage leading to nothing" reminds us that private fascism is not a male prerogative and promotes sympathy for Robert (110, 257, 258). But his betrayal of Stella and his embrace of political fascism are none the more forgivable for all of that. Robert, ironically, seeks rescue and validation in the very ideology that has destroyed him and terrorized Stella. His impossible situation thus perfectly refracts Bowen's own self-negating position as supporter of masculinist traditions that necessarily and remorselessly abandon her.

As in the case of Mrs. Drover (in "The Demon Lover"), the story of Stella's eventual breakdown completes a story begun in World War I and hinges on an invalidation of her being and experience. Just before her capitulation to Harrison, Roderick forces Stella to recall the events of her first marriage, a story whose original plot was immediately revised for public consumption so that blame would once again be deflected onto a faithless woman. During the Great War, Victor was wounded and fell in love with an older woman, his nurse.[23] Unable to admit the possibility that his rejection of Stella may have more to do with his wounding than her inadequacies, Victor attacks her. Despite what she may think, he asserts, she has never loved him, for she has not "the remotest conception of what love [is]" (*HD* 223). Furthermore, "any other woman . . . could have made him forget the nurse"; instead, Stella's "shortcomings [have] had the reverse effect." Thus pronounced a failure as a woman and a wife by a self-proclaimed authority, Stella accepts his judgment, not realizing she has any alternative. Later, when everyone assumes she must be at fault in the matter of divorce, she likewise accepts the "story about my guiltiness," preferring to "sound a monster than look a fool" (222, 224).

Deeply wounded by the aptly named Victor, not until the next war does Stella love again. Robert Kelway similarly invalidates her experience and, even if inadvertently, completes her violation. This time Stella feels doubly betrayed, first, because he says "there is no country," while she has all along derived solace and strength from the "war-warmed impulse of people to be *a* people . . . the curious animal psychic oneness . . . so deeply shared" (*HD* 275). While the war alienates Robert, it galvanizes Stella's sense of community. She feels most acutely, however, the pain of personal betrayal. Because Robert has lied to her, has been an "actor" in their personal drama, Stella can be sure of nothing. She again undergoes a jarring change of perspective and cannot reconcile what supposedly was and what actually is.

Finally, Robert does not even grant her the notion of betrayal, which is all she has to account for her despair. Echoing Hemingwayesque rhetoric, Robert abrogates the concept of betrayal and other abstractions: "Don't you understand that all that language is dead currency? . . . Words, words like that. . . . I . . . became absolutely certain they mean nothing. What they once meant is gone" (*HD* 268). Robert's invalidation of Stella is complete; he leaves her nothing. Nevertheless, she insists, "There still must be something that matters that one has forgotten. . . . The more wars there are, I suppose, the more we shall learn to be survivors" (317). But Stella's survival requires a reversal of tactics, a movement from resistance to capitulation. In her final meeting with Harrison, she contemplates with equal indifference the only alternatives she sees left to her: death under the rain of German bombs or collaboration with the male "enemy" in two possible forms, both of which signify the classic completion of a woman's story. She offers her body to Harrison and plans to marry a "brigadier," thus indicating unconditional surrender to her submissive position within the sexual/militarist economy. Stella has become a spoil of war.

As she had anticipated, her tale's "beginning, in which was conceived the end, could not but continue to shape the middle part of the
story," during which she had "felt in her . . . a . . . helpless progress towards disaster" (*HD* 133, 134). With little insight into their deepest motivation and although consciously at odds with one another, Robert and
Harrison together finish what Victor started, resurrecting his ghost and
driving Stella once again to comply not only with the hazardous plot of
heterosexual romance (or the "continuous narrative of love"), but with
the fiction that she is a "bad" woman (99). For at the inquiry regarding
Robert's death during his flight from Harrison, Stella protects Robert's
reputation by sacrificing her own.

Stories from the past return to haunt Stella even in the guise of the
future through her son's repossession of Mount Morris, whose unhappy
history is unearthed in the process. In Nettie Morris, Cousin Francis's
purportedly insane wife, we see Stella's predecessor similarly enmeshed in
both the ongoing narrative of men, women, and war and double-edged,
self-fulfilling fictions about deviant women. During World War I Nettie
found she could no longer bear her suffocating existence as mistress of
Mount Morris: "Day after day was for me like sinking further down a
well—it became too much for me, but how could I say so?" (*HD* 216). So
she left and eventually committed herself to a private home for the emo-
tionally disturbed, where she withdrew from the world. To avoid returning to Francis and his tradition-bound estate, she accepted society's verdict
that she was an aberration among women. Friends repeatedly told her, "If
you keep on not going back to Mount Morris when Francis asks you to
and everybody thinks you should, people will come to the conclusion that
you are odd" (213). Spying refuge in this label, Nettie decided, "'Then
that must be what I am.' Because once that came to be known, nothing
more could be expected." The only escape Nettie saw open to her was
to authorize another false story—a story of insanity ending in self-
incarceration. Ironically, this dead end provides her only safe house. As
Nettie quite sanely explains to Roderick, to whom she happily abdicates all
privileges and rights to Mount Morris, "[H]ere I am, and you can't make
any more stories out of that" (214).

Like Stella, then, Nettie thinks of life as a script predetermined by
cultural/narrative conventions that fix choices for everyone. Of Francis's
thwarted potential and narrow obsession with tradition and patrilineal
continuity, Nettie observes, "Who knows what might not have come of a
different story, if there could have been one. As it was, he had to go out
looking for a son" (*HD* 209). "Such a pity," she continues, "that there
should have to be any stories. We might have been happy" (214). But of
course there must always be stories, the means by which we make sense of
the world and our place in it. In *The Heat of the Day* (as in *Between the*

Acts), life is a book or a drama in which actors play out scripted roles; but in contrast with Woolf, Bowen does not clearly advocate dispensing with dysfunctional plots and starting anew. Falling silent in the midst of their "rasping wordy battle," Stella and Harrison, "though fated to speak again, could be felt to be depersonalized speakers in a drama which should best of all have remained silent as it essentially was" (139, 140). Considering what they *do* say when they speak again and again, one is tempted to conclude that despite Bowen's dense narrative and abundance of dialogue, nothing can be said that could change the drama's outcome.

Or perhaps it is because of Bowen's fidelity to "realism" that the novel reinforces the idea of narrative destiny. Stella, who "felt herself . . . going to a rendezvous inside the pages of a book" (87), and Nettie, who dismisses the possibility of a "different story," seem in agreement with the narrator, for whom the "rules of fiction, with which life to be credible must comply," constitute recognizable parameters for lived reality (140). But this yardstick sets epistemological and ontological limitations even greater than those faced by Burdekin and Smith, who at least saw radical potential in narrative experimentation. "Rules of fiction" can prove a catch-22 when one assumes, like Bowen, that the novel imposes "orthodox demands," including strict adherence to verisimilitude. She consequently worked under a "steadying" rather than a liberating influence (*MT* 130). Thus, despite the novel's marked resistance to the frequently onerous scripts of women's reality, *The Heat of the Day* ultimately conforms to the weighty pressure of literary realism, which naturalizes and congeals life as it is. The resulting internal disconsonance palpably contributes to the novel's sense of "struggle" and "strain" (Lee 164).

A third female character embodies both the conceptual limitations imposed by Bowen's chosen novel form and her tendency to sabotage her own "resistance writing." Appropriately bearing two traditionally male names, Louie Lewis embraces and enacts the phallogocentric injunction that "in the beginning was the word; and to that it came back in the long run" (*HD* 151). Naïve and inarticulate, socially and politically disenfranchised, Louie, whose husband's absence leaves her without identity or purpose, finds "peace" only in reading newspapers. She privileges their censored ordering of reality over independent inquiry and self-determination: "What a mistake to have gone by the look of things!" Allowing headlines to decide "every event's importance by the size of the print . . . Louie . . . discovered that she *had* got a point of view, and not only a point of view but the right one." Moreover, she finds in the newspapers' propagandistic, hegemonic voice a welcome catalogue of definition:

> Was she not a worker, a soldier's lonely wife, a war orphan . . . a home- and animal-lover, a thinking democrat . . . a woman of Britain,

a letter writer, a fuel-saver, and a housewife? She was only not a
mother, a knitter, a gardener . . . or a sweetheart. . . . Louie now felt
bad only about any part of herself which in any way did not fit into
the papers' picture; she could not have survived their disapproval.
[152][24]

Of course, Bowen here mocks Louie and her eager claim to this
series of stock roles. Nevertheless, with good reason readers have tended
to identify Louie as one of the novel's redemptive figures to whom the
future is entrusted.[25] Barbara Watson, to cite one example, quite astutely
reads *The Heat of the Day* as a novel of epistemological uncertainty, a state
highlighted rather than created by the war. But she also quite reasonably
sees in Louie an unproblematic guarantor of much-needed continuity.
The novel's conclusion, in which Louie has returned to her pastoral roots,
conventionally brings the reader full circle; in both season and time of day,
the novel ends exactly three years after it opens. Now a widow, Louie lifts
up her infant son to behold the promising vision of three swans flying
overhead where there had recently been warplanes. As Harriet Blodgett
has noted, the upbeat thrust of this conclusion is unmistakable. Louie has
not only survived the war unscathed, but the baby's life has "taught her
sense" and made her life "now complete" (329). Louie and the novel find
classical completion together; things change but, paradoxically, everything
stays the same. The future *has* been placed in Louie's instinctively maternal
hands, but the "sense" she makes out of life comes straight from the
ready-made fictions Bowen otherwise finds false and dangerously limiting.
The baby's name provides the final and most obvious clue that something
is amiss. Thomas Victor, whose father is unknown, nevertheless to Louie
bears an uncanny resemblance to her war-killed husband, also named
Thomas. Louie thus reincarnates her husband and, even more ominously,
Stella's ex-husband, both of whom (like the demon lover) suspend or
undermine the epistemological and ontological integrity of the women
they claim. Adumbrated by Stella's capitulation, this conclusion represents
on Bowen's part a move from resistance to reinscription of the male-
dominant status quo.

Louie's subplot parallels that of Roderick, Stella's son, the other
supposedly redemptive character making claims on the future. Roderick's
youthful innocence and good intentions tend to overshadow the textual
evidence that he completes the male triad, whose shared goal is (re)asser-
tion of unattenuated male authority. Thus, as Barbara Watson points out,
in the novel "hope" seems finally to "lie in preservation [Roderick]
and generation [Louie]" (132). The polarized, complementary, and mutually re-creative fates of these two characters—apotheosis through male

mastery or female motherhood—could not be more normalizing and are clearly disconsonant with the "other" plots' subversively aberrant women's stories. Furthermore, this disjunction reproduces Bowen's own struggle with the problem of literary and personal inheritance, for Roderick and Louie respectively embody the very "shortcomings"—patrilineage and maternity—that force Bowen's break with her ancestral continuity and are presumably related to her compensatory adherence to a conservative literary form.

The ambivalence that produces the novel's competing discourses most poignantly resides in Stella, the character most like Bowen herself. Both Stella and her creator are the same age as the century. In a letter (of January 1941) to Virginia Woolf, Bowen confided that she felt "a sort of despair about my own generation—the people the same age as the century, I mean—we don't really suffer much but we get all sealed up" (*MT* 218). For Bowen, a woman of the generation caught "*entre les guerres*," an era of brightest hopes and darkest disillusionment, of unsettling change and depressing sameness, World War II constituted a personal and epochal midlife crisis. As Stella knows, "The fateful course of her fatalistic century seemed more and more her own: together had she and it arrived at the testing extremities of their noonday," an allusion to the novel's title (*HD* 134). Much had been lost but the gains remained unclear or elusive; a midcourse correction seemed called for, but toward what? Bowen captures this sense of abandonment and lack of direction in "The Disinherited" (1934), about whose paradigmatic character the narrator comments, "The old order left him stranded, the new offered him no place" (*CS* 388).[26]

Stella, having gained unprecedented financial independence and sexual freedom—having escaped from the parlor into the world—likewise feels lost between what has been and what could be. As she explores Cousin Nettie's drawing room at Mount Morris, which recalls the symbolic space of the patrilineal "lasting order" Bowen envisioned for Bowen's Court, Stella looks into the antique mirrors with "some sense of herself missing" and observes a face that wears "the look of everything she had lost the secret of being" (*HD* 173, 174). Drawn to the familiarity and stability of the illusory past, she nonetheless finally "turn[s] away from it," repudiating the trap it represents. Stella knows she is saved from the fate of Cousin Nettie ("and who now knew how many before her") because "the fatal connection between the past and future [had] been broken. . . . It had been Stella, her generation, who had broken the link" (174, 176). Like any fundamental change, however, this one is painful; she feels "its broken edges . . . grating inside her soul." The difficult and awkward period between the past and the future she must endure has left her, she seems to feel, with "freedom in nothing," but this is merely the transition, not the end result: "That her own life should be a chapter missing from this book need not mean that the story was at an end—at a pause it was, but perhaps a pause for the turning point?" (175). The question remains unanswered.

Bowen had previously articulated this tension between continuity and transformation (or collaboration and resistance) vis-à-vis the war's unsettling force in one of her best and longest stories, "Summer Night" (1941). As William Heath observes, this particular tale anticipates the "intellectual history rendered in *The Heat of the Day*" (105) and, I would add, her personal struggle. All the female characters strive to cope with stifling restraint by exhibiting personally aberrant behavior engendered, Bowen implies, by the provocative ambiance of the war. Emma, married to a man called simply "the Major," is on her way to consummate a love affair, her first. The old and mostly ignored Aunt Fran, habitually passive and uncomplaining, uncharacteristically responds to the Major's patronizing with anger and pentup resentment: "It's never me, never me. . . . Whatever *I* see, whatever I hear it's 'nothing.'. . . I am never told . . . . I am never allowed to go and see!" (*CS* 597). Emma's young daughter Vivie at the same time senses "anarchy . . . all through the house." In a scene charged with sexual tension, she runs naked through rooms in which "human order seemed to have lapsed" (596). Having tattooed her body with colored chalk, "she ben[ds] right down and squint[s], upside down between her legs, at the bedroom" (597). Armed with this inverted perspective, she dances on her parents' bed in unconscious defiance of authority and bankrupt sexual arrangements: "The springs bounced her higher and higher; chalk dust flew from her body . . . on to the two cold pillows that she was trampling out of their place. The bed castors lunged, under her springing, over the threadbare pink bridal carpet of Emma's room." Restless and uneasy on this evening in which thoughts of the distant war preoccupy the Major, the women of the house protest the usually subdued patterns of their lives.

But well established patterns are not so easily disturbed. Emma's clandestine rendezvous disappoints because of her would-be lover's "imperturbable male personality" (588). His "authoritative male room" and "stern, experienced delicacy" in the matter of romantic liaisons cools Emma's ardor and kills the "adventure . . . at its root" (603, 604, 605). When old Aunt Fran discovers naked Vivie, tattooed like a heathen and jumping on her parents' bed, she berates her, "Do you not know what is wicked?" (598). She rolls Vivie up in her mother's pink eiderdown "until only the prisoner's dark eyes, so like her mother's, were left free." Thus the heritage of submission and conformity passes from generation to generation.

The imprint of the past cannot be erased or even dimmed for Aunt Fran, despite her frustrated outburst, because she cannot question, much less reject, the deeply inculcated belief that women who challenge the traditional and supposedly God-ordained order of things are unnatural or evil. She stifles Vivie's rebellious exuberance in atonement for having resentfully lashed out against the consequences of that unimpeachable order for women like herself. To subdue Vivie, whose name signifies life itself, is to contain the "violence of the stranger within [Fran's] ribs," the repressed self who was the source of "the evil . . . moment when she had cried, 'It is never me!'" (598, 599). Utterly ashamed and self-admonishing, Aunt Fran chooses to "abase herself . . . for them all"—for all those who would betray the past lifelessly contained in her "musty" keepsakes from which the "original virtue had by now almost evaporated" (599, 598). "The blood of the world is poisoned," she mourns, "even the heroes shed black blood. . . . [W]ho shall stem the black tide coming in? There are no more children: the children are born knowing. . . . There is not even the past: our memories share with us the infected zone; not a memory does not lead up to this. Each moment . . . holds the war in its crystal" (599). War-begotten unrest, loss of innocence, and especially any change that threatens to invalidate Aunt Fran's life and very being—these constitute the evil for which the war here, as in *Bowen's Court,* becomes an objective correlative. "What's the matter tonight," she wonders, "is there a battle? This is a threatened night" (599).

"In the Square" (1941), in contrast, posits and celebrates precisely those avenues of personal release and social transformation that seem blocked in "Summer Night." When an old friend pays a social call on Magdela, a woman he hasn't seen since before the war, he finds little of the past intact. Surrounded by ruins, relics "belonging to some ages ago," Magdela senses the process of transformation and its longterm potential (*CS* 609). With the nuclear family dispersed and day-to-day priorities rearranged, her house has become a sort of commune. And her drawing room, once the "room of a hostess" is now "dead" (610)—rather like Nettie's, but in this instance the drawing room's demise optimistically signals revitalization. "Who would think this was the same world?" Magdela asks (611). "Sometimes I think I hardly know myself," she pensively admits, but adds, "You know, I am happy" (615). The story ends as she asks her visitor his impressions of London: "Do you think we shall all see a great change?" But Magdela has already answered the question for herself: "[S]o much has happened. . . . So much more than you know" (612).[27]

Thus, though Bowen may revere and often privilege the past and continuity, destabilized by the wars and the subsequent move toward socialism, her position is not nearly so straightforward nor her outlook so dark as some have concluded.[28] The good old days syndrome that seems to pervade her texts is belied by the repeated uneasy admission that (again, as in *Bowen's Court*) much about those days wasn't so good. In "Summer Night," for example, a passionate though displaced call for escape from old conceptual paradigms and inadequate forms of expression (which mirrors Virginia Woolf's similar call in *Between the Acts*) struggles against complacency, insensibility, and stagnation. Justin Cavey, whose words, significantly, fall on deaf ears (for his male audience won't hear him and his deaf sister can't), speaks out for a "new form for thinking and feeling" (*CS* 589). The war, he argues, has been "an awful illumination; it's destroyed our dark; we have to see where we are. Immobilized . . . and each so far apart that we can't even try to signal each other" (590). Efforts at connection and communion are further hampered by outworn modes of representation: "what we say doesn't even approximate to reality; it only approximates what's been said. . . . And our currency's worthless—our 'ideas.'. . . We've got to mint a new one." But reconceptualization and rebirth are contingent on "annihilation" of those ways of seeing and being that isolate and ex-communicate, such as the concept of a "self" in isolation (591). "Scrap 'me,'" Justin declares, "scrap my wretched identity and you'll bring open some bud of life. I *not* 'I'—I'd be the world . . . and I'd *think*. I might see . . . I might even love."

Justin Cavey, advocate of the truly new, stands in contradistinction to Aunt Fran, guardian of the menaced status quo. Both recognize the war's pivotal potential. Together they provide yet another figuration of Bowen's dilemma. If the "musty" old cultural forms, to which Aunt Fran desperately clings and in which Bowen finally seems immured, undermine or normalize the otherwise subversive stories of women like Nettie and Stella, how, then, does the storyteller open a congenial space in which the "other" story can unfold without being compromised by an imposed shape, the "old currency"?[29] Bowen clearly had misgivings about tampering with forms—especially the classical realist novel—which she thought suited to her temperament and/or to the nature of (a) reality. But she also believed that "as a generation, we writers are in a transitional, learning stage . . . the old simplicities of the world are gone. . . . Our century, as it takes its frantic course, seems barely habitable . . . we have to survive while we learn to write" (*SW&A* 81). Toward that end, even Bowen sometimes took old inimical stories firmly into her authorial control and refashioned them, repudiating the masculinist ideology they enclose and affirm.

When Stella, for example, contemplates Roderick's future as master of Mount Morris, she welcomes the solidity and meaningfulness of his destiny. But fresh from her epiphanal visit to Nettie's drawing room, crowded with the ghosts of silent women whose eyes flash "candid and clear . . . warnings," Stella matches "Cousin Francis's egotistic creative boldness" in appropriating a son for his future with a boldly creative act of her own (*HD* 175). She cannot deny marriage, the telos of romance; instead, in order to modify the future she rescripts the primal creation of woman. Looking into the unknown, Stella conjures an image of Roderick's wife-to-be. Her vision of "that future creature came into being mistily . . . the daughter-in-law curled forming like ectoplasm out of Stella's flank. Unmistakably, however, from the bride's fluid anatomy stood out *eyes*—unspent and fearless" (175). The ancient stories, in which women invariably constitute not the I but the Other, are dangerously inadequate to accommodate the transformations set in motion when the women of Stella's (and Bowen's) generation broke that fatal link between past and future female ways of being. Sensing this, Stella unconsciously rewrites the creation myth and from her own mind and body creates a new Eve—autonomous, courageous, and woman-born.

Stella's reclamation of female generativity bespeaks Bowen's periodic assertion of her own creative authority. The final story in her wartime collection stands as a brilliant example of the resulting mythopoesis. In "Mysterious Kôr" (1944), Pepita lives in a London whose appearance suggests the male modernist wasteland—"shallow, cratered, extinct" (*CS* 728). But Pepita, strolling through the desolate landscape with her soldier lover, sees no wasteland; she sees Kôr—a mythical city "with no history," a city "altogether different" from bombed out London (729). Pepita knows of Kôr from an obscure poem, a line of which—"the world is disenchanted"— once set her to "hating civilization" (730). Since the war began, however, she has "cheered up," for like Stella, she knows the war could be a crucial turning point: "This war shows we've by no means come to the end. If you can blow whole places out of existence, you can blow whole places into it. I don't see why not. They say we can't say what's come out since the bombing started. By the time we've come to the end, Kôr may be the one city left: the abiding city. I should laugh."[30]

Arthur, her lover, typically tries to invalidate her interpretation of the poem, claiming it means, "Kôr's not really anywhere." Gently but with conviction, she rebukes him: "What it tries to say doesn't matter: I see what it makes me see. Anyhow, that was written some time ago . . . when they thought they had got everything taped" (*CS* 730). Refusing such certainty and closure, Pepita unhesitantly rewrites the myth of Kôr to meet her needs and to express her hopeful vision. It thereby provides her with sustenance others lack. "I don't know how other girls manage," she says. "I always think about Kôr." Although abandoned for millennia, Kôr is "very strong; there is not a crack in it anywhere for a weed to grow in; the corners of stones and monuments might have been cut yesterday, and the stairs and arches are built to support themselves" (729). Indestructible, self-sustaining, and unfettered by history, Kôr awaits those who believe in it.

The clarity and confidence of Pepita's mythic vision almost converts Arthur, who admits that new realities begin as dreams: "from the way she saw it I saw it, too. . . . [W]hy not want Kôr, as a start?" (738). Pepita loves Arthur and includes him in her dream. But Arthur's mythical name signifies the wrong kind of story, the kind that professes egalitarian and chivalrous ideals, but in truth recapitulates the dominance/submission paradigm and ultimately engenders only deceit, distrust, sorrow, and war. Thus, her vision does not depend on Arthur, but transcends him. That night, as she lies in the magical light of a powerful moon, a sign of female generativity, Pepita has "an avid dream, of which Arthur had been the source, of which Arthur was not the end. With him she looked . . . down the wide, void, pure streets. . . . With him she went up the stairs down which nothing but moon came. . . . He was the password, but not the answer: it was to Kôr's finality that she turned" (739-40). All wars find surcease on the moonlit streets of this mythical city, which, paradoxically, owes its resurrection to the war-induced vision of a woman true to the "other" story—not the culturally inscribed one she has been brought up on, but a reinscription of her own making.[31]

Similarly, "Mysterious Kôr" itself represents the mythic vision of Pepita's creator, who in this case refused fidelity to a deeply resonant story from her past, for Bowen's tale is a powerful revision of H. Rider Haggard's *She* (1884). That Bowen chose this particular tale and recast it as she did at this precise moment in history reveals a great deal about her response to the war. For Bowen, *She* had multiple and overlapping significance: a fictional enactment of an ancestral compulsion, her introduction to "adult" myth—or, more accurately to "masculinist mythology" (Gilbert and Gubar, *Sexchanges* 5)—and, perhaps most importantly, her awakening to the enormous power of the written word. The text of "Mysterious Kôr," then, provides a crucial signpost by which we can map a flareup of unmitigated resistance.

In 1947 Bowen devoted a radio broadcast to her meditations on *She*, which she first encountered in 1912, the year she became aware of her "grudge against actuality" and the need for adult myths (*SW&A* 229). Appalled by geography's "absence of prospect," which left no new country to discover, and depressed by history's ample testimony to the "uniformity of the human lot" (230), Bowen turned to fiction and stumbled upon *She*. Its "soaring unrealism" seemed a timely response to her longing for hidden places and unknown histories just waiting to be uncovered (231). Fascinated by Kôr, the ancient ruined city, and She, whose "triumphant obstination" and "proud, ambitious spirit" seemed to assure fulfillment of Her personal and political desires, Bowen experienced "the first totally violent impact [she had] ever received from print" (234, 235, 236). Many years and many stories later, World War II reawakened her quiescent recollection of this fabulous tale, which emerged metamorphosed after its long incubation in the chrysalis of her now "overcharged subconscious."

Like a mythic Bowen's Court, Kôr is the point of origin and return for an individual quest impelled by inheritance and tradition. "Ruled by a continuity that [he] cannot see," Haggard's hero Leo Vincey, like Bowen, must contend with his legacy. Despite Bowen's disclaimer that she "saw little point in Leo" (234), he represents, on the one hand, all she cannot be but guiltily feels she should have been and, on the other, everything she resents and would repudiate, especially the imperious assumption of male authority and inevitable conquest figured by his name. Accordingly, he encounters and ultimately defeats a vindictive but beguiling woman with monstrous powers, ruler of an alien culture in which women live in "perfect equality with men" (Haggard 173). As Gilbert and Gubar argue, She represents an "objectification of primordial female otherness," both the classic femme fatale and the mythic New Woman (*Sexchanges* 7). Daring to "oppose herself against the eternal Law," She "would have revolutionized society, and even perchance have changed the destiny of mankind" (Haggard 276). But a phallic preemptive strike (in the form of an erect "pillar of fire") consumes Her, reducing She-Who-Must-Be-Obeyed to her ostensibly true form, that of a hideous, helpless beast who then dies. Haggard's story, Gilbert and Gubar conclude, thus confirms the "inexorability of . . . patriarchal law" (20).

Bowen's revision of Haggard's tale indicates that, consciously or not, she appreciated its ideological significance and its potential for subversive reformation. As conflicted at every turn as Bowen was during the war, her recollected response to this "historic" story was no doubt varied and complex (*SW&A* 236). But her discovery that its "magic" inhered not in its characters but in the act of *writing*, her "revelation" of the incomparable "power of the . . . inventive pen" seems to have inspired her to rescript this story when all that had been "germinating" during this war compelled and authorized her to do so (236-37).

Pepita's self-justification, "If you can blow whole places out of existence, you can blow whole places into it," articulates England's optimism, born of both hope and desperation, that the war's disorder and destruction would paradoxically engender true reconstruction. J.B. Priestley, for example, wrote that because war "compel[s] us to change not only our ordinary, social and economic habits, but also our habits of thought," it portends a "glorious beginning of a new world order" (*PS* 38). In *Their Finest Hour* Alan Kendall observes that "people were aware that the war had created tremendous opportunities, and that mankind had been given a challenge. . . . It was as if the areas of devastation had suddenly opened up immense vistas" (90). And *Mass Observation* (a social survey organization) reported that people generally believed the war meant that "nothing was ever going to be quite the same again. The blitz had been 'the end of *a* world'" (quoted in Calder 293).

Though none of these cultural historians had anything like Bowen's Kôr remotely in mind, photographer Cecil Beaton inadvertently provided a poetically just image for the demolished order giving way to make room for the new: "Milton's statue has been flung from its plinth," he recorded in his diary during the blitz (quoted in Hewison, *Under Siege* 28). As if to free Bowen (and others) to explore her own version of paradise regained, Milton is dethroned. Accordingly, the whole and pristine landscape Bowen recreates in "Mysterious Kôr"—in which women and men can once again walk in "perfect equality"—gracefully and immutably displaces both Adam and Eve's mythical garden and the postlapsarian wasteland of war. In Bowen's urban Eden the emphasis shifts from individuals or countries battling for power and preeminence to a symbolic location—a consciousness—that transcends recorded history and physical geography. In accordance with her youthful ideal, Bowen's literary revision thus truly denies those very limitations—the "absence of prospects" and history's dispiriting redundancies—that Haggard's fantastic narrative at first blush seems to deny but, instead, emphatically reconstitutes. In Bowen's antidotal reconstruction of Kôr, new territories—new states of consciousness—*do* await discovery: history need *not* repeat itself endlessly. Kôr's citizen and sustainer, an ordinary woman, does not seek to subject but to share. The "triumphant obstinance" of her will strives to convert rather than to coerce. Significantly, the vision of She that Bowen recalls in her radio broadcast resembles Stella's image of the future mistress of Mount Morris, the succeeding female generation; for Bowen cannot picture Her face except for "two eyes burning their way through . . . layers of gauze" (236). By association, then, even an Anglo-Irish patriarchal stronghold holds the potential for mythopoeic transformation.

To conclude, however, with Bowen's subversive, utopian vision would be misleading and unfaithful to her wartime writing as a whole. Ultimately, in her consideration of the war's transformative potential, she remained as divided and equivocal as ever. In "I Hear You Say So" (1945), her only story set immediately after the war's end, Bowen continues to draw from and transform mythic material, but her narrative's psychic climate is cautious and imprecise. To be sure, as dusk falls, "no miracle seemed impossible" (*CS* 751). The unexpected song of a nightingale, which portends London's postwar reawakening, moves one woman to wonder, "suppose the world was made for happiness, after all?" (753). But as the unseen bird "sang into incredulity like the first nightingale in Eden," its song's implicit promise of peace and paradise carries the burden of too much frustrated longing, too much irrevocable loss. It thus prompts a tragic denial of hope: "We're not made for this, we can't take it." In others, the bittersweet song variously evokes disbelief, indifference, or resentment. As one listener observes, "it's too soon. Much too soon, after a war like this" to feel, to plan, to begin anew (755).

Only Ursula, a young widow whose husband was killed in the war, listens to the nightingale's song with "profound happiness" (757). Although she regrets the "irreparable loss" of her life with Roland and the future they had hoped would yield a "magic recapturing of the past," news of his death has triggered welcome release from that over-determined future and from the martyred "narrow form" of Saint Ursula, the legendary British princess with whom she is identified. Saint Ursula and her eleven hundred virgin handmaids were killed by the Huns (757, 756). But in this Ursula's here and now, rather than sacrificial virgins the Germans have killed Roland, whose epic precursor pursued martial glory unto death—his and that of hundreds of others. For Britain, Bowen seems to imply, Saint Ursula's legend no longer pertains, Roland's song no longer resonates. Roland's grandmother finds this tragic. And even for Ursula, the brief nightingale's song, with its almost intolerable promise of rebirth, remains elusive and indecipherable. As the last notes fade, Ursula looks at the carpet beneath her feet, "wondering if a secret were in its pattern." But she can discern no portent, no sign of what war's end will bring, for "naturally, it was too dark to see" (757).

Bowen's search for the causes of war and some clue to its outcome appropriately began with the pattern she discerned in Bowen's Court, the construction of which provides a self-reflexive metaphor for the writing process: "A good deal that . . . Henry Bowen could not foresee was built into Bowen's Court as the walls went up. In building as in writing, something one did not reckon with always waits to add itself to the plan. In fact, if this (sometimes combative) unexpected element be not present, the building or book remains academic and without living force" (*BC* 31-32). Although feelings of loss, guilt, and impropriety moved her to deny knowledge of the unexpected element—the "resistance writing"—that permeates her wartime texts, by her own criterion they are charged with "living force." For although the loyalties of a writer such as Bowen to her "strongly personal and . . . inherited sense of life" are "involuntary . . . and . . . the more powerful for that," she also pledged fidelity to Graham Greene's injunction that, for writers, "disloyalty" must be a "virtue" (*SW&A* 67, 63). Still, betrayal of one's "hereditary influences," she explained a few years after the war, necessarily creates a "crisis . . . felt in [one's] personal . . . and aesthetic being" (*SW&A* 68). World War II triggered precisely this crisis in Bowen, who observes that its "glaring ordeal" seemed "to seek out and demand truth" ("On Writing" 11). Like the characters in *The Heat of the Day,* though, she "at once dread[ed] and desire[d]" that truth, which murkily emerges from a discourse double-voiced in the extreme (11). Despite her sometimes passionate resistance, Bowen's wartime writing poignantly illustrates Stella's plaint that one "never was out of reach of the power of what had been written first" (*HD* 133).

4

Re-Plotting the War(s)
Virginia Woolf's Radical Legacy

Prof Huxley . . . warns us that "any considerable alteration of the hereditary constitution is an affair of millennia, not of decades." [Thus],
as science also assures us that life on earth is "an affair of millennia,
not of decades," some alteration in the hereditary constitution may
be worth attempting.
                                        —Virginia Woolf, *Three Guineas* (1938)

In one sense, Virginia Woolf spent a lifetime trying to "tell the truth
about war" (*TG* 97). Even before the 1930s, war and suggestions of its
deepest origins as well as its far-reaching, often insidious consequences
broke through the seemingly placid surface of her narratives with significant frequency.[1] Always implicit in her censure of war was her awareness
of the need for deep-seated change, not only in gender relations but
throughout the web-like structure of human existence. For, like Burdekin
and Smith, Woolf traced the roots of war to divisive, adversarial habits of
mind—paradigms of difference and opposition of which the male-female
dichotomy seemed the most fundamental. Her deceptively simple anti-
dote, to "live differently," entails a complex and sophisticated philosophy
that informs her entire "oeuvre" and evolved over a lifetime. Still, the approach of World War II, which at once carried the threat and promise of
change, naturally created a sense of urgency and intensified Woolf's inner
dialogue. Somewhat paradoxically, the possibility of life-affirming change
never so thoroughly informed her consciousness and her art as in the years
preceding the war. Nevertheless, as others have noted, this advent of yet
another, even more destructive world war inevitably and insistently forced
Woolf to confront many questions regarding the possibility and nature of
any true deviation from history's endless refrain of violence.

As James Naremore has argued, her penultimate novel reveals the
ambivalence and irony the approaching war engendered for Woolf in this
regard.[2] In *The Years* (1937), which spans the two pre–world war eras,
a great deal—and yet nothing—appears to change. Referring to Nurse

Cavell's maxim that "Patriotism is not enough," a phrase open to interpretation as either a critique of jingoism or an expression of war's traditional rhetoric of sacrifice, young Peggy North cynically concludes, "It didn't come to much" (336).[3] In other words, neither the bitterly ironic antiwar sentiment nor the dutiful sacrifice of life and limb changed anything at all, as the imminent resumption of overt hostilities too eloquently testified.

Yet in *The Years* change is on everyone's mind, never more intensely than when the two wars disrupt the complacent rhythms of everyday life. While waiting out an air raid during World War I, Eleanor Pargiter shares in a toast to "the New World," in which, finally, "We shall be free" (292, 297). "Do you think we're going to improve?" she asks. Yes, she is told, "It is only a question . . . of learning . . . to expand; to adventure; to form—new combinations" (295, 296). Twenty years later, on the eve of World War II, Eleanor still dreams of "something different . . . another kind of civilisation" (335). Similarly, her nephew North wistfully meditates on the possibility of "a different life," one made possible by a psychic metamorphosis, a "new ripple in human consciousness" (410). But to think, to see, to live differently by forming "new combinations"—such efforts are repeatedly thwarted, as becomes painfully clear during the Pargiter family gathering that ends the novel. Yet, in the final scene the new day conspicuously dawns, seeming to promise "extraordinary beauty, simplicity and *peace*" (435, emphasis added). Woolf thus ambiguously ends on a brighter note than circumstances seem to warrant. Though faced with discouraging realities, she refused to relinquish the eventual possibility of life-affirming changes in human consciousness, of a "different" life. As Eleanor's niece Maggie joyously exults, "Nothing was fixed; . . . life was open and free before them" (382).

Of course, Woolf did not always share such happily unsullied optimism, especially not as she observed the increasing menace fascism represented. But she continued to place the same hopeful question before her readers—"Do you think we're going to improve?"—and to refine her own tentative, partial answer. In her final novel, *Between the Acts* (1941), once again the possibility of change becomes a foremost concern. The village pageant's quick progression through centuries of history prompts the audience to consider, "D'you think people change?" (121). And at its conclusion, they ask whether the pageant meant "that if we don't jump to conclusions, if you think, and I think, perhaps one day, thinking differently, we shall think the same?" (200). Or are we doomed, they wonder, to "answer to the infernal, agelong and eternal order. . . . And obey[?]" (119).

Here Woolf voices the possibility of failure and pointedly leaves the questions unanswered, for in 1941, the war's "darkest hour," she found assertions of hope against evidence to the contrary harder to come by.[4] In *Three Guineas* (1938), her sardonic and sometimes angry analysis of the fascism inherent in patriarchal culture, Woolf had encouraged "complete indifference" to war (107). One can hardly remain indifferent, however, to a war that threatened, as Woolf put it, "the complete ruin not only of civilisation in Europe but of our last lap" (*WD* 289). One cannot remain indifferent to the fall of France, the Blitz, the constant threat of Axis invasion, and the daily possibility of death. Understandably, the realities of war colored her perceptions and enlarged her experience, inducing at times profound ambivalence and doubt.

The dark side of Woolf's wartime responses has led some commentators to conclude that she experienced a profound crisis of faith, which led to a surrender of previously held ideals, especially her hope for a transformed future.[5] Indeed, Woolf's last novel has frequently been read not only as an elegy for everything Woolf cherished but (to quote Herbert Marder) as "the longest suicide note in the English language" (467): *Between the Acts* as an indication of Woolf's "bankrupt" faith and mournful longing for England's traditional past (Zwerdling 305); a renouncement of the efficacy of language (and, by implication, literature) (Sears); a reflection of her "deep pessimism about the human condition" (Squier 188); an assertion of the triumph of misogyny (Marcus, "LSM"); and, finally, even a relinquishing of Woolf's feminist resistance to the cultural centrality of masculinism (Moore).

To be sure, the war did induce a crisis that led Woolf through a maze of introspection and re-analysis. The Axis threat forced her to reexamine both her espousal of pacifism and eschewal of patriotism. The war clearly intensified an ambivalence she had always experienced, if not acknowledged: her antipathy toward the inequities inherent in England's patriarchal culture and a deep-seated affection for a culturally specific way of life. Worse, war's thickening desolation tended to cloud Woolf's inner vision of reality as "a unity that rubs out divisions" and her related belief in "the capacity of the human spirit to overflow boundaries and make unity out of multiplicity" (*TG* 11, 143.) Perhaps most troubling of all, the pattern of war following war forced her to question her faith in the political efficacy of writing, and intensified her normally periodic doubts about the ultimate worth of her own work.

Nevertheless, her wartime novel suggests that although shaken and bruised, Woolf did not, ultimately, soften her critique or abandon her radical views. Quite the contrary, the war, which signified yet another chapter in civilization's perverse romance with self-annihilation, mandated even more vigorous exposure of and resistance to masculinist culture and a continued championing of her feminist philosophy. Transformation of

patriarchal ways of seeing and being—living differently—became imperative. In fact, she found in World War II a unique opportunity: the violent
eruption of fascism could precipitate not only its own demise, but the beginning of the very psychosocial transformation she had long been working toward. Thus, despite feelings of ambivalence, doubt and, in the worst
moments, despair, Woolf redoubled her efforts to tell the truth about war
and refused to betray the future by writing failure into its script.

Accordingly, like Burdekin and Smith, she exposes and critiques the
foundational inter-dependence of sexual and martial politics and plots.
Throughout the fabric of British culture represented in *Between the Acts*—
in its institutions, history, traditions, and art, as well as in its families and
individual "subjects"—Woolf discerns interlocking patterns of fascism,
imperialism, and geopolitical war. More explicitly than Burdekin or Smith,
Woolf argues (in *Room*) that without the continuous reestablishment and
validation of masculinity as an opposite and superior reflection of the
"feminine," there would be no war. She thus found the seemingly ineluctable masculine/feminine divide to be fundamental to a whole system of
hierarchized binary opposites. But hierarchical structures are inherently
unstable. The sex-gender system, for example, must be both self-defining
and self-perpetuating, systematically imbuing male and female with the
symbiotic subjectivities Woolf deemed essential to the making of war. This
is precisely, Woolf implies, what renders the "story" of men, women, and
war vulnerable to change.

Woolf attempts to model this change by introducing a *third alternative,* positing the existence of an unoffical "Outsiders' Society," whose
duty is to "live [and write] differently," in part by maintaining a "complete
indifference" to war (*TG* 106, 107). If "Outsiders" fail to cultivate "indifference" to the "false and unreal positions taken by the human form,"
humankind's potential "power to change and create new wholes" will
remain thwarted (114). Not to "live differently" is to "follow and repeat
and score deeper still the old worn ruts in which society, like a gramo-
phone whose needle has stuck," grinds out it deadly refrain (105)—a
metaphor to which she returns in *Between the Acts.*

As the very act of writing *Three Guineas* indicated, however, her
advocation of indifference constituted a deliberately extreme political strategy that, taken literally, few people—least of all Woolf—would have
wished to practice. Rather, "complete indifference" came to suggest a trope,
an expansive philosophical position "between the acts" of, on the one
hand, support for the twin goals of defending democracy and fighting fascism and, on the other, a critique of the habits of mind that make war seem
inevitable—a mediating space in which one could dwell *in difference,* that
is, "think differently" (9). The relative freedom of this Outsiders' space

allowed Woolf to reconcile an intensified attachment to her cultural roots—patriarchal and tyrannical as they were—with profound political convictions to which she had become even more committed. This reconciliation, realized in *Between the Acts,* successfully supports the dialectic "between a writer and the spirit of the age" that Madeline Moore argues Woolf fails to sustain (152). Woolf's denouncement of masculinism and female complicity in essays such as "Thoughts on Peace," in her wartime letters and speeches, and in *Between the Acts* indicates that after a lifetime of struggle, Woolf could not and did not, as Moore states, "[relinquish] her center in a female world, and cast her lot in with the men" (152).

In a revealing diary entry (November 1940) with provocative implications, Woolf positions herself outside of and in deconstructive opposition to the male literary/historical tradition. She claims a "double vision" that enables her to perceive the elusive nature of both the "word structure," the edifice of language that shapes reality, and "the man who makes it" (*D* 340). In her reading of male cultural texts, Woolf claims to have discerned "[l]ittle boys making sand castles . . . destructive of [their own] architecture." Male writers (she cites T.S. Eliot and H.G. Wells among others), privileged "tower dwellers" all, similarly construct the literary canon, walling in those like themselves and shutting out all others.[6] Woolf has no faith in their constructs and has renounced the religion in which "man is . . . God." Her cultural heresy places her in a "position . . . quite unlike" that of the destructive "boys." Indeed, she sees herself as "the sea which demolishes . . . [their] castles." In this passage Woolf exudes a calm self-confidence and clear sense of purpose consonant with the hopeful aspects of her ambivalence—her belief that writing has transformative potential and that her work, especially within the circumference of the war, is of "more importance than ever" (*WD* 320). Although she speaks of demolishing sand castles, her choice of metaphors clearly implies that her sense of power connotes not simple destruction, but a cleansing rejuvenation, emblemized by the healing, transformative, and life-giving power of the sea. Furthermore, when considered from within the larger context of Woolf's philosophy, the reference to demolishing constructs in which she has no faith alludes not only to the literary tradition that initially prompted her comments, but to the entire edifice of patriarchal civilization, which threatens to crumble due to innate flaws.

A similarly dissenting perspective had surfaced months earlier, when she was discussing the future with some male friends, including Eliot. She found "all the gents. against [her]," all predicting "this war means that the barbarian will gradually freeze out culture. Nor have we improved. . . . So I flung some rather crazy theories into the air" (*D* 268).[7] Although discouraged and uncertain, Woolf advanced her "crazy theories" in defiance of the inevitability of barbarism, the impossibility of deviating from history's violent course. No doubt scoffed at by the "gents.," Woolf's earnest defiance came to life in *Between the Acts*—a work whose pages constitute not fragments shored up against the ruins, but a "rambling capricious but somehow unified whole" whose purpose was to "explore this possibility of seeing the great world from a new angle" (*WD* 279, *D* 182). Self-consciously critical of cultural, literary, and historical convention, Woolf tentatively posits the possibility of an alternative to the ostensibly immutable drama of human be-ing—the story of "loving arms." To this end, she realized her most passionate attempt to formulate a non-antagonistic epistemology, and to reeducate the human imagination toward the crucial "new combinations" she saw as fundamental to meaningful change. In this way Woolf did what she could to prepare the foundation for a rebuilt civilization without phallic towers and the self-destruct mechanisms they house—a futile gesture, perhaps, but not a surrender.

The deftness with which Woolf expands the parameters of war in *Between the Acts* even as she establishes it as her primary subject provides an illuminating example of her method of "indifference." As has frequently been noted, the novel's title suggests, among other things, the interval between the two world wars, a fact which establishes war's centrality to the novel as a whole. More specifically, Woolf sets *Between the Acts* in a time between but also determined by the acknowledged major acts of history, and in a space between but also including both the domestic and the public. She thus attempts to heal the fissure she observes in her culture's value system, which imbues literature and determines its worth. Since masculine "values . . . prevail," critics privilege books that "deal with war" over those that "deal with the feelings of women in a drawing-room" (*Room* 77). *Between the Acts* deals with the love/war plot(s) at once and inseparably, thus critiquing and obviating this paradigmatic dichotomy. As we shall see, in so doing Woolf creates a legible space that employs the antagonistic parameters of literary discourse *in order to transform them,* thus effecting an escape from the insidious confines of normative plot and history.[8]

Although the war is almost never specifically mentioned, its shadow darkens the landscape, evoking ire in some and dread in others. Giles Oliver's "vision of Europe, bristling with guns, poised with planes," and his awareness that "at any moment" these weapons could be turned on the countryside he loves provoke him to violence and frustrated rage (53). William Dodge, in contrast, passively dreads what seems to him the inevitable "doom of sudden death hanging over us" (114). Representing the possibility of a different response, *Between the Acts* negotiates these two extremes: jealous, angry aggression, which represents the focus of Woolf's critique of patriarchal ideology, and passive acquiescence to the "inevitable," which reflects her fears for the future. As the chameleon-like narrator explains, "The future shadowed their present" (114). But, Woolf insists, the shape of the future is not necessarily already written. As she explores this unfamiliar territory, Woolf harnesses her ambivalence and plots her ideological position.

Woolf's newly intensified feelings for England—its countryside, its traditions, and its culture—surface repeatedly in *Between the Acts,* perhaps most conspicuously in the characters' deep attachment to their land and its history.[9] Her fond depiction of the grounds at Pointz Hall and her choice of the traditional English pageant together evoke the pastoral tradition.[10] Her strong suggestion of a spiritual correspondence between people and nature may similarly seem indebted to conventional Romanticism. Lucy Swithin's preoccupation with the past and concern with origins, the numerous references to the persistence of the past in the present, as well as the narrator's frequent historical allusions and occasionally nostalgic tone all suggest a profound sense of cultural roots and unbroken continuity.[11] The barn to which the audience retreats for tea, for example, is described as "the Noble Barn, the barn that had been built over seven hundred years ago and reminded some people of a Greek temple" (99). To this "fine old Barn," Lucy Swithin claims, the same swallows return every year (101). Such images evoke an almost religious sense of ritual and renewal, both of which, on the eve of England's entrance to the war, were genuinely threatened.[12]

To conclude, however, as Alex Zwerdling has, that *Between the Acts* therefore articulates Woolf's "acute longing for an earlier, more civilized phase of English culture," one that is, for example, "feudal rather than democratic" (308, 309), does not acknowledge her antipathy for the overwhelming patriarchal bias in England's history and culture or the novel's equally strong resistance to blind entrapment in the patterns of the past.[13] Indeed, in contrast to T.S. Eliot, Woolf feared not that England's "once vital cultural tradition . . . ha[d] lost its authority and connection with the present" (Zwerdling 316), but, conversely, that this authority and connection were proving altogether too tenacious. However nostalgic Woolf may have been for a more peaceful time, she nevertheless balanced the novel's occasional tone of tender longing against the deliberate insertion of undercutting ironies. A cesspool, for example, is the disconcerting topic under discussion on the pastoral summer night on which the novel opens. Moreover, too often the relics of the past signify not the comfort of tradition and continuity, but the indelible imprint of invasion and conquest. From the air one can see, "plainly marked, the scars made by the Britons; by the Romans" (4).[14] Preserving their heritage of violence, the Olivers honor mementoes of war: "under a glass case there was a watch that had stopped a bullet on the field of Waterloo" (7), ironically a site synonymous with irrevocable loss.

Furthermore, emphatically resisting the "herd impulse" to idealize all things English, Woolf once again foregrounds the fascist nature of England's cultural hegemony—in both the larger real-life drama and the pageant it at once frames and mirrors (*WD* 291). Through the pageant, moreover, she excoriates the past for its tendency—which has condemned the present and jeopardizes the future—to repeat itself endlessly. Miss La Trobe immediately recognizes Pointz Hall, which lies "in the very heart of England," as "the very place . . . for a pageant" (*BA* 16, 57). And rightly so, for it has been and remains a theater for generations of tyranny— brother against sister and husband against wife. Bart Oliver and his widowed sister Lucy Swithin enact codified roles from the Victorian Age. A retired officer, Bart dreams of his idealized youth in India, but conjures only images of sterility and violent death: "no water . . . in the sand a hoop of ribs . . . and in his hand a gun" (17). He terrorizes his grandson in a perverse effort to teach him to be manly and dismisses Isa, his daughter-in-law, as inadequate for his son Giles's happiness. Further, he disparages, bullies, and silences Lucy, whom he has arbitrarily renamed Cindy (also "Sindy" in the text), thus asserting his ultimate authority to name her (like Eve) an avatar of moral error (21). In short, he is a patriarch of the old order, shamelessly oblivious to the psychic violence with which he maintains his privileged position. Finding sustenance only in his violent past and dedicated to maintenance of the status quo, Bart feels he "must respect the conventions" (203).

Lucy exhibits qualities that hold the potential to resist Bart's assumption of power. She has an active, curious intelligence and a rare capacity for perceiving reality in terms of fluid boundaries, connection, and mutuality. Lucy is the only one, for example, to note that geographical barriers (such as the English Channel) shift with time and that the supposedly progressive "march" of history is in one sense an illusion accomplished by changes of costume and scenery. Her unusually broad and inclusive perspective enables her to perceive the fallacy of insisting on "natural" and immutable barriers and categorization, to appreciate similarity and connection over difference and division. However, although Lucy tends to ignore the conventions Bart rigorously upholds, she ultimately deradicalizes her "one-making" by displacing it onto conventional religious mysticism. Woolf's depiction gently mocks Lucy's retreat from the conflict of the real world into the too easy comfort of religiosity:

> Mrs. Swithin caressed her cross. . . . She was off . . . one-making.
> Sheep, cows, grass, trees, ourselves—all are one. If discordant, pro-

ducing harmony—if not to us, to a gigantic ear attached to a gigantic head. And thus—she was smiling benignly—the agony of the particular sheep . . . or human being is necessary; and so . . . we reach the conclusion that *all* is harmony, could we hear it. And we shall. Her eyes now rested on the white summit of a cloud. [175]

Looking heavenward rather than to the attainment of a more harmonious life on earth, Lucy employs a readily available coping mechanism that enables her to "ignore the battle in the mud" (203). As Rachel Blau DuPlessis has noted, Lucy cannot divert her "religious spirit from its present servitude" toward "a spiritual commitment to the world as it might be" (*TG* 113, *WBE* 173).

Although she intuits that "we have other lives"—that the roles we play represent only one inadequate possibility—she is divided between a repressed truancy and learned deference to patriarchal authority (*BA* 70). As she and Dodge watch the audience assembling for the pageant that will chronicle England's history and literature, for example, she espies a "strapping clergyman . . . striding . . . with the air of a person of authority." "'Is it time . . . to go and join—'" she begins to ask, but leaves "the sentence unfinished, as if she were of two minds" (74). Drawn to the pageant and all that it ordinarily signifies, but deterred by the clergyman—always in Woolf's writing a symbol of patriarchal power and authority—Lucy hesitates. This fleeting moment neatly captures what seems to have been Woolf's own war-induced ambivalence. But, unlike Woolf, Lucy demurs only momentarily and for reasons she never dares to understand. Although she carries the symbolic hammer with which Isa envisions a raped woman resisting her violators, Lucy's token resistance is confined to using the hammer without permission. Moreover, nailing up the pageant announcement becomes the initiatory act in a ritualistic scene so habitual that year upon year "the same chime followed the same chime" (22). Resolving her conflict by aligning herself with the unimpeachable authority of the patriarchal God, and cowed by her brother's truculent ridicule, Lucy loses the opportunity both to assert her holistic vision as a constructive alternative to masculinist ways of ordering reality and to resist psychic and physical violence against women. Instead, she participates in the reproduction of historical patterns that condemn her to a "tragic" role (214). Lucy thus represents the failure to develop one's potential to "think differently."

Giles's role in the ongoing drama is that of a contemporary though less complacent version of his father. "Hirsute" and "virile," he can barely suppress violent anger at his forced passivity in the face of the war (106). Inwardly raging at everyone but his father, who with masculine solidarity remains "exempted from censure," he finally finds relief in the bloody crushing of a snake choking on a toad (53). His bloodstained shoes come to signify the "pure, self-assertive virility" (106)—here clearly exacerbated by the war—that Woolf foresaw in *A Room of One's Own* and identified with geopolitical fascism. His private violence and his alienation from Isa, his wife, stem not only from his emotional response to the impending war, but also from his conscious resentment of traditions, which have made him a slave to the "ghost of convention." Capitalism's success ethic, for example, has trapped him in meaningless work from which he gets no satisfaction (46). Since becoming a stockbroker, a self-perpetuating but utterly creationless role, he has felt "afflicted": "he was not given his choice. So one thing led to another; and the conglomeration of things pressed you flat" (47).

Once again Woolf emphasizes her conviction, expressed in *Room* and *Three Guineas,* that men are victims of their own tyrannical power and the closed, self-destructive system it supports. The snake that Giles kills provides an arresting metaphor for this situation. Just as civilization is choking on its own paradoxically life-denying culture, so too "the snake [is] unable to swallow." And just as these self-annihilating ways of seeing and being resist transformation, "the toad [is] unable to die. . . . It was birth the wrong way round—a monstrous inversion" (99). Significantly, it is Giles who crushes the snake, but the tragically ironic motivation for this symbolic act is not his unconscious desire for regeneration but his conscious need for violent and deadly action. Like his father before him, Giles does not question cultural conventions, though they sometimes "enrage" him (46). Also like his father, Giles locates the source of his unhappiness not in the system, but in various "unmanly" scapegoats—Lucy, on whom he "hung his grievances . . . instinctively" (46); Isa, at whom he directs his "pose of one who bears the burden of the world's woe, making money for her to spend" (111); and William Dodge, a homosexual who "conveniently" gives "Giles another peg on which to hang his rage" (60). Finally, continuing the patrilineage, Giles diverts his "anger disguised and complex" into aggression (*Room* 32). "Ancient instincts . . . fostered and cherished by education and tradition" enslave the Oliver men ("Thoughts" 175).

Like Giles, Isa inherits much from her models of previous generations. In her initial meeting with him, she had become "entangled" in his fishing line and had "given over" (*BA* 5, 48). Now "afraid . . . of her husband," Isa hides from him her poetry and her innermost self (50). Unable to actualize her desires or an independent personality, "abortive" Isa (15) embodies the squelched creativity of enforced domesticity that Woolf repeatedly condemns in earlier works. Although Isa "loathed the domestic, the possessive; the maternal," she remains their "captive" and dutifully dons the assigned psychic costumes of wife and mother "as if she . . . got out of one dress and put on another" (19, 105).

Nevertheless, in contrast with Lucy, Isa sometimes consciously rebels. Silently sneering at Giles's masculine posturing ("Silly little boy, with blood on his boots"), she refuses to act as his magnifying mirror (111). Moreover, she repeatedly envisions the rape she had read about earlier that day—troopers luring an unsuspecting woman into the barracks, her screams, her struggle. This story of violation, which explicitly links violence against women and military aggression, at times seems more "real" to Isa than the everyday stories that unfold around her. Exactly the same age as the century and thus its representative (like Stella Rodney), Isa recognizes the sickness that plagues her and her times and seeks a "remedy" for their condition (19). She wearies of the "burden" of the past "laid on [her] in the cradle"—the burden of subservience ("Rise up, donkey"), of victimization, of silence, of sterility ("The pear was hard as stone") (155). Still, though she exhorts herself to remember "the brawl in the barrack room when they stripped her naked," Isa struggles with ambivalence (156). Her inability to disengage from the drama of heterosexual romance, in which her role has become instinctive, compromises her rebellion.[15] Giles, as the "father of [her] children"—a "cliché conveniently provided by *fiction*"—evokes "pride; and affection" alongside her anger and contempt (14, emphasis added; 48). Conflicting emotions of love and hate, of possessiveness and repudiation, divide Isa, at once reinforcing and belying the fiction of domestic romance that, with cruel irony, defines her existence and remains her only "glory."

Male-centered Mrs. Manresa ("how they bored her—her own sex!" [106]) experiences no such conflict. Eager diversion for Giles, she is attracted and aroused by his assertive virility; his bloodstained shoes somehow "proved his valour for her admiration" (107). Enthusiastically fulfilling the role of seductive queen to her "sulky hero," she feels "in conspiracy" with Giles (107, 55). The true nature of her conspiracy lies in her willingness to serve as a magnifying "looking glass," that two-way mirror without which the "glories of all our wars would be unknown" (*Room* 35, 36). The depiction of Mrs. Manresa, with her red nails and her vain preoccupation with primping, clearly echoes Woolf's description (in "Thoughts on Peace") of women who are "slaves . . . trying to enslave"—"painted women . . . with crimson lips and crimson fingernails" (174). Though seeming to flaunt societal convention, Mrs. Manresa stands guilty of pernicious collusion with "Hitlerism."

To underscore her critique of the fascist nature of patriarchy and of the past's tendency to repeat itself, Woolf creates a surrogate, Miss La Trobe—an Outsider whose artistic vision reveals the truth as she perceives it, no matter how discomfiting. La Trobe's satirical critique of England's past society illuminates Woolf's depiction of the present. With its playlets, its interpolated narration, and its snatches of poetry and musical refrains, the pageant comprises a series of brief plots and implied narratives. Together they both parody and revise the drama of English history, whose many acts have differed only in plot detail, not in deep structure. Revising the position of Stephen Daedalus, the alter ego of her exact contemporary and male modernist counterpart, James Joyce, Woolf defines history as a nightmare from which she is trying to awaken others. A *Between the Acts* in miniature, La Trobe's pageant unconventionally moves between the sort of milestones by which history has been measured. Colonel Mayhew's query, "Why leave out the British Army? What's history without the Army. . . ?" bespeaks his failure to perceive the pageant's challenge to the very definition of history as the "Biographies of Great Men" and a sequence of wars (157).[16] Like Burdekin, Woolf prefigures Hayden White, Foucault, and others in her awareness of history as a highly structured and over-determined fiction, a drama at once authored by and authorizing "master" myths and dominant ideologies.

The plot of heterosexual romance with its minor variations represents one of the two major strands of the pageant's (history's) story. The other is war. If Colonel Mayhew were not hindered by a kind of tunnel vision, he would see that exclusion of the army by no means indicates the absence of war. Like Woolf, La Trobe has simply recontextualized war, foregrounding its usually obscured domestic origins. Accordingly, a connecting bridge of contiguous public/private experience forges these two strands—romance and war—into a double helix configuration of endless, mutually reflective internexus.[17] The various elements and strands of the pageant thus complete one another, just as the pageant and the novel's "real-life" drama interact and form a mutually constitutive whole.

The plot of domestic romance, with its various stages of courtship, marriage, and family, receives special attention in the pageant's three short plays, which parody popular dramatic forms of the Elizabethan, Restoration, and Victorian periods, respectively.[18] As James Naremore has similarly noted, all enact narratives of lovers united, each foregrounding and satirizing various roles codified in this apparently timeless story: the Prince, lover as lord, and his beautiful, adoring princess; lovers who play foolish courtship games of faithless love modeled on fictional romances; conniving materialists who trade women—or, if they are women, sell themselves—for capital in the form of dowry; mothers who scheme to marry off their daughters; sheltered wives who live their impoverished lives through their husbands; women who internalize patriarchal values and regard marriage as the acme of bliss. All this Woolf dramatizes within the omnipresent context of geopolitical tyranny, signs of which include an all-male rendition of "Rule, Britannia" and a duplicitous villain in jackboots.

Typically for Woolf, the Victorian period bears the brunt of her most scathing satire. Similar in tone and substance to stage satire à la Gilbert and Sullivan, the scene is dominated by the "huge, symbolical figure" of Budge the publican. His chest bedecked with medals, he imperiously flourishes a truncheon while proclaiming the broad extent of his authority and boasting that "all Her Majesty's minion . . . [must] obey the laws of God and Man" (*BA* 162). Having given "Man" equal billing with God, Budge adds,

> the natives . . . require protection and correction; we give 'em what's due. But . . . our rule don't end there. . . . Over thought and religion; drink; dress; manners; marriage too, I wield my truncheon. . . . The Ruler of an Empire must keep his eye on the cot; spy too in the kitchen; drawing-room; library. . . . Let 'em [the working class and the colonized] sweat at the mines; cough at the looms; rightly endure their lot. That's the price of Empire; that's the white man's burden. [162-63]

With one well-placed blow Woolf censures patriarchal arrogance and tyranny and exposes the hierarchical values that gird up the system of white male privilege. She also deftly demonstrates the seamless continuity between public policy and domestic training.[19] In the segment's conclusion, Budge imagines the "breadwinner," come to "'Ome, Sweet 'Ome," gathering his children about his knee so that they can together build a brick "tower . . . with our flag on top" (172, 173). Elsewhere in the pageant (and in Woolf's writing), building with bricks serves as a trope for the construction of a civilization she finds phallic, divisive, aggressively nationalistic, and ultimately destructive. And the home, with its traditional family unit, forms this civilization's center, its breeding ground. Moore's identification of the Victorian segment of the pageant as the "domestic prelude to worldwide violence" is most apt (169).

Woolf's disclosure of the mutually formative nature of systems of gender and war comprises the pageant's most crucial narrative thread, which remains unbroken through the several intervals. Men and women making war becomes the pageant's subtext, composed of fragments of popular culture and myth. La Trobe repeatedly inserts two particular refrains, one a "popular tune," the other a well-known nursery rhyme. The "pompous . . . bray[ing]" tune alludes to the coming war and captures the valorized image of the soldier: "Armed and valiant / Bold and blatant . . . See the warriors—here they come" (79). The same tune marks the pageant's first interval, during which Giles finds and crushes the emblematic snake and toad. As Jane Marcus has noted, within this space between the pageant's acts allusions to "sister swallow" invoke the story of Procne and Philomela, of rape and attempts to silence its victims.[20] This in turn echoes the story of rape that haunts Isa's consciousness. The interval closes with an ironically lyrical suggestion of the apocalyptic fate awaiting men and women living and loving as enemies, endlessly reproducing the adversarial archetype of war:

> I love till I die . . .
> For all are dancing, retreating and advancing,
> The moth and the dragon fly. . . .
> For this day and this dance . . .
> Will be over, over, over,
> And the ice will dart its splinter, and the winter,
> O the winter, will fill the grate with ashes,
> And there'll be no glow, no glow on the log. [117-18]

Songs that valorize soldiering and war, stories of female violation, and poetic renditions of romance's *danse macabre* combine, finally, with the nursery rhyme's timely intrusion to remind us of the psychosocial constructions Woolf hopes to disinherit, the plots that shore them up, and the fundamental split that threatens civilization from within: "The king is in his counting house / Counting out his money, / The Queen is in her parlour/ Eating bread and honey" (115). With England about to open yet another bloody chapter of history's seemingly changeless narrative, one scene in the pageant briefly recounts the futility of loving arms: "Palaces tumble down . . . Babylon, Ninevah, Troy. . . . And Caesar's great house . . . all fallen they lie. . . . Agamemnon . . . Clytemnestra" (139-40). The mythic and actual past—martial conquest and marital betrayal—haunt the present in ways we prefer not to acknowledge; instead of exorcising these ghosts, we emulate them. And thus we repeatedly reenact their story—nation against nation, man against woman—again and again: "all changes . . . but we remain forever the same" (139). Like the seemingly immutable view from Pointz Hall, the "repetition was senseless, hideous, stupefying" (67).

La Trobe's fugue-like pageant having duly warned us of the teleological nature of history's suicidally repetitious plot, Woolf then offers her ultimate challenge. The present, in particular the war, represents one more interval between the acts of history. The pageant's final scene, framed by repetition of the King/Queen nursery rhyme and spoken by a communal voice "that wept for human pain unending," conveys the image of "Civilization . . . in ruins; rebuilt . . . by human effort" (181). A man with a hod on his back builds a wall, assisted by a woman handing him bricks. After the war, civilization can be rebuilt. But in what manner and to what end? To replicate the prewar structure? Or to introduce fundamental change? Although some of the audience think of this scene as a "flattering tribute" to human persistence and ingenuity, the scene's framing indicates that La Trobe's meaning is cautionary, even admonitory. For once again man—"little boys . . . making sand castles"—is building civilization. And once again woman is assisting, handing him the bricks. Without revision of this paradigmatic scene, without a new blueprint, the foundations of civilization will remain self-eroding. For all its architectural elegance, the castle of the king and his attendant queen cannot keep chaos and dissolution forever at bay.

La Trobe's elaborate metaphor has, of course, a double implication, the more overt of which, as signified by the wall-building scenes, plainly indicates that humanity is caught (to mix La Trobe's metaphor with Woolf's) within the ultimately destructive strictures of a tragic drama of its own making. As the pageant's final segment, "Present Time, Ourselves," begins, Giles, Dodge, and Isa all think how "damnably unhappy" they are (176). "[C]aught and caged" in both the interior drama of the pageant and the subsuming drama of life, they are "prisoners; watching a spectacle." All long to escape the conventions that lock them into an outworn narrative, to break out of the straightjacket of the past, and to prepare to build a new, sane future. As Isa observes, "Surely it was time someone invented a new plot, or that the author came out from the bushes" (215). They are characters in search of a new author and a more viable story.[21]

On completion of the "Present Time" segment, the focus returns to the larger drama's final act, in which Giles and Isa become the authors of the novel's unwritten conclusion. In this highly ambiguous and conspicuously open-ended scene, wife and husband finally confront one another: "enmity was bared; also love. Before they slept, they must fight; after they had fought, they would embrace. From that embrace another life might be born" (219). Thus, the fundamentally paradoxical nature of human relationships (and, by proxy, the human race) ends Woolf's incursion into the drama of life, which for Isa and Giles now begins anew ("Then the curtain rose. They spoke."). In the midnight shadows they grow "enormous" and time reverts to prehistory: "The house had lost its shelter. It was night before roads were made, or houses. It was the night that dwellers in caves had watched" (219). As Giles and Isa turn to one another, the fate of civilization seems to lie with them.[22] Will they reenact the same wretched roles in the same timeless drama? Or will they espy the author in the bushes, unmask him, and rewrite the plot? Woolf leaves these questions unanswered. To write the next act would be both presumptuous and premature. We must be the authors of our own stories and our own lives; we must speak the lines Isa and Giles do not. Like La Trobe's audience, "We're the oracles."

Still, protestations against didacticism in art aside, Woolf—analyst of history and culture, critic of patriarchy, and advocate of change—aspires to be our teacher and guide.[23] For her dual tropes (the masculinist construction of civilization's walls and inscription of its master plots) imply not only that we are caught within cultural constructs that threaten our survival, but also that certain unsettling moments in social and literary history are especially propitious for the deconstruction and re-creation of life's unsatisfactory plots and the edifices that at once manufacture and contain them. By tunneling through the unwholesome foundations of what we "miscall civilization" (*BA* 188), Woolf does her utmost to "demolish" culture's phallic towers; at the same time (to borrow an apt phrase from Wayne Booth), she seeks to "re-educate our imaginations" (174) through continued application and refinement of her "new combinations" (*Years* 296).

Although Woolf's preoccupation with the dissolution of boundaries and the consequent free play of mergence and connection variously inform her life's work, perhaps nowhere does she explore the multiple possibilities more fully and more urgently than in *Between the Acts*.[24] Rejecting masculinist ways of knowing that define reality in terms of hierarchy, separation and opposition (Otherness), conflict, objectivity and certitude, Woolf gradually evolved an alternative, feminist epistemology and poetics. In 1939 her alternative mode of knowing—based on mutual inclusion, the dissolution of dualisms, and the acceptance of paradox and ambiguity—was for her the key that could unlock humankind's potential "to change and create new wholes" and thus at last to silence history's deadly refrain—to displace the ideology of conflict with one of connection and mutuality.

When Woolf spoke of wholeness and "unity out of multiplicity," she seems to have been imagining not some Romantic (transcendent, idealist) union. Rather, she sought to effect a radical paradigm shift away from the discrete distinctions by which we cognitively and psychologically compartmentalize (and control) reality. Thus, she was constantly experimenting with what for Burdekin and Smith proved more or less inconceivable—a revolutionary yet realizable mode of ordering reality that fundamentally frustrates dualisms by introducing paradoxical and shifting third possibilities (such as her "indifference" to war). These potential third terms create and inhabit a space that belies boundaries and incorporates the original two terms, beginning with those of subject and object (and masculine and feminine). The consequent dissolution of difference is not meant to be total and absolute but, rather, to provide an alternative that renders the concept of simple binary opposition meaningless. The denotation shifts from discrete difference to fluid and ambiguous mutuality.[25]

But as Woolf makes clear in *The Years*, though indeterminate, this state of being achieves not the bland, static sameness of "rice pudding," but the perpetual dynamism of "the bubble and the stream" or "myself and the world together"—North Pargiter's wistful description of the "new ripple in human consciousness" for which he longs (410).[26] As Patricia Waugh argues, Woolf's oft-quoted "'I' rejected: 'We' substituted" (*WD* 279) calls not for denial of individual identity per se (as illusory as such a coherent state of being may be), but for rejection of what Jessica Benjamin has identified as "the one form of individuality ['our culture knows']: the male stance of over-differentiation, of splitting off and denying the tendencies toward sameness and reciprocal responsiveness. In this 'false differentiation,'" Benjamin continues, "the other subject remains an object. . . . This way of establishing and protecting individuality dovetails with the dualistic, objective posturing of western rationality" (quoted in P. Waugh 22).

As Jane Flax similarly argues in her corrective feminist analysis of the historically masculine "discipline" of philosophy, being cannot be separated from knowing, Plato and the Cartesian split notwithstanding (see Flax, "Political Philosophy and the Patriarchal Unconscious"). In her call for a feminist epistemology that would illuminate how profoundly the widespread implications of such dualistic thinking have "permeated . . . our concept of knowledge" and have been "elevated into abstract theories of human nature," Flax reissues Woolf's implicit challenge to develop altered ways of knowing as the necessary basis for a "more adequate social practice" (268, 269). Flax's outline for the "beginning of a feminist theory of knowledge" provides an academic reformulation of Woolf's prototypical feminist philosophy and historiography. A divided psyche (subject/object, male/female) in which the "'other' must be dominated and/or repressed rather than incorporated into the self while simultaneously acknowledging difference" is unhealthy (Flax 269). Moreover, this "unhealthy self projects its own dilemmas on the world and posits them as the 'human condition.'. . . The apparently irresolvable dualisms of subject-object, mind-body, inner-outer, reason-sense, reflect this dilemma" (269-70). To redress such reductionism, Flax continues, "all concepts must be relational and contextual. Ways of thinking . . . must be developed which do justice to the multiplicity of experience, the many layers of any instant in time and space" (270-71). Finally, "feminist theory and practice . . . requires simultaneously an incorporation, negation and transformation of all human history. . . . Nothing less than a new stage of human development is required in which reciprocity can emerge for the first time as the basis of social relations" (270).[27]

Like North Pargiter, who recognizes the unhealthy state of human subjectivity and intercourse, Isa encounters barriers between herself and others and thus longs for a relaxing of boundaries, a dissolution of difference defined in opposition—prerequisites to making viable connections: "What do I ask? To fly away, from night and day, and issue where—no partings are—but eye meets eye" (83).[28] The "I" to "I" moments realized by Isa, Lucy, and William Dodge—their mutual sympathy and unspoken bonding—replicate in miniature the connections that intermittently flow among the members of La Trobe's pageant and the audience. Though at times "conspirators" and "truants" together or part of a harmonious collective reluctant to disperse, none is capable of attaining a "bubble and stream" consciousness except fleetingly. Divisive ways of knowing—staid habits of hierarchy and otherness—combine with mostly unacknowledged yearnings for wholeness, connection, and mutual inclusion to produce an untenable paradox: "Their *minds* and *bodies* were too close, yet not close enough. . . . We're too close, but not close enough" (65, emphasis added). Although this repetition appears to be a simple rhetorical device for emphasis, the subject shift creates quite different denotations for each sentence—in the first instance, an internal split, and in the second, alienation among individuals. Together they stress the doubly problematic nature of difference and connection. Nevertheless, simultaneously the immediate repetition closes the gap between we and they, self and other.

Throughout *Between the Acts,* suggestions of fluid subjectivity abound. The pageant's actors, for example, are clearly recognizable as themselves and as their characters, sustaining both identities—the "I" and the "not I"—at once. And at the pageant's end, the actors "lingered; they mingled. There was Budge the policeman talking to old Queen Bess. And the Age of Reason hobnobbed with the foreparts of the donkey. . . . Beauty was on them. Beauty revealed them" (195-96). Individual yet communal, connected in a web-like pattern in which differences of rank, time, gender, and even species have lost their significance, the actors are transfigured and the audience captivated: "What a pity—must they change?" The casting of a woman in the role of Reason, moreover, pointedly cuts to the heart of the arbitrary and deadly habit of differentiating human nature along gender lines. When woman and reason are thus reunited, "the armed warrior lays his shield aside" and wayfarers need not fear "the poisoned snake," for "heavenly harmony" attains (123, 124)—a harmony brutally absent in the earlier enmity-charged image of the choking snake and half-consumed toad locked in mutual destruction.

As the pageant's creator, La Trobe signifies (if imperfectly) another variation on the healing of this breach.[29] In contrast both to "abortive" Isa, entangled in domesticity and romantic clichés, and to the equally sterile Bart and Giles, enslaved by convention and their public personae, La Trobe resembles neither of the two portraits that dominate the Oliver home. She has taken the part of neither the silent, nameless "lady" nor the arrogant "talk produc[ing]" male Oliver ancestor, who together embody culturally codified gender polarization and who, as a result, "in real life . . . had never met" (36). Instead, La Trobe resembles a figure of indiscernible gender in a third (and much less conspicuous) painting, one in which "[p]ossibly . . . there was a little figure—a woman . . . or a man?" (214). This painting posits yet another third alternative, one that signifies not the union of masculine and feminine, which assumes a priori gender dichotomy, but "a third sex beyond gender," a denial of this dichotomy at the metaphysical level (Gilbert and Gubar, *Sexchanges* 365).[30] In short, as Toril Moi claims, Woolf's concept of androgyny ultimately does not affirm but rejects and "deconstruct[s] . . . the death-dealing binary oppositions of masculinity and femininity" (13). Thus, again unlike Isa, who never completes her secret poems, or the Oliver men, whose actions destroy worlds, the "androgynous" La Trobe magically *creates,* demonstrating the bewitching and formidable power of the artist: "she was one who seethes wandering bodies and floating voices in a cauldron, and makes rise up from its amorphous mass a *re-created world*" (*BA* 153, emphasis added).

Unlike La Trobe, William Dodge, another potential Outsider (in Woolf's sense of political resistance), feels diminished by his homosexuality and denies his power to create. Attracted to Giles's masculine "virility," William thinks himself "a half-man . . . a flickering, mind-divided little snake in the grass" and, therefore, deserving of Giles's contempt and violent impulses (73). His constitutional insuitablity for both the marriage and the war plots might behoove him, with La Trobe, to seek alternatives that would obviate his self-loathing. But, having absorbed the ethos of masculinism and implying that he "believe[s] in history," Dodge acquiesces to the immutability of his culture's master plots and is therefore forced to accept the inevitability of both his despised marginality and war (175). Rather than admit to being an artist, the aptly named Dodge claims to be a clerk, a cog in the reproductive social machinery. He thus relinquishes the possibility of release from his anguished position. Entranced by a woman's portrait, he fixes on the static truth of representational art; his eye ("I") thus never perceives art's transformative potential.

In sharp contrast, as DuPlessis similarly argues, at every level in *Between the Acts* Woolf continues her quest to "break the sentence" and to "write a new plot"—that is, to dismantle the differentiating and antagonistic habits of mind underlying dominant literary conventions and to create narrative methods more consonant with the "expanded," connective consciousness she advocates.[31] While Woolf employs some formal techniques in common with male modernist and postmodernist writers, she does so with her own (feminist) agenda in mind. The shifting narrative point of view, for example, is not simply "communal" or "collective," but *protean.*[32] The "voice that was no one's voice" and yet everyone's, separately and together, slips effortlessly from individual to group consciousness, from inner to outer, from identity to anonymity while privileging none (181).[33] Clear-cut distinctions, rigid boundaries, the either-or paradigm, linear progress, telos—all these dissolve and (over)flow; all resist containment and thwart expectation. Noting the discrepancy between the infinitely various, fluid nature of existence and the obsessive efforts to bind, measure, and canalize it, Bernard (*The Waves*) remarks, "But it is a mistake, this extreme precision, this orderly and military progress; a convenience, a lie. There is always deep below it . . . a rushing stream of broken dreams, nursery rhymes, street cries, half-finished sentences and sights. . . . There is nothing one can fish up in a spoon; nothing one can call an event. Yet it is alive too and deep, this stream" (255-56). Through Bernard, Woolf not only proffers a glimpse of her own reciprocal ontological and aesthetic theories, but, more specifically, previews in some detail the slippery "bubble and stream" dimension of *Between the Acts*.

With its embedded nest of plays within plays, its poetry and snatches of music and song, its nursery rhymes and choral interpolations, and, finally, its mercurial narrative voice and point of view, *Between the Acts* actively resists categorization by genre (DuPlessis has called the novel "intergeneric" [163]). The pageant within likewise comprises an exotic hybrid of the traditional and the avant garde—the pastoral masque as absurdist drama and street theater.[34] Moreover, the boundaries of the pageant are in constant flux, as nature and the audience intermittently take their part in serendipitous creation, intermingling throughout and contributing to the pageant's indeterminate beginning and end.[35] Two deliberate narrative strategies enhance this merging of "spectators and spectacle," to borrow Bowlby's phrasing (152): first, La Trobe's inclusion of the audience in the pageant, when their reflected images quite aptly *become* the narrative; second, and even more startling for a Woolfian artist, her shift from the representational to a presentational and didactic mode for her warning and affirmation in the last act. The interfacing edges between art and reality blur and fuse, each becoming the other.

Indeed, the entire pageant (signifying England's history and literary tradition, with their intertwined romance and war plots) and the contemporary life-drama unfolding at Pointz Hall (embodying the social, historical, and literary present) become mutually constitutive and inseparably coextensive. Thus, throughout *Between the Acts* Woolf tirelessly forms and strengthens "new combinations" between ostensible antitheses. Incessantly introducing reintegrative third terms—alternative perceptions and configurations of mergence and reciprocity—she "cuts the knot at the centre"—the ontological knot that holds such pairs (past and present, fact and fiction, observer and participant, and so on) in contradistinction (91). Thus, like La Trobe, Woolf too "makes rise up . . . a re-created world."

Moreover, through La Trobe's more direct methods, which transform the audience from passive or merely reactive viewers to active participants and, most importantly, *creators* of the drama that signifies their lives and portends their futures, Woolf invites collaboration with her larger project. While the "expository" mirrors still reflect the startled and evasive community, a "voice . . . no one knew" delivers an unexpected peroration—La Trobe's final warning and affirmation, which is ultimately a recapitulation of Woolf's vision (186). Exhorting the audience to join in "break[ing] the rhythm and forget[ting] the rhyme," the anonymous voice asks that "we . . . consider ourselves. . . . Liars most of us. Thieves too. . . . Consider the gun slayers, bomb droppers. . . . They do openly what we do slyly. . . . A tyrant, remember, is half a slave" (187). Unflinchingly confronting her own guilt, La Trobe seems to speak directly for Woolf, who remained painfully aware of her complicity.

Alluding once again to cultural construction, La Trobe urges reevaluative introspection: "Look at ourselves, ladies and gentlemen! Then look at the wall, and ask how's this . . . great wall, which we . . . miscall civilization, to be built by . . . orts, scraps and fragments like ourselves?" (188). Typically, however, an affirmation of redeeming humanity follows, attesting to kindness, affiliation across difference, and principled resolve. Nevertheless, the "anonymous bray of the infernal megaphone," which too crudely translates the fractured, flickering images caught by the mirrors, makes the audience resentful and resistant (188). "Reality [is] too strong" (179); suggestion and example prove more efficacious. Direct confrontation is effectively displaced with an act of creation that absorbs discord and transmutes it into soothing and complex harmony, transporting the audience despite themselves:

> The tune began. . . . Then down beneath a force was born in opposition; then another. On different levels they diverged. On different levels ourselves went forward . . . but all comprehending; all enlisted. The whole population of the mind's profundity came flocking . . . and dawn rose; . . . from chaos and cacophony measure; but not the melody of surface sound alone controlled it; but also the warring battle-plumed warriors straining asunder: To part? No. Compelled from the ends of the horizon; recalled from the edge of appalling crevasses; they crashed; solved; united. [189]

The multiple significance of Woolf's richly allusive language harks back to the close of *The Years,* when the dawn promised reconciliation and new beginnings, and forward to the non-closure of *Between the Acts.* In this end/beginning, Isa and Giles embody the possibility of turning the seemingly disparate and opposed ends of the human horizon back toward one another, away from the abyss at the outer edges to a central place where they meet, merge, and restructure the raw materials of life (and, thus, narrative). "From that embrace *another* life might be born" (219, emphasis added)—not simply one more life enacting a familiar and tragic role, but one in which it is possible to "live differently." Thus, I cannot accept one reader's condemnation of Isa for sleeping "with the enemy" ("LSM" 90). The realization of Woolf's inclusionary vision of peace requires that men and women re-educate themselves not to perceive one another oppositionally, as enemies. To win the battle of the sexes is to lose the war as Woolf ultimately defines it. Having explored the issue of geopolitical war in terms of gender conflict, she ultimately locates the battleground in the metaphysical, the psychosocial, the narrative, and, finally, in the linguistic.

Woolf attempts to reconceive the terms of war and wrest them from the lexicon of sterility and death with which we have built impenetrable walls of combative difference. As Patricia Waugh has argued, difference, if re-visioned, can connote unexpected forms of mergent life.[36] From this perspective, an otherwise internally contradictory passage assumes an oxymoronic logic: "Then suddenly the starlings attacked the tree. . . . In one flock they pelted it like so many winged stones. The whole tree hummed. . . . The tree became a rhapsody, a quivering cacophony, a whizz and vibrant rapture, branches, leaves, birds syllabling discordantly life, life, life, without measure, without stop devouring the tree" (209). Woolf co-opts lexical items with usually antagonistic significance (attacked, pelted, devouring) and mixes them freely with items of supposedly opposite connotation in order to suggest alternate meaning and to construct a highly paradoxical context vibrant with rhapsodic *life*—one in which different elements remain separate and yet "combine to create new wholes." The "bird-buzzing, bird-vibrant, bird-blackened tree," like the pageant's final melodic cacophony, thus images a rather more sophisticated version of the "bubble and stream" ontology suggested in *The Years;* for in the tree/bird mergence, paradox and discord are accounted for and assume the function of contributing to the life-affirming whole.

Significantly, a woman's reverence for the dead (carrying flowers to her husband's grave) disrupts this image for "living differently," as the past once more imperils the future. Repeated caveats against female collaboration with the ongoing reproduction of the past attest to Woolf's conviction that women, especially women artists, are perhaps uniquely suited to inhabit that potential third space from which they can model and encourage radical change. Despite personal and artistic doubts, La Trobe does just that. Even before leaving the grounds, she gives free reign to her creative urges and prepares once again to try to impart her vision. She cannot, it seems, do otherwise. And, as other readers have noted, the scene she conjures is precisely the final, impressionistic scene between Isa and Giles: "It would be midnight; there would be two figures. . . . The curtain would rise" (210). Although she can only hope for limited success, La Trobe nonetheless sets out to write a new script for the primordial couple—a script with an altogether different plot, signifying a new beginning and a different end. But the words Isa and Giles would eventually speak remain tantalizingly unknowable.

While the (non)conclusion's ambiguity inarguably reflects the profound uncertainty of the times, as well as Woolf's personal doubt about the future, in another sense it points to an essential facet of Woolf's feminist epistemology. As sardonically related in *A Room of One's Own,* an experience in the British Museum, where she goes in search of the missing truths of women's lives, illuminates two contrasting ways of thinking about knowledge. In vain Woolf peruses the plethora of mostly absurd "truisms" about women, all written by men. The grunting male scholar beside her, however, happily extracts "pure nuggets of the essential ore [of truth] every ten minutes or so" (28). It becomes quite clear that both their methods and their assumptions differ.

The male reader has been "trained in . . . some method of shepherding his question past all distractions till it runs into its answer as sheep run into the pen" (28). With her usual keen wit, Woolf is of course implying that such narrowness of inquiry along conventional and premarked pathways—veins of preconceptions and received truth—yield only the illusion of truth.[37] While he formulates the "neatest abstracts," Woolf's "notebook rioted with the wildest scribble of contradictory jottings. . . . Truth had run through my fingers," she mockingly laments. "Every drop had escaped" (30). Truth has eluded her in part because it has first escaped the declamatory male writers to whom she is forced to turn, but also because her idea of truth differs from that of her grunting neighbor. For him truth takes the rigid, definite, readily graspable form of "nuggets"; for her, truth is liquid, elusive, its shape dependent on the context. He arrives at truth by direct assault along prearranged lines; she explores truth from multiple directions, through its gaps and contradictions.

Thoroughly inculcated with the masculinized ("objective") theory of knowledge, in which ambiguity and uncertainty are undesirable and discomfiting, the audience in *Between the Acts* finds fault with the pageant for its failure to parcel out definitive nuggets of truth. "How difficult to come to any conclusion!" one complains (164). Immediately on the pageant's indeterminate ending, the audience turns to one another in search of measured meaning. Finding no clear-cut answers to their questions, they wonder, "[I]f we're left asking questions, isn't it a failure, as a play? I must say I like to feel sure if I go to the theatre, that I've grasped the meaning. . . . Or was that, perhaps, what she meant? . . . that if we don't jump to conclusions, if you think, and I think, perhaps one day, thinking differently, we shall think the same?" (200). One representative observer remains blind to the value of being left with questions and of the contextual truths—including the truth about war—that can emerge from a less rigid approach to knowing. Page, the local reporter (whose name is as apt as his profession), plans to "collar Miss Whatshername and ask for a synopsis" (150). Oblivious to La Trobe as a human being and to the pageant's multiple, overlapping nuances, his approach does violence to both the person and her creation. He confidently, assiduously jots down factual details; with these notes and the ambushed author's synoptic "nugget," Page expects to capture the pageant on paper and to pass it on, in hard copy, to his readers.

In marked contrast, throughout *Between the Acts* Woolf continually embraces paradox, ambiguity, multiple significance, and fluid forms of knowing and being. She calls on her readers not only to read the lines on the page but to explore the little-known spaces between—between the lines, the acts, the designated moments of history, the "I" and the "not I" and so on. Moreover, by necessity but also by design she relinquishes control of the outcome to her reading audience. With all the re-creative energy she can muster, she encourages them—the oracles, architects, and fiction-makers of the future—to participate in their own radical acts of (re)creation—to form "new combinations" and to conceive that untapped space in which "perhaps one day" we will "live differently" and realize the "dream of peace; the dream of freedom" (*TG* 143).

Thus, despite the ambivalence, doubts, and periodic despair engendered by the war, Woolf neither relinquished her ideals nor abandoned her purpose. Even at the time of her death, she was working on her latest manuscript, "Anon," another revision of "common history," whose title recalls both Woolf's assertion that "Anon was a woman" and La Trobe's anonymous final warning and affirmation.[38] In her last *Writer's Diary* entry, Woolf acknowledged her "despondency," but, appropriating a military metaphor, she resolutely declared, "I will go down with my colours flying" (351). That is precisely what she did. For *Between the Acts* constitutes not an epic lament—the "longest suicide note in the English language"—but a leap of faith, the final legacy of a visionary artist and woman committed to peace and to change.[39]

5

A Different Story

Doris Lessing's Great Escape

There is love among the ruins; after strife
There is life.

      —Muriel Grainger, "Love among the Ruins of London"

"War," Doris Lessing once declared, has been the "most important thing" in her life (quoted in Fishburn, *Life* 5). Her fiction repeatedly affirms this observation, for even more than in Woolf's oeuvre, war in its multiple guises insistently marches across the pages of Lessing's texts, leaving ruin in its wake. Of all the writers included in this study, none is so quintessentially a child of violence as Lessing—born out of the psychic ruins of World War I and, through her writing, reborn with great difficulty out of the grim and glaring holocaust of World War II. Her father a maimed veteran of the Great War, her mother his flag-waving, self-martyring nurse, Lessing is the daughter of a literal embodiment of history's intertwined war/romance plot.

Her *Children of Violence* series (1952-69) and *The Golden Notebook* (1962), which together comprise a roman à clef of epic proportion, enact these twin plots only to expose, demythologize, and rescript them.[1] In this way, these six novels provide a gloss on, and an extension of, the issues we have been exploring. In fact, Lessing sometimes seems in dialogue with the earlier writers in quite specific ways. Like Stevie Smith, she leads her conflicted protagonists over the frontiers of war into a confrontation with ontological insecurity and the enemy within. Like Katherine Burdekin, from an analysis of the culturally institutionalized reproduction of the ideology of conflict Lessing extrapolates a fascist future in which men and women systematically if unknowingly collaborate in their own ultimate self-destruction. Like Elizabeth Bowen, Lessing posits gender-specific connections between the two world wars and finds that issues of colonialism necessarily complicate already vexed questions about the mutually formative systems of gender and war. And like Virginia Woolf, Lessing attempts to disrupt this pattern by foregrounding the endless refrain of history—the "nightmare repetition"—with its insidiously symbiotic plots of war and romance. Moreover, Lessing encourages (again, like Woolf) a transformation of consciousness by exposing that symbiosis and modeling the epistemic shift that they both believed would "cut the knot" and extricate us from the Möbius-strip logic of dichotomous thought.

All this is not to say that Lessing simply recapitulates what has already been written. To be sure, the perhaps surprising number of parallels with these writers clearly indicates that, consciously or not, many women intellectuals of the war era were seeking answers to the same sorts of questions. Their work thus constitutes an ongoing stream within the female literary tradition.[2] As one would expect, however, Lessing adds her own currents and eddies to the alternately cascading, meandering literary flow. For among these writers Lessing's material and historical position is unique. "[W]hatever I am, I have been made so by Central Africa," she wrote in *Going Home*, an account of her first visit to Africa after years of self-exile (90). As a child of colonized Africa, she was perfectly positioned to observe that issues of imperialism, class, and, above all, race could not be dissected out of the cultural matrix, but were each an inseparable strand of an intricate braid—the "whole pattern of discrimination and tyranny and violence" that she depicts in *Children of Violence* (Newquist 58). More than any of her foremothers, therefore, Lessing's "cultural struggle" against the increasingly dysfunctional dominant order "derive[s] from and draw[s] upon diverse subordinated and oppressed groups"; she consequently articulates that struggle from more "complex and interlocking positions" (Sinfield 34). Although her African (and Marxist) roots impel her to include people of color and the working class as well as women in her representation of that struggle, war nonetheless once again functions as a trope for the whole and as the narrative thread that weaves the widely different novels considered here into a tapestry of protest and subversion/conversion. In so doing, Lessing passionately demonstrates her belief that art has an essential didactic dimension.

In production for more than twenty years after the war ended, Lessing's retrospective retelling of the war(s) also takes into account historical circumstances the earlier writers were for the most part spared: the proliferation of nuclear weapons, the realignment of overt hostilities in the so-called Cold War, communism's unconscionable political and personal repression, the curtailment of personal liberties in supposedly democratic nations such as Britain and the United States, the continued institutionalization of racial oppression, and the increasing militarization of the world's political economies.[3] Thus, while she wrote with full knowledge of the outcome of World War II, she was historically privy to a clearer sense of perpetual war as the condition of modernity than were her predecessors.

She consequently suffers from profound anxiety about humanity's survival: "We are already living [Armageddon]," she once declared (Torrents 13).

Referring to the ongoing violence of the twentieth century, Lessing has remarked, "The human imagination rejects the implications of our situation. War scars humanity in ways we refuse to recognize" (Raskin 76). Above all, Lessing's self-appointed task as a writer has been to scrutinize those scars, to reveal us to ourselves through the stories that we tell, and to teach us that we can—must—"force ourselves into the effort of imagination necessary" to disinherit our legacy of violence ("SPV" 9). For Lessing's history as a quintessential child of violence and her consequent assessment that since World War II we have been living Armageddon has been tempered by her equally strong and somewhat paradoxical conviction that "We are living at one of the great turning points of history" ("SPV" 7). "We all have extraordinary, non-rational capacities," Lessing believes; more, she foresees a crucial epistemic shift: "We're just on the verge of a complete revolution in how we make sense of things" (Torrents 12, Driver 22). Thus, although she sees some violent apocalypse as inevitable, she refuses (like Pepita in Bowen's "Mysterious Kôr") to abandon her vision of new life rising out of the ashes: "Some terrible new thing is happening. Maybe it'll be marvelous. . . . Maybe out of destruction there will be born some new creature. . . . What interests me more than anything is how our minds are changing, how our ways of perceiving reality are changing" (Raskin 66).

As it did for Woolf, then, World War II crystallized Lessing's conviction that "something new was demanding conception" (*MQ* 53), something which would enable us to "live differently," something almost incommunicable because straining the limits of discourse. Nevertheless, Lessing has been determined not only to articulate this "something new," but to model it via her persistent retelling of war stories. For she has astutely identified storytelling as a key site for both the validation and subversion of dominant ideologies and conceptual paradigms—as a "resource for . . . acquiescence," certainly, but also for "revolt" (Sinfield 31). We tell stories, Lessing once said, because "it is the way we structure reality" (Ziegler and Bigsby 206). She seems always to have understood that, as Alan Sinfield explains, "stories are lived. They are not just outside ourselves, something we hear or read about. They make sense for us—of us—because we have been and are in them. They are already proceeding when we arrive in the world, and we come to consciousness in their terms. . . . They become common sense" (24-25).

Challenging prevalent notions of reality, of common sense, *Children of Violence* and *The Golden Notebook* accordingly constitute a recursive series of literary revisions, a linked chain of familiar history, stories, and myths, refashioned and retold. These novels, precisely as does *Between the Acts,* carry the burden of the past and assume responsibility for the future. They comprise an unending effort to revise, both one by one and all at once, the interlocking strands of history's master narratives and thus to escape the "nightmare repetition," the "series of prisons called race, class, male and female" (Ziegler and Bigsby 199). In short, Lessing's war fictions suggest ways to restructure reality and to change the future with the stories that we tell.

One personal story of an hallucinatory vision, related in an interview, captures the essence of both her motives and her transformative storytelling process. In a drug-induced state of hyper-consciousness, Lessing imagined herself "both giving birth and being given birth to. . . . I was both [the mother and the baby] but neither" (Newquist 58).[4] Her psyche, she explains, was transforming her real birth, "painful and bad" by all reports, "into a good birth" (59). But the metamorphosis is not easily accomplished, for the new being "did not want to be born. First, there was the war . . . and the smell of war and suffering was everywhere and the most terrible cold. . . . The baby did not want to be born to those parents." More, it suffered "a sort of cosmic boredom." This Everybaby, "born many times before," was "exhausted" and dispirited by the "mere idea of 'having to go through it all again.'" War thus constitutes both the pressing motive for transformation and its primary obstacle. Nevertheless—miraculously, inexplicably—the rebirth proceeds and "the pain, the boredom, the cold, the misery (and the smell of war) diminished, until I was born with the sun rising in a glow of firelight" (60).[5] Above all, the "creature being born . . . was immensely ancient . . . and it was neither male nor female, and it had no race or nationality."

Lessing's utopian vision, born of an altered state of consciousness and typically enmeshed in a discredited discourse (in this case, that of a drug-enhanced vision), calls for an altered state of Being—one in which differences in time, gender, race, and nationality melt away before the annealing dawn of a fiery new age. In a rebirthing process that eludes rational explanation and defies its own obstacle-laden improbability, the new, protean subject (like the characters in La Trobe's pageant) paradoxically transforms and is transformed. Lessing's sense of phoenix-like life emerging from the ashes becomes explicit in her fiction. By narratively rendering Otherness ontologically untenable, rupturing the barren cycle of violence, and asserting the possibility of an organic cosmic peace, she seems finally to palliate—or defy—her despair at humanity's penchant for self-destruction. But the phoenix allusion does injustice to Lessing's hopeful revisionary story, for this mythic bird, endlessly reborn only to perish again and again, never breaks free of the circularity that constitutes the crux of its tale. This myth thus presents still another counterproductive story in need of revision, one that purports to offer hope and compensation, but actually reinscribes an inescapable cycle of conflict and violent self-immolation—in short, the history that Lessing would leave behind.

Her rebirth story's final vision of a bright new epoch recapitulates the seemingly unwarranted optimism, adumbrated by *The Years'* conclusion, of Woolf's final "leap of faith." But Lessing's faith that we can undermine the staying power of old stories and recreate reality by learning more flexible and inclusive modes of consciousness exceeds Woolf's by far. Indeed, Lessing's revision of the future may finally seem like a quixotic gesture of desperation flung in the face of experience. Of course, that may be the point. Her writing tirelessly testifies to her conviction that "we are survivors if nothing else" (Ziegler and Bigsby 207). Anna Wulf's lover, Saul Green, optimistically predicts in *The Golden Notebook,* "We're going to be saved by what we seriously put on our agendas. . . . We've got to believe in our beautiful impossible blueprints" (638). And so believe Lessing does.

The *Children of Violence* sequence opens with the adolescent Martha Quest doggedly trying to resist the normative stories she was born to, stories effortlessly perpetuated by adults. She counters their stories by flaunting Havelock Ellis, whose story of sexuality she imagines has some revelatory power to free her from the preceding generation's repression, homogeneity, and conventionality. Martha looks to this purportedly shocking (and therefore potentially disruptive) text, rather than elsewhere, because she images "herself . . . in the only way she was equipped to" (*MQ* 7)— through the beguiling lens of the "literature that was her tradition" (2), which includes ample nonfiction. She does not yet fully understand that the stories which have most insidiously shaped her consciousness, while (re)inscribed between the covers of books, are those lived and told (relived) with mesmerizing repetition by everyone around her.

In the opening scene of *Martha Quest,* Mrs. Quest and Mrs. Van Rensberg discuss their children, their (native) servants, their homes—the "dull staple of their lives" (*MQ* 2). Their husbands, resolutely sitting "on the other end of the verandah" with "their backs . . . turned on the women," talk about their work, the government, and the "native problem." Playing her expected role of "'young girl' against [the adults'] own familiar roles," Martha seems merely an observer caught between these two discursive positions. She responds with irritation and bitter resentment that "they should have been saying the same things ever since she could remember." The women's stories of domesticity and the men's of public affairs are equally familiar to Martha, who has "listened to such talk for a large part of her life" until "the two currents ran sleepily on inside her." She is an unwilling and helpless participant in life as they tell it, with its seemingly natural, unbridgeable divisions by gender, class, and race.

But Lessing throws into question all the stories Martha has grown up with by foregrounding the nature of storytelling itself—inevitably a process of censorship and reconstruction that demonstrates the disparity between lived experience and its representation. Lessing also highlights the narrators' tendency to rely on storytelling patterns deeply etched into cultural and individual consciousness through frequent repetition, and the function of such stories in the incessant process of cultural (re)production. As Mrs. Quest and Mrs. Van Rensberg nostalgically recall their lost girlhoods, defined by episodes of courtship and romance, they share "not the memories of their behaviour, but the phrases of their respective traditions" (5). Their stories are "heavily, though unconsciously censored," for "[t]radition demanded . . . a cautionary tale" (6), especially in the presence of the malleable young. In this way stories of romance, the family, state politics, and the past—all filtered through an unquestioned assumption of essential divisions between male and female, black and white, rich and poor—interlock and cohere into the narrative structure that ultimately will afford Martha (and Lessing) the "resources for both acquiescence and revolt" (Sinfield 31).

Another storytelling scene distills the essence of the complementary male and female strands of British culture's progenitive narratives in precisely the contrapuntal terms of the war/romance plot. As the Quests trade stories with the British McDougalls, with whom they share identical assumptions, codes of behavior, and a sense of history, their stories more completely capture the simultaneously beguiling and coercive reproductive function of familiar fictions than do the consciously censored tales exchanged with the Afrikaaner Van Rensbergs. To Martha's one side, Mrs. Quest recounts stirring tales of nursing the war-wounded, invoking place names saturated with over-determined significance and resonant with obligatory emotion. On Martha's other side, the men nostalgically "share memories of the trenches" (*MQ* 25). Caught between them, Martha listens, "absorbed in these twin litanies of suffering in spite of herself, for they had been murmuring down her childhood as far back as she could remember, and were twined with her deepest self." Simultaneously captivated and repulsed, Martha measures "the effect on herself of the poetry of suffering":

> the words "no man's land," "star shells," "Boche," touched off in her images like those of poetry; no man's land was the black and wasted desert between the living forces; star shells exploded in coloured lights, like fireworks, across her brain, drenched in reminiscence;

Boche was fearful and gigantic, nothing human, a night figure; the tripping word "Gallipoli" was like a heroic dance. She was afraid because of the power of these words, which affected her so strongly, who had nothing to do with what they stood for. [25]

As conveyed by her parents, storytelling agents and oral historians of their culture, actors who embody the violent drama's leading roles, the Great War at once looms grotesque and romantic, familiar and alien, repellent and enticing. As if to underscore the paradoxical perception and reconstitution of the war experience, Mr. Quest ironically calls the war, which he mentions at every opportunity (to regale it, denounce it, or both) the "Great Unmentionable." Furthermore, as if to affirm the underlying (if unconscious) purpose of most war stories, he predicts that Martha will be unable to extricate herself from the pattern of violence that snares generation after generation: "You'll fight, too, you'll see" (25).

Even after Martha flees her parents and the "ancient role" they would have her play, their stories shadow her (*MQ* 70). On hearing Mr. Quest recount his story about being wounded at Passchendaele to her landlady, Martha quails before the evocative power of his words:

In spite of herself . . . she was seeing, too, the landscape of devastation, shattered trees, churned and muddy earth, a tangle of barbed wire. . . . She understood that the roar of a starting car outside had become the sound of an approaching shell. . . . She was weighted with a terrible, tired, dragging feeling, like a doom. It was all . . . so horribly familiar, even to the exact words her father would use next, the exact tone of his voice, which was querulous, but nevertheless held a frightening excitement. [90]

Despite Martha's self-conscious resistance, her father's words recreate for her the terrible reality of war with his own overlay of seductive mythologizing.

Like Lessing's own father (an "officer in the 1914-1918 war" ["My Father" 83]), Mr. Quest compulsively adds his recreated experiences to the pool of war stories, which inevitably formed a deep body of myth whose function was to lend meaning to events of mind-boggling proportion—to simplify, order, justify, and preserve them. Lessing reports that her father's "war memories were congealed in stories that he told again and again, with the same words and gestures, in stereotyped phrases. They were anonymous, general, as if they had come out of a communal war memoir" (86). As indeed they had, for the disillusioning nature of World War I and the consequent outpouring of myth-debunking literature tarnished but never eradicated the ancient ready-made forms of perception

and representation through which many of the onlookers and even some
of the participants continued to view war, although now with an overlay
of wrenching irony.[6] Even Mr. Quest, who lost a leg to the war and who
thinks of "himself as a peace-loving man," wishes only to be left "in peace
to think about the war, in which he had lost his health, and perhaps something more important than health" (*MQ* 19, 20).[7] And while "he might
talk of that war with the bitter, savage consciousness of betrayal, yet there
was always an undercurrent of burning regret. Then he had been alive.
'The comradeship,' he would exclaim, 'the comradeship!'. . . And then the
terrible '*It was the only time in my life I was really happy*'" (*PM* 69). Although the crippled Mr. Quest has been symbolically castrated by the
Great War (like the ex-officer in "Songs My Father Sang for Me" and
Robert Kelway in *The Heat of the Day*), as World War II approaches, he
can only envy his son, "who (lucky devil) would be allowed to fight in this
new war" (*MQ* 238).[8]

At the same time, the myths resurface even in Martha's resisting
imagination, refashioned slightly to accommodate her own participation.
As she daydreams, her "blood quickened at the idea" of volunteer nursing: "she was picturing herself a heroine in the trenches; she was leaning
over a wounded man in the slime and debris" (*MQ* 168). Aghast at her
complicity with what she has denounced, she angrily acknowledges that
"these highly coloured fantasies of heroism and fated death were so powerful she could only with a great effort close her mind to them." Martha
perfectly demonstrates Lynne Hanley's observation that war stories are
"particularly potent in shaping our imagination, indeed our very memory,
of war" (*War* 4). Moreover, Martha intuits the significance of Hanley's
assertion that "how we imagine (or remember . . .) war has a great deal to
do with our propensity to make war" (*War* 4).

But Martha is somewhat more successful in exorcising romantic notions about war than she is in escaping its domestic double, the even more
tenacious and less frequently challenged story of heterosexual romance. As
others have noted, Martha repeatedly falls victim to her fairy-tale notions
of female passivity, gender complementarity, and idealized love. Waiting
"to be released by love," she moves from man to man in hopes that one
will save and complete her (*MQ* 157). In an editorial aside, the narrator in
A Ripple from the Storm acknowledges Martha's widely shared perception
of women as mere potential, blank pages awaiting inscription, chameleons
responsive to the male environment:

> There is a type of woman who can never be . . . "themselves" [*sic*]
> with anyone but the man to whom they have . . . given their hearts. If
> the man goes away . . . [s]he mourns for the temporarily extinct

person she can only be with a man she loves. . . . She lives with the empty space at her side, peopled with images of her own potentialities until the next man walks into the space . . . creating her, allowing her to be her "self"—but a new self, since it is his conception which forms her. [*RS* 38]

To silence the dissenting, "honest voice of her femininity" (*RS* 155), Martha entertains consoling "fantasies of the faceless man who waited in the wings of the future, waiting to free the Martha who was in cold storage" (230). "[F]inal heir to the long romantic tradition of love, [she] demanded nothing less than that the quintessence of all experience, all love, all beauty, should explode suddenly in a drenching, saturated moment of illumination" (*MQ* 184).

That the idealized "image of a lover . . . offered a woman by society . . . remained intact and unhurt" despite her several unsatisfying and even unpleasant romantic entanglements demonstrates the staying power of this particular fiction (*PM* 27), which for some time survives her persistent "feeling of being caged and trapped" and her repressed suspicion that marriage was simply "a gigantic social deception" (*PM* 28, 36). Thus, with actions so automatic that she believes they are instinctive, a "compliant" and "enthusiastic" Martha "took every step into bondage" while "three parts of herself stood on one side, idle, waiting to be called into action" (*PM* 250). After two failed marriages, Martha still aspires to an essentialist ideal, one keyed to the ostensible qualities of a "*real* man" who would recognize the "real" Martha and help her to become it, a man she "can really be married to" (*RS* 89, *Ll* 93). Douglas Knowell and Anton Hesse inevitably fail to pass muster not merely because of their actual faults (which are many), but because they cannot live up to Martha's impossible masculine ideal. Although the sleeping princesses waiting to be awakened, the damsels in distress, are legion, the princes prove lacking in charm, their armor dented and dingy.

That Martha (exactly like her mother) seems eager to embrace the assigned roles of wife and mother despite their tacitly shared sense of depletion and entrapment leads Martha to fear they are both "mere pawns in the hands of an old fatality" (*PM* 94). Like characters in novels (which, of course, they are), Martha and her parents seem "doomed individuals, carrying their doom *inside* them, like the seeds of a fatal disease" (95). Martha struggles to expel the seed, to find a cure—to confound the "Logic of History" as distilled in its ubiquitous stories of war and romance (*PM* 289). Indications that these plots feed one another, grow out of the same logic, and are even at times fundamentally indistinguishable abound throughout the *Children of Violence* series and *The Golden Note-*

book (written between *A Ripple from the Storm* and *Landlocked*). The very title "Children of Violence" conveys the double significance of the heritage of conflict, the miscreated progeny of social/sexual intercourse in its most inclusive sense. Like Lessing, Martha "was as much a child of the 1914-1918 war as she was of" her parents (*Ll* 196). As Lessing has explained, "The idea is to write about people like myself, people my age who are born out of wars and who have lived through them, the framework of lives in conflict" (Newquist 57).

On the most mundane level, war promotes marriage and marriage, war. Infected with a "terrible urgency" as the war approaches, the once determinedly single Sports Club members impulsively begin to pair off and marry in feverish haste (*MQ* 246). Their marriages, including Martha's, signify the "first infection from that brutal sentimentality which poisons us all in time of war" (247). To complete the cycle, both the notion and reality of marriage seem only to feed the men's appetite for war. In 1938, as anticipation of war becomes more acute, the ostensible "wild oats" misbehavior of the Sports Club men, known as "wolves," assumes a more sinister taint. The traditional celebration of premarital freedom from responsibility becomes more desperate and uninhibited, as though the war implicitly promised and validated both release from unwanted commitment and release of sublimated hostility: "they all behaved like licensed lunatics, as if there were no future, as if they had no plans to become important men . . . with wives and children. . . . [T]he wolves decided life owed them a holocaust" (152). Written in 1952, lexical choices like lunatic, wolf, and, above all, holocaust cannot help but impress upon the reader their murderous and historically fascist connotations.

Its phrases assiduously repeated with litany-like devotion, the adversarial discourse of courtship in vogue with club members lends linguistic validation to the men's state of perpetual adolescence and the women's acceptance of infantilization: "kid" is the mandatory form of address for the "wolves," "baby" for the "girls." "Baby, baby, you'll be the death of me," one wolf complains to Martha (*MQ* 150). Stinging from his rebuke, Martha dutifully reminds herself that she "must remember he would die for her, she killed him." The barely veiled implications of this language reassert the woman-directed animosity felt by a number of World War I veterans and occasionally expressed openly in the literature of that war (as in Sassoon's "Glory of Women," for example). As Gilbert and Gubar, among others, have shown, this resentment was perpetuated and used to great advantage by state propaganda, which often incited men to war either by calling on them, in the name of female goodness, to sacrifice life and limb, or by goading them to revenge their wounded manhood, treacherously impugned by faithless whores.[9] The club wolves preemptively avenge themselves by objectifying women whom they pass from man to man as the compliant recipients of symbolic assaults in the guise of sex. One man after another draws Martha aside to kiss her in "a small ceremony of hatred": "Abruptly, without any sort of preface, she was held rigid against his hard body, whose lower half pushed against hers in an aggressive but at the same time humble way; and her head was bent back under a thrusting, teeth-bared kiss" (*MQ* 157). At once supplicating and threatening, this Draculean embrace captures the dual and paradoxical nature of men's traditional relation with women, brought into relief and intensified by the war.

With the declaration of war, the immediate recall of the Great War's cultural markers signals that World War II resumes history's ongoing saga of violence as if without interruption. As the band plays "Tipperary" and "Keep the Home Fires Burning" (thus both anticipating nostalgia and evoking it), a general solemnly invokes "1914. That date, and the words Verdun, Passchendaele, the Somme, were like a bell tolling, and led to . . . 'this day, September the third, 1939'" (*PM* 121, 122). This infamous historical signpost thus becomes "another note of the solemn bell pealing the black dates of history," and World War II another measure in the insistent refrain. The Great War's rhetoric of chivalry, analyzed by Paul Fussell in *The Great War and Modern Memory*, is soon recalled to duty for the mythologizing of the Battle of Britain.[10] Flourishes like "'Knights of the Air' and 'our boys'" feed "a need for heroism, starved so long . . . it was as if the gallant youth from 1914 had donned a uniform the colour of the sky and taken wing" (*PM* 163).

The war similarly initiates resumption of the ancient roles of the warrior and his woman who waits, immortalized in Western literary tradition by Ulysses and Penelope. Douglas's and Martha's disparate responses to their respective parts, however, demonstrate dissonances that highlight the reciprocal relation between war and gender identity as a process of cultural construction rather than a "natural" function. "[J]ust as he was playing a role which was surely inconsistent with what he thought—the young hero off to the wars for adventure—so she began speaking in the ancient female voice," which makes "anxious demands for his love." But the voice also deflects onto Douglas, as representative male, culpability for war as an ongoing enterprise: "there would be wars so long as men were such babies" (*PM* 68). In this way Martha conveniently effaces her own susceptibility to war's "dangerous undertow of excitement" and her reflexive tendency to serve as "magnifying mirror" for Douglas's war-inflated sense of self. He becomes "stern, subdued, authoritative. Martha was only too

ready to find this impressive" (*PM* 120). But soon the men's reactive posturing (described in terms of violent sexuality)—"stiff as ramrods, with
their fists clenched"—seems "rather ridiculous" (121). As the husbands
don uniforms and drill, a gulf forms between them and their wives, who in
"derisive silence" watch them become "strangers" and "willing savages"
(*PM* 132). The bonding husbands assume the stance of "men escaping
their wives"; each woman is reduced to "the wife of one of the lads. That
was all" (133). War captures and externalizes their gender-encoded adversity.

Because Douglas and his friends cannot resist war's alluring tale of
the ultimate escape, adventure, and validation of their masculinity, they
welcome the warrior role and self-consciously defend it, though their "official tone carries no conviction any longer, not even to the people who
use it" (*PM* 68). They deny the "truth about war," preferring the lie. Because it is unthinkable to repudiate their function as "sacred witness" to
the warriors' courage, the women silently smile and resist the eventual
realization that

> the condition of being a woman in wartime . . . was that one should
> love not a man, but a man in relation to other men. . . . [A]nd it was
> precisely this thing, dangerous and attractive, which fed the intoxica-
> tion of war . . . drugged them all into losing their heads. You love not
> a man, but that man's idea of you in relation to his friends. But that
> had been true . . . long before the war. [*PM* 238][11]

Martha recognizes that war only intensifies woman's objectification as
Other, against which men define themselves as the only true subjects. Despite her self-awareness—or, rather, to protect herself against it—Martha
fully participates in this process; out of guilt and revulsion at her role, she
too stifles the truth and revives the lie: "she hastily began to re-create that
coarsened soldier [Douglas] into something masculine and strong and
attractive" (*PM* 239).

Like her sister war novelists, Lessing ultimately indicts not men but
the historical/cultural matrix to which the men proffer their tragically self-
victimizing but determined support. As colonizers, hardy and hardened
men among men (especially in contrast to the pale and "effeminate"
Brits), Douglas and his friends have perhaps less to gain by donning the
war's cloak of masculinity than their English counterparts, and more to
lose. When Douglas is discharged because of an ulcer just before the fighting begins, he suffers an overwhelming sense of failure, shame, and loss—
in short, emasculation. The discharged "colonials, so tough, masculine,
violent," alternately exhibit bellicose hostility and tearful "self-pity" (*PM*

220). For any so-called weakness or inadequacy on their part not only calls into question their ostensibly exceptional virility, but also deprives them (as they see it) of the pleasure and validation afforded by the intense, exclusively male experience of "the real thing"—life as only war can make it. "It seemed that his whole life had led without his knowing it to the climax of being with those men, his fellows, his friends, parts of himself, in real fighting, real living, real experience at last. And he was out of it" (*PM* 223).

The adventure story of a lifetime goes on without him, consigning him to the tedious role of civil servant in the exceedingly banal theater of domesticity. "Never again would he know the comradeship of men. Never. Never. . . . What he felt for Martha was nothing, nothing at all compared with his year among soldiers. Rage filled him. He was filled with a need to tear, to destroy. . . . Next morning . . . he would step straight off the plane into domesticity and the office from eight until four" (224).[12] Worse, if (as Nancy Huston has suggested) war—*agon* writ large—has proved the paradigmatic narrative by which we make sense of history and even life, then to be excluded from one's privileged place in that story is to be erased from history, to have not lived at all. His absence from war thus not only invalidates Douglas's masculinity but nullifies his subjectivity, his very existence.

Paradoxically, then, war tends to guarantee ontological stability for participating men even as it casts women (like Pompey Casmilus) who refuse the role of female Other into an ontological void. Lessing, like Smith, turns to the female soldier as a singularly instructive example of a woman in war's double bind. Bobby (an emblematically androgynous name), "one of the girls from the Sports Club" who joins the army, deals with her new identity by adopting a quasi-male persona. Her "mannish" mannerisms and studied use of obscenities dismay and irritate Perry, who peevishly implies that Bobby has thwarted his desire to look on a (real) woman after long sexual deprivation (*PM* 216). He nevertheless (or, more accurately, he therefore) belligerently lays claim to her. Bobby has assumed behaviors she thinks "suitable to her role as a female soldier," but finds her position insupportably vexed (225). When confronted by the expectations of men who knew her in her former "feminine" role, she tries to maintain the soldierly camaraderie she so clearly enjoys. But her "eager determination to hear every detail" of Douglas's training experience makes it evident that she can play the soldier only "by proxy" (226). And despite Perry's abuse, she responds to his challenge by resuming her former position as placating sexual respondent. At one moment compliant and compassionate, at the next professional and flaunting her "free manly stride," Bobby openly displays both her psychosexual ambivalence, here again sharpened by the war, and the futility of pretending to be one of the guys (233). Her attempts to become more "masculine" earn her the epithet "bloody skirt," an instance of male naming that re-feminizes Bobby in terms of biology (menstruation), the traditional costume of sexual accessibility, and perhaps even violent assault (218). Martha's own efforts to join the war effort are immediately forestalled by Douglas, who at once re-affirms and throws doubt on her femininity by asserting the "unsuitability of danger for women" in "that anonymous voice of authority" which "even intelligent and liberal-minded men" fall back on when "their own personal authority is threatened" (*PM* 92).

Significantly, Martha's first wedding coincides with Hitler's invasion of Bavaria and Moravia, and her second (also war-induced) marriage is intended to last only for the war's duration. As in all the fiction we have studied, the geopolitical conflict in *Children of Violence* unfolds off-stage and functions as foil and sometimes agent for war's domestic counterpart— couples at war—every variety of which inhabits center stage with numbing regularity, most conspicuously in *A Ripple from the Storm*. Claire Sprague has noted that the title of this numerically and thematically central text refers both to the distant war with the Nazis and the various domestic wars obviating any peace at home.[13] One may tend to assign the geopolitical war greater import and thus to designate it the center of the storm, its repercussions rippling out to take their toll even on the home front. But this view is too limited, for the novel's center of disturbance can as easily be located in the many domestic and personal skirmishes of which World War II proves as much effect as cause. The deceivingly peaceful eye of the storm, Africa's home front, ostensibly a safe haven, becomes both the inner and outer boundary of an intense and capricious system of destruction.

While the quarrelling Quests recede to the background and other older couples, such as the Van der Bylts and the Maynards, politely do battle behind the facade of stolid respectability, the younger generation wars more openly. Martha and Anton Hesse, Piet and Marie du Preez, Maisie and Andrew McGrew, Colin and Marjorie Black—all "fight a losing battle . . . in the no-man's land between image and the truth," mired in the "savage discrepancy" between the stories with which they order their lives and their actual experience (*RS* 193, *MQ* 72). Individually, these couples merely play out the same old story of gender asymmetry and marital discord. As a group, however, they are of particular interest because through them Lessing illustrates not only the overlap and mergence of the personal and political, but also the enormous discrepancy between, on the one hand, a supposedly revolutionary theory (in this case, communism) and its rhetoric of equality and, on the other, actual practice. Of all the stories communism is meant to rewrite, the tale of a man and a woman, told and retold, most stubbornly resists erasure.

Communism seduces Martha not only with its call for justice and equality, but with its philosophical analysis, which in part recalls her own intuitive musings on the web-like nature of reality (which, in turn, resemble the collective feminist philosophy that emerges from these war narratives as a whole): "the infinite complexity of events, each acting and interacting, so that there is no phenomenon in the world which is not linked with and affects every other" (*RS* 54). Speeches such as this one by Anton, however, amount to little more than lip service, for by their actions many of the men who mouth these ideals consistently repudiate any connection between their personal lives and the party's goals or between abstract party principles and concrete human need, thus perpetuating essentialist gender/race differences and dichotomous opposition at every level.

As Carol Gilligan has demonstrated in *In a Different Voice*, discrepancies such as those that plague Martha's group signify more or less gender-specific approaches to ordering reality and defining appropriate moral action. Attitudes and behaviors that seem to indicate the stereotypical contrast between head and heart more complexly figure two different modes of psychological development—a tendency toward abstract reasoning and strict adherence to principles and regulations, on the one hand, and an ethic of responsibility and compassionate connection on the other. When Anton rebukes Martha, who spends much of her time trying to help native Africans with "personal problems," and condemns her actions as inconsistent with the party's official class analysis, Marie du Preez objects. "Logically I agree with you. When you put it logically," she tells him, "no one could disagree. But humanly—there is something wrong. . . . The Coloured people . . . are human beings and so are we" (*RS* 81).[14] Similarly, when Anton decrees that Jimmy cannot associate with a "Coloured woman" because, first, it would harm the party and, second, there could be no exceptions to established policy, Martha "felt him to be logically right; she felt him to be inhuman and wrong. There was no way for her to make these two feelings fit together" (99).

Caught in this double bind, the women find themselves helplessly conflicted and, what is more, vulnerable to male ridicule. Marie's husband, who laughs at her objection, comments, "Women. She feels it is wrong, and so that's enough" (*RS* 81). He disguises his derision with affectionate teasing of the sort that effectively keeps women on the defensive and in doubt of their own judgments. When Marie speaks on the "question of women's rights," the party men, supposed advocates of universal equality, completely undermine her authority with their facetious comments and derisive grins (*RS* 186). These men have never learned to perceive women as true comrades; for them women remain the objectified sexual Other. If a woman is beautiful, they desire and dismiss her. Like the post-adolescents of the Sports Club, they treat women as "bits of property," even quarreling over ownership (*RS* 230). Jimmy, one of the youngest group members, embodies the most naïve of the men's politically inconsistent attitudes. While clearly preferring women who make themselves attractive to men, he criticizes the female group members as helplessly bourgeois for wearing makeup. Worse, he idealizes women who "sacrific[e] themselves for their families," a position that prompts Martha to snap, "Good, then let's arrange things so that women have to work eighteen hours a day and die at fifty, worn out so that you can go on being sentimental about us" (*RS* 94). Jimmy shows his hand in spades when he tells Martha, "You bourgeois girls, you need a good working class husband to teach you a thing or two."

For the women, in contrast, communism means "real equality" between the sexes (*RS* 154). In the Soviet Union, they imagine, people "would understand at once why [women] needed to be given work which would absorb the best of themselves, why they need time for study. 'Under capitalism,' they rationalize, 'women have to diminish themselves,' thus parroting the party line. When not indulging in this "fantasy," however, and when provoked into letting down their guard, Martha and the others articulate the unwelcome realization that, of all the battles to be won, the battle of the sexes seems the most fundamental. When Marie du Preez meets resistance from all the men in her audience, regardless of race, she exclaims, "If there's one thing that teaches me there's no such thing as colour [it] is that men are men, black and white" (*RS* 186). Marjorie Black similarly remarks, "As far as I can see when we get socialism we'll have to fight another revolution against men—lot of hidebound reactionaries, that's what they are!" (*RS* 247). And (recalling embattled relationships in evidence throughout this study) Martha realizes with dismay that "her husband [Anton] provoked in her only the enemy, feelings so ancient and, it seemed, autonomous, they were beyond her control" (*Ll* 112). Like Pompey Casmilus, Martha begins to trace her experience to what she fears may be its logical and terrible conclusion: enmity between the sexes, so ancient, primal, and vast, may prove immutable.

At times, then, Martha and the other white women privilege gender over race as the signifier of subjugated Otherness. Still, she senses some congruence. And the narrator insists on a root connection. As Martha prepares to leave Douglas, she confusedly notes that his "hysteria" strikes exactly the same note as does the newspaper when it complains that outsiders "did not understand the sacrifices the white population made" for the blacks (*PM* 334). The "connection" Martha senses is the self-righteous posturing of those who rationalize the domination of others by disguising it as caretaking. If questions of gender inequality repeatedly recede into the background while debates about how to achieve racial justice dominate every agenda, the text renders separation of these issues inescapably ironic. The scene in which Marjorie Black's angry speech on the position of women intrudes on the designated subject (the status of blacks) is only one of many indications. Lessing contextualizes Martha's first wedding, for example, not only in terms of Hitler's territorial aggression, but of Britain's as well, by calling attention to the location ("the capital city of a British colony in the centre of the great African continent" [*MQ* 246]). She thereby stresses the marriage's metonymical coincidence with both militaristic aggression and racist imperialism. Similarly, Martha's second marriage is conspicuously overshadowed by endless arguments concerning the question of "racial prejudice" (*RS* 175). The mostly futile struggle for an end to the "colour bar" constitutes yet another of the several overlapping storms alluded to in *A Ripple from the Storm* and the third element in the series' gender-war-race triad.

Just as most of the men unself-consciously reveal their hypocrisy vis-à-vis the women comrades, the public voice of the colony, the *Zambesia News,* discloses its complicity with fascism in its "reluctance" to "remind its readers about the atrocious nature of Hitler's Germany" until it could no longer be altogether ignored. Indeed, "it showed real indignation only over Hitler's capacity for absorbing other countries" (*PM* 69). With scathing irony, the narrator comments that "the authorities' first concern was to explain to [the Blacks] through wireless and loudspeaker why it was their patriotic task to join their white masters in taking up arms against the monster across the seas in a Europe they could scarcely form a picture of, whose crimes consisted of invading other people's countries and forming a society based on the conception of a master race" (*PM* 120).

As the war-induced "dangerous undertow of excitement" sucks Martha into a sort of mob hysteria, she participates in an orgy of "enjoyable cynicism . . . being fed by everything about her." Night after night "she joined the swinging circle of intoxicated dancers controlled by the thudding of the drums" (*PM* 69). Clearly, the true savages are those who revel in the seductive, frenzied rhythms of war. When the men finally leave for active duty, the expression of their almost gleeful anticipation of battle betrays not only the sexual work of war, but this war's significance as a struggle for dominance between two oppressive, racist powers. From the roof of the train, the grinning soldiers stretch out their arms to the adoring "female chorus," which faithfully acts the part of sexual cheerleader (*PM* 160).[15] Then, as if to express the racist element of their soldierly duty, the men do a war dance and sing "Hold Him Down, the Zulu War-rior." The male communists hypocritically condemn the British colonizers as "bloody white fascists" and "rapacious imperialist exploiters" while they continue to exploit and diminish women (*RS* 14, 246). Similarly, the settlers think of themselves as iconoclastic "crusaders against tyranny" while they tyrannize blacks (*PM* 299). Neither group appreciates the ex-treme irony of its position.

It is perhaps too easy to condemn such straightforward hypocrisy. But Lessing insistently reminds us that the war raised more distressing questions of moral ambiguity and shared responsibility. As a Jewish victim of Nazi barbarism and a helpless observer of colonialism's racial cruelty, for example, Thomas Stern (Martha's lover) illuminates the much more vexed issue of whether one is justified in resorting to violence to quell injustice or whether by doing so one becomes (like Pompey) indistin-guishable from the enemy. Toward the end of the war, an Allied news-reel depicting German prisoners throws into focus war as both a self-perpetuating process and a moral dilemma. As lines of "defeated men . . . in the last extremity of hunger, cold and defeat," crawl across the screen, a "sneering" announcer jeers his contempt for the "übermensch" (*Ll* 48-49). "Take a good look," he incites the audience. "We have fought the good fight and won." Images of decimated, burning German cities fill the screen. While the newsreel discomfits Martha, it only feeds Thomas's hate. Having lost friends and family to Nazi slaughter, he can feel no pity for Germans. Victimized by violence, saturated with it, Thomas cannot purge it from his soul: "When Thomas and [Martha] touched . . . in the touch cried out the murdered flesh of the millions of Europe—the squandered flesh was having its revenge" (*Ll* 159).

But Nazism is not the only spring that feeds Thomas's torrent of rage, for he has been helplessly implicated in a variation of the racial hatred by which he has also been victimized. The white South Africans' abuse of Blacks during the war was not so overtly homicidal as the system-atic persecution of the Jews, but only because, as Thomas (like Pompey) learns, "There are national styles in murder" (*Ll* 142). Thomas's superior, Sergeant Tressell, a "bastard . . . out of sheer indifference," thwarts Thomas's every effort to ensure minimally humane treatment of the Afri-cans conscripted for war work (140). A horrified accomplice to depriva-tion, disease, and even death, Thomas fosters an overpowering hatred for this man who "finally made [him] understand the world" (141). Tressell, whose murder, Thomas admits, "would be the greatest pleasure I could imagine" (144), comes to embody (like the Holocaust) a principle of evil that poisons the heart and mind and destroys human connection. Martha knows that Tressell, a fascist of the British variety, "was an enemy too strong for her" (146); she cannot save Thomas from his own hatred and vengeful violence. Their lives lacerated by racism, nationalism, hatred, and war, Thomas and Martha cannot sustain their love: "it was all much too painful and they had to separate" (*Ll* 159).

Martha's attempt to dissuade Thomas from his determined militancy with well-intended clichés—"violence does not achieve anything," it will violate "everything you believe" (*Ll* 194, 193)—seems a meaningless gesture in the context of genocide and atom bombs. He can only mockingly ask her, "So, you don't believe in violence, is that it?" (195). Finally, in *Landlocked,* the series' penultimate volume, comes the climactic moment when Lessing articulates the fundamental human dilemma that defines her life's work: how can we repudiate and purge the legacy of violence in which we are so profoundly and cruelly immured?

> Having lived through a war when half the human race was engaged in murdering the other half, murdering more vilely, savagely, cruelly, than ever in human history, what does it mean to say: I don't believe that violence achieves anything?
>
> Every fiber of Martha's body, everything she thought, every movement she made, everything she was, was because she had been born at the end of one world war, and had spent all her adolescence in the atmosphere of preparations for another which had . . . inflicted such wounds on the human race that no one had any idea of what the results would be.
>
> Martha did not believe in violence.
>
> Martha was the essence of violence, she had been conceived, bred, fed and reared on violence. [*Ll* 195]

Thomas and Martha exemplify Lessing's provocative conclusion that no one is truly innocent. As Pompey Casmilus similarly learns in *Over the Frontier,* and as Miss La Trobe admonishes in *Between the Acts,* "[T]he gun slayers, bomb droppers . . . do openly what we do slyly. . . . O we're all the same" (*BA* 187). Because of World War II, Lessing has said, "We now know what we are really like," and we must account for and reckon with the "ambiguities of complicity" (Ziegler and Bigsby 199, "Vonnegut" 140).[16]

This soul searching constitutes a key element in the two closely related projects that Lessing finds essential to escaping the Logic of History and ending war: developing new modes of consciousness and recognizing that our stories offer the "resources for both acquiescence and revolt." In her novels about war Lessing manages to model these inseparable processes on multiple levels, for while her characters enact and discuss these strategies in her writing, she herself demonstrates them through her writing.

World War II (and, by extension, war in general), Lessing tells us, was the result of a dysfunctional habit of mind she often calls, simply, a "failure of imagination . . . of sympathy" (*Ll* 187). Her healing prescription entails a shift in focus, a widening of our perceptual gaze to include the kinds of (suspect) knowledge shunted to the periphery of human understanding. Or, to put it another way, the kinds of knowledge associated with the "negative" ("female") side of the "hierarchical dualisms [that] . . . lie at the foundations of western epistemology and moral thought" (Wilshire 95). As Donna Wilshire has pointed out, "knowledge (accepted wisdom)" and "ignorance (the occult and taboo)" head up a long list of supposed oppositions which, going beyond the mind/body, reason/emotion, individual/social splits, also includes

> order/chaos
> objective/subjective
> literal truth, fact/poetic truth, metaphor
> seeing, detachment/listening, attachment
> permanence, ideal (fixed) forms/change, fluctuations
> goals/process. [95-96]

Lessing repeatedly demonstrates that, as Wilshire argues, these contradistinctions express and reinforce "value judgments that have unnecessarily brought about human alienation from self, other, and planet" because "they have disastrously limited what we think is desirable and worth knowing." Like Wilshire, Flax, and other contemporary feminist thinkers, Lessing dissents from Cartesian rationalism, positing instead the idea that knowledge "comes from many kinds of knowing working together or taking turns," that "no one manner of knowing—not disinterested cognition [if there were such a thing], intuition, inspiration, sensuous awareness, nor any other—is sufficient unto itself to satisfy our need to know ourselves and the world" (Wilshire 92). Accordingly, in a Woolfian (and proto-Derridean) enterprise, Lessing envisions an epistemological/ontological process by which one can elude the "metaphysical logic of dichotomous" thought (Felman 3). She thereby hopes both to encourage and to provide appropriate tools for the reexamination of history and its lifeless plots, for release from history's self-sustaining cycle of absolute difference, antipathy, and discord, and, finally, for consequent self- and cultural transformation.

In 1984, Lessing admonished an interviewer for presenting her with preclusive alternatives: "Why do you make it 'or, or, or?' It could be 'and, and, and.' You don't have to have an either/or" (Stamberg 4). Appositely, Martha's fundamental quest is a realization of her youthful revelation on the veld when she ephemerally achieves that "difficult knowledge" which emerges from an experience of "slow integration," when everything "became one, shuddering together in a dissolution of dancing atoms"

(*MQ* 53, 52). In the lifelong struggle against the "sickness of dissolution" that follows, Martha slowly accretes understanding and strategies that equip her to overcome the formidable obstacles she faces. First she must conquer the "fear" that resists "a new sort of understanding" (*FGC* 489, 357). She has to unlearn the "rigid formulas" that distort her perceptions and limit her inquiry (*FGC* 359). She must learn to reconsider the mundane, for it is "through banalities" that the "most interesting discoveries" are made (*FGC* 37). So-called normality, she discovers, is a "condition of disparateness," for the "compartmented, pigeonholed" human mind compulsively "separated, and divided" (*FGC* 61, 33, 79). With this knowledge Martha finally "understood *really* . . . how human beings could be separated so absolutely by a slight difference . . . that they could not talk to each other, must be wary, or enemies" (79).

But Martha comes to this understanding behind the scenes, as it were. Until well into *The Four-Gated City*, there remains an enormous disparity between what the narrator acknowledges and Martha's profoundly felt but incompletely formulated understanding of the interlocking patterns repeatedly inscribed through the earlier texts' pointed juxtapositions and ironic commentary. Indeed, Lessing temporarily displaces Martha's full understanding of the gender-race-war matrix onto a surrogate in a different novel, Anna Wulf, another manifestation of Martha Quest and of Lessing. Apparently having reached, in *Ripple from the Storm*, a literary and philosophical impasse, before continuing *Children of Violence* Lessing wrote *The Golden Notebook*. In this intensely introspective novel, she confronts the many questions *Children of Violence* had so far raised about the interconnected, fluid nature of reality, the necessity of additional ways of knowing, the nature and function of storytelling, and, finally, her consequent doubts about realism as her chosen vehicle for social commitment—in short, her increasingly prohibitive suspicion that in telling Martha's life story she was somehow at odds with her own enterprise.

What Lessing consequently viewed as the shortcomings of the "conventional novel" (discussed in the Preface to *The Golden Notebook*) can be more broadly defined as realism's reliance on assertion of the oppositional, hierarchical condition of the status quo, the transparency of language, and the logic of rationalism—in general, the meaning-making systems that falsely render our over-determined sense of reality as natural and inevitable.[17] As Catherine Belsey has observed, classic realism is "intelligible as 'realist' precisely because it reproduces what we already seem to know" (47). Or, as Shoshana Felman explains it, realist texts and their commensurate reading strategies are "designed as a stimulus not for knowledge and cognition, but for acknowledgement and *re-cognition*, not for the *production* of a question, but for the *reproduction* of a foreknown answer—

delineated within a pre-existing, pre-defined horizon, where the 'truth' to be discovered is reduced to the natural status of a simple *given*" (10). Conventional novels, Lessing has (paradoxically) complained, "always . . . lie" (quoted in Pratt and Dembo 11).

Gayle Greene has identified Lessing's problem as how to create a self-consciously subversive discourse out of signifying systems unavoidably "inscribed within the culture she would oppose" (82). This presents a more than awkward dilemma for a writer committed to realism, who must then wrestle with questions that anticipate poststructuralist notions of the interdependence of language, fictional form, mechanisms of power, subjectivity, and social reality. In *The Golden Notebook,* Lessing steps off stage in order to reconsider and to clarify her assumptions before raising the curtain on *Children of Violence* once again. In as much as it interrogates literary realism and its relation to philosophical systems fundamental to war, *The Golden Notebook* is a metafictional comment on and thus an integral part of the Martha Quest series. Sprague and Tiger have observed that between *Ripple* and the last two volumes of the series "falls the great shadow of *The Golden Notebook*" (8). But rather than demarcating an obscurance or a gap, it functions as both a bridge and an illumination of the whole.

During the *Golden Notebook* interval, as Lessing has explained, she realized that her "philosophy was absolutely inadequate"—that is, that her thinking about thinking and about art had been divorced from her own experience and what she was to discover she was really "thinking and feeling" (Ziegler and Bigsby 200). Writing *The Golden Notebook* was the pivotal "crystallizing process" out of which "all sorts of ideas and experiences I didn't recognize as mine emerged" (quoted in *SPV* 27). "I was learning as I wrote," she continues. "The actual . . . writing . . . was really traumatic: it changed me." By way of Anna's creation and the telling of her story, Lessing meticulously enacts her frustration with the ideological/epistemological prison of traditional storytelling and then forges that trauma into the vision of interconnection and shape-changing integration that eventually surfaces in *Landlocked* and thoroughly informs *The Four-Gated City.*

Anna Wulf's only novel, a story of gender and race antagonism on the African home front during World War II, is aptly entitled *The Frontiers of War.* In Anna's story, the seemingly discrete elements of race and romance, whose edges blur but only fleetingly merge for Martha, pointedly coalesce against the larger canvas of war, thus providing a miniature reprise of *Children of Violence* up to this point. At the novel's conclusion, romantic jealousy, racial difference, and the war seemingly conspire to doom the lovers to their separate and gender-encoded fates. Unable to bear her loss, Anna's heroine sacrifices her body to men and to commodification, ironically choosing prostitution to express her independence. Her act simultaneously embodies self-punishment and despoliation. The "Ace pilot," in contrast, immediately turns his eye to a greater purpose, the mythically glorious "death that awaits him" in war (*GN* 59). Both are victims of this familiar love/war story, but the black woman's fate conventionally signifies an ignominious, self-immolating defeat, and the white male's a praiseworthy and meaningful assertion of the heroic self. In this way, Anna's novel does indeed reproduce a definitive male/female opposition valorized in stories of both war and miscegenation.

Doing their part to censor the stories we hear (see) and to obscure the mutually informative nature of the novel's intertwined themes, screenwriters edit out the all-important racial plot, play up the "melodramatic sexual relationships," and rename their clichéd and whitewashed script *Forbidden Love* (*GN* 60). Their misappropriation proves ironically fitting, however, in light of the novel's tacit assertions of war-intensified assumptions of difference (gender, race, class), which poison love—and all human relations—at the root. But while manipulators of popular culture attempt to extract the racial component from the cultural matrix, Anna refuses their silencing gesture, explaining, "This war was presented to us as a crusade against the evil doctrines of Hitler, against racialism, etc., yet the whole of . . . [colonized] Africa was conducted on precisely Hitler's assumption—that some human beings are better than others because of their race" (*GN* 65).

The popular perception of her novel only confirms Anna's notion that the "novel has become a function of the fragmented society, the fragmented consciousness" (*GN* 61). More, it feeds her fears that because she is utterly self-divided, barred by "education, sex, politics, [and] class" from "completion," she lacks the "qualities necessary" to form a "new sensibility . . . a new imaginative comprehension" (61). Despite her best intentions, *The Frontiers of War,* she concludes, fails to tell the truth about war or race or anything else. As a conventionally tragic interracial/wartime romance, it merely repeats ancient lies, not only promoting "racist voyeurism," but, worse, invoking a "dangerous delicious intoxication . . . of war itself . . . the death that we all wanted, for each other and for ourselves" (*GN* 153).[18] Inspired and informed by "the unhealthy, feverish illicit excitement of wartime . . . a terrible lying nostalgia lights every sentence" (63). To her mind, then, the novel is "immoral," for nostalgia—the insistent recollection of self-destructive, self-deluding fictions—represents a powerful form of "nihilism, an angry readiness to throw everything overboard. . . . This emotion," Anna contends, "is one of the strongest rea-

sons why wars continue. And the people who read *Frontiers of War* will
have had fed in them this emotion, even though they were not conscious
of it. That is why I am ashamed, and why I feel continually as if I had
committed a crime" (64).

But Anna's guilt over the culturally reproductive function of her
novel does not by itself account for her writer's block. The war behind
her, tragic love stories reappear to the point of obsession in Anna's own
life and in the fictional free-writing with which she tries to distance and
come to terms with the plot of heterosexual romance. In the Yellow Notebook, devoted to fiction, Anna jots down brief plot synopses for numerous projects that she will never complete. With one parodic exception, all
depict variations of the wounded-woman-in-love theme, starkly illuminate
her own dysfunctional relationships with men, and imply the most muted
of protests against gender-based asymmetries that invariably leave the
woman "diminished" or "destroyed" (*GN* 534).[19] Anna's artistic crisis is
not merely a block but a stutter—the inability to tell any story except that
of women victimized by their love for men and by their own romantic notions. Not until Anna can reject the role of victim, accept the ambiguities
of her own complicity, and imagine other plots does Lessing choose to
return to Martha's story, ready to take it in a new direction. As will
Martha, Anna finds that madness, dreams, and intuitive epiphanies—marginalized or discredited ways of knowing—combine with rational analysis
to develop multiform ways of "making sense" of her life as a woman and
of her writing.

As Martha's more intellectual surrogate, Anna too seeks liberation
from the nightmare repetition: "I want to be able to separate in myself
what is old and cyclic, the recurring history, the myth, from what is new,
what I feel or think that might be new" (*GN* 472-73). She envisions the
latent potential in similarly receptive individuals as "a gap in a dam"
through which "the future might pour in a different shape—terrible perhaps, or marvelous, but something new" (473). But Anna herself remains
ill-prepared and at a loss as to how to breach the dam, the wall of consciousness behind which forgotten or undiscovered truths glimmer dimly,
because she remains epistemologically enslaved by seemingly timeless,
overlapping fictions of men, women, and war.

As Saul Green, in an uncensored eruption of masculine egotism, ha-
rangues Anna about how to raise a girl to be a "real woman," Anna's
"watcher" comes to see his repeated assertion of privileged knowing and
human (male) being in opposition to femaleness as a deadly assault: "I, I,
I, I, I—I began to feel as if the word *I* was being shot at me like bullets
from a machine gun. For a moment I fancied that his mouth . . . was a
gun of some kind" (556). Anna's figures suggest that she perceives Saul's

insistence, by means of which he conspicuously reiterates language that splits the I from the Other, as the source of a war-like violence with which men bully and subject women. The next time Saul's "I, I, I, like a machine-gun ejaculating regularly . . . spew[s] out hot aggressive language, words like bullets" (628), Anna not only recognizes his "I, the naked ego" (629) as "I against women" (630), but she conflates it with a nightmare in which she "knew, but really knew, how war waited" (629).[20]

But this notion proves too one-sided, as Anna discovers during a crisis sparked by a seemingly random coincidence of love and war stories. As she anticipates the inevitably unhappy conclusion to her love affair with Saul (who sneaks off "like a prisoner escaping" [586]), she similarly de-spairs of the newspaper's predictable reports of "a war here, a dispute there" (588). Contemplating these seemingly disparate events in tandem, Anna is suddenly

> invaded by . . . the fear of war . . . of the real movement of the world towards dark, hardening power. I *knew* . . . that whatever already is has its logic and its force, that the great armouries of the world have their inner force, and that my terror . . . was part of the force. . . . *And I know that the cruelty and the spite and the I, I, I, I of Saul and Anna were part of the logic of war,* and I know . . . these emotions were . . . part of how I saw the world. [588-89, latter emphasis added][21]

Moreover, Anna knows "finally, that the truth for our time was war, the immanence of war" and, most importantly, that "war was working in us all, towards fruition" (591, 594). Anna's new knowledge forms the crux of an understanding that Martha finally shares but never quite articulates.

Rather than a surrender to fear or despair, this realization indicates a "kind of shifting of the balances of [her] brain . . . [a] realignment" that enables her (at least for the moment) to dispel the man as warmonger/woman as victim dichotomy and to reintegrate the "principle of destruc-tion" she had been projecting onto men (588). In a dream she accordingly becomes the "malicious male-female . . . figure, the principle of joy-in-destruction: and Saul was my counterpart, male-female, my brother and my sister. . . . We came together and kissed, in love. It was terrible. . . . Be-cause I recognized . . . the caress of two half-human creatures, celebrating destruction" (*GN* 594-95). For the first time she sees through male and female role-playing to the life-denying "gender symbiosis" that prevents their full humanity and creates instead miscreants, who, as in the mermaid and minotaur metaphor employed by Dorothy Dinnerstein, together seem determined and destined to "meet death half-way" (*MM* xii, 149). To put it in Dinnerstein's words, Lessing attributes the institutionalization of war, humanity's "drift . . . toward despotism in societal authority" (*MM* 163), and our precarious existence "at the edge" of nuclear and/or environmental apocalypse to a "male-female collaboration to keep history mad" (*MM* 276). That the collaboration is unconscious neither palliates its consequences nor lessens our responsibility for its cessation.

This "new knowledge," partial and periodic as it proves to be, leads Anna through a series of waking and sleeping dreams that closely resembles Pompey's dream-like journey over the frontier of militarism and masculine being. In these dreams, Anna at first identifies with victims of ideological coercion: "an Algerian soldier stretched on a torture bed . . . the British conscript . . . killed for futility . . . a peasant" (*GN* 596). But her shifting consciousness insistently illuminates the shadowy underside of her self-righteous revolutionary zeal:

> I was not Anna, but a soldier. I could feel the uniform on me. . . . But I didn't know who the enemy was, what my cause was. . . . Yet Anna's brain was working in this man's head, and she was thinking: Yes I shall kill, I shall even torture because I have to, but without belief. Because it is no longer possible to organise and to fight and to kill without knowing that new tyranny arises from it. Yet one has to fight. [600-601]

Anna's cross-dressing and assumption of a male body not only reaffirm her earlier vision of shared responsibility for war, but also image the integration of both male/female and victim/victimizer (thus portending Martha's vision in *The Four-Gated City* of herself as both Nazi and concentration camp fatality).

For Anna the writer (as for Lessing), this mergence of the Self and the Other, this Escheresque way of thinking about being, has expressive repercussions. Significantly, this dream scene begins with Anna's abortive attempt to record the supposedly nostalgia-free *facts* of her life in the Blue Notebook, in order to hold chaos and fragmentation at bay. Instead of a pen, however, Anna finds she grasps a gun in her hand. She cannot accept the paradox of "unity out of multiplicity" and rewrite her life until she comes to grips with that gun—at once the phallic apparatus of death, the polyvalent symbol of her own involvement, and an instrument of scripts. Appropriately, her recurring dream of soldiering is succeeded by a dream of romance, still defined, however, in terms of strict opposition. She watches herself "playing roles, one after another, against Saul, who was playing roles. It was like being in a play, whose words kept changing, as if a playwright had written the same play again and again, but slightly different each time" (*GN* 603-4). Another manifestation of the paradigmatic couple (like Isa and Giles), Anna and Saul "played against each other every man-woman role *imaginable*" (emphasis added). Her dream captures the essence of the stuttering Yellow Notebook, evidence of her "failure of imagination." Faced with such redundancy, Anna admits to her writer's block and at last begins to locate its source in her frustration with the maddening repetition of the stories with which she has ordered (determined) the material of her life.

Anna eventually succeeds in reconceiving her life because the real and the imagined, the rational and the intuitive, the conscious and the unconscious at last come together and work in concert. This lifesaving process emerges from that tantalizing landscape in which all these supposedly antithetical modes of knowing and being kaleidoscopically flow into protean patterns—her dreams. Anna watches her life unfold as if it were a film. Alternately speeding up and slowing down, the images are "rough, crude . . . [and] rather jerky," for they lack the polish of a consciously manipulated, edited narrative (*GN* 634). When the film slows down, she "watched, absorbed, details" previously unnoticed. When it speeds up, those things "to which the pattern of [her] life had given emphasis, were now slipping past, fast and unimportant." All the seemingly noteworthy events—the designated major moments of her life story—"had given place to what was really important"—what happened between the acts, so to speak. Lessing thus calls into question the ways in which lives are shaped into stories just as Woolf interrogates conventional notions of history. In each case, it is a matter of shifting emphasis, of adjusting one's focus and one's rhythm.

Finally, the film re-vision of Anna's life moves "beyond [her] experience . . . beyond the [dividing, canalizing] notebooks, because there was a fusion; and instead of seeing separate scenes, people, faces, movements . . . they were all together" (*GN* 635). As the film slows for the last time, it offers a series of seemingly unrelated images—a hand dropping a seed into the earth, a rock slowly worn away by dripping water, a man standing on a moonlit hillside with "his rifle ready on his arm," and a woman choosing life over suicide. In this closing comment on the form/content of Anna's life, time, implicitly synchronic and diachronic at once, becomes timeless. The two images which conventionally connote death or decay are held within the embrace of two acts of life, the first setting new life into motion, the latter refusing to cut the life process short. Thus does the story of Anna's life, including the events depicted in *The Frontiers of War,* become a paradoxical but ultimately life-affirming vision of growth and dissolution together, of awaiting death and deferring it—all part of the inclusionary whole.

Anna makes a gift of her dream's single image of war—the man on the hillside, rifle in hand—to Saul, whose task is to turn it into a re-vision of his own, a rescription of the (male) war story. A similar task will fall to Martha/Lessing when *Children of Violence* resumes. In *The Golden Notebook*, however, Anna/Lessing accepts the challenge Saul presents with his opening line for the story that signals and enacts the cure of her writer's stutter. The sentence, "The two women were alone in the London flat," portends a tale of insulated domesticity, but in the skillful hands of a transformed Anna/Lessing it becomes instead *The Golden Notebook* itself, which not only subsumes Saul's story of war, but endlessly denies the limitations implicit in the content and structure of the opening/reopening sentence he provides her (639, 3). *The Golden Notebook*, then, is a novel about war—geopolitical war, war between the sexes, and the struggle to salvage life and redirect the future by revising our maladaptive stories. It exemplifies the "self-consuming artifact" described by Stanley Fish, the literary text that turns back on itself, thus (as Jeanette King similarly argues) denying telos and origin, having no center and no margin, no hierarchy of discourse.[22] Moreover, in this war story, Lessing's tour de force, one cannot clearly differentiate the novel's subject, author, and narrator, who become one another and yet remain themselves. Like *Between the Acts*, Lessing's text effaces the line between fiction and reality. Wholeness consists of interfused, reciprocally informing fragments that encourage the reader to take nothing for granted, to reconsider radically what has come before, and to develop a shifting, inclusionary perspective capable of seeing both the parts and the whole while appreciating the futility of seeing them as separate. Finally, with its interleaving of the classically realist (and ironically titled) "Free Women" sections and the disruptive "notebooks" sections, *The Golden Notebook* demonstrates the would-be subversive storyteller's dilemma: how to speak intelligibly both within and against known discourse, how to weaken and permeate the borders of a discursive "reality" from which one can never be altogether free. Paradoxically, Lessing escapes this dilemma by embracing it, relying on and exploiting realist methods while destabilizing them, thus once again proving the efficacy of both/and over either/or.

In this way Lessing frustrates the demands of literary realism and paves the way for the less formal break with realism and more subtle revision of timeworn stories that she executes in the last two volumes of *Children of Violence*. Having worked through and demonstrated how all of her transformative strategies (admitting to the ambiguities of complicity, dilating one's consciousness, revising stories) overlap and merge, in *Landlocked* and *The Four-Gated City* she elaborates on her new epistemological framework and completes the deconstructive project begun in the earlier volumes—the transmutation of her own stories into a "resource for . . . revolt" (Sinfield 31).

As the ironic conclusion of *The Golden Notebook* implies, however, meaningful change seems a hopelessly impossible task for the human organism, ostensibly locked in a prison of impaired consciousness that keeps us at war with ourselves and each other, an organism "whose essential characteristic is the inability to diagnose its own condition," though it cost our very survival (*FGC* 430). Nevertheless, Lessing once again prefigures Dinnerstein in her implicit belief that our very capacity for consciousness makes us, in Dinnerstein's terms, a "self-created, self-responsible species" (*MM* 23). "We are what we have made ourselves," Dinnerstein argues (22), and that same capacity for consciousness gives human beings the unique (so far as we know) capacity for shaping our own evolution. Lessing concedes, however, that the obstacles are enormous.

From the beginning, for example, Martha despairs of the limitations of language, a self-creating, self-limiting system—a conceptual feedback loop. How does one step outside this loop, either to "destroy the words *black, white, nation, race*" with a herculean "effort of the imagination," or to communicate experiences that fall outside linguistic borders, or, most fundamentally, even to conceive of "something new" (*MQ* 47, 53)? "Our whole language, the way we think," Lessing has complained, "is set up for putting things in departments" (Bikman 26). Still, other than silence, what choice do we have? We must all rely on language, slippery, treacherous, and prescriptive as it is. How, then, to interrupt the loop, to turn language back on itself? "Words, words, words," Martha muses, "If the words come, the reality will afterwards?" (*FGC* 515). Lessing acts on the faith that the answer to Martha's question could be yes, that we can write a new script for the future if we can only see/say it.

In *Children of Violence*, Lessing rather murkily traces the exclusionary habit of mind that plagues Martha and that divides humanity along the unstable fault lines of nationality, race, gender, and class, to a process of individuation and repression. During one of Martha's interior journeys into madness and self-discovery, she encounters and grapples with the "self-hater"—that is, a denied aspect of her "self" split off and projected outward in a deadly negation of human potential (*FGC* 511). Although Lessing is not clear on the source or moment of this formative event, she sees the split as remediable. Martha eventually reintegrates her other/selves in a perilous process of self-confrontation. This decidedly nebulous enterprise is doubly paradoxical: If the self-hater proves too fully disarticulated, too strong, insanity and/or surrender to hate could result. Less clearly, both in order to absorb/transform the Other and in the process of absorbing/transforming, Martha accesses a remote reservoir of shared consciousness that heals her psychic division (or amputation) and uncovers the repressed knowledge of interconnectedness. Martha admits the paradox of mutual inclusivity, the "I" and the "not I" together, when she writes, "The tortured and the Torturer. Am being both. . . . [S]moke from a gas chamber in concentration camp. Then first separate but becoming the same, the ragged bit of refuse (me) pushed into the gas chamber and the uniformed woman (me) who pushed" (*FGC* 510). "I am what the human race is," she adds. "I am 'The Germans are the mirror and catalyst of Europe' and also: 'Dirty Hun, Filthy Nazi'" (511). Martha here not only acknowledges her "ambiguous complicity," but executes the either/or deconstruction and the both/and reconstruction necessary for reparation. The resulting modified consciousness allows for both an individual's "permanent" self (227), which has "no sex" (221), and an oceanic "impersonality," part of a universal consciousness into which (potentially) anyone can tap (369).[23] Martha's breakdown and "self-healing" repeats and extends the same process attempted by Anna, who is less consistently successful at "dismissing false dichotomies and divisions" (*GN* Preface in *SPV* 28).

Lessing characterizes Martha's chaotic and arduous process of self-recovery as a journey without maps into an unknown territory, a "country which lay just beyond, or alongside, or within the landscape [one] could see and touch" (*FGC* 355), thus once again recalling Pompey's journey across similar borders. Martha's journey, no less surreal, proves far more productive, however, for it models extra-rational modes of perception and dissolution of difference that enable Martha to defeat her "Devil" (515), while at journey's end Pompey/Celia remains poised at Hades' door. As Patricia Waugh has pointed out, although once clinging to a strong sense of an *individuated* "real self," Martha has come to see herself in exactly the same fashion as La Trobe hoped her audience would view themselves—as a "faceted mirror" in dialogue with her various selves (and with willing others), as "a dispersed, relational subjectivity which is both part of and separate from others and could form the basis of a new collective mode of social living" (201). In the Preface to *The Golden Notebook*, Lessing somewhat differently explains that "the way to deal with the problem of 'subjectivity,' that shocking business of being preoccupied with the tiny individual who is at the same time caught up in such an explosion of terrible and marvelous possibilities, is to see him [*sic*] as a microcosm and in this way to break through the personal, the subjective, making the personal general . . . transforming a private experience . . . into something much larger" (*SPV* 32). She also understands that while we perceive our-

selves as—and to that extent are—discrete individuals, our sense of subjectivity is historically and culturally produced: "While there is something in
me which I recognize is uniquely me . . . at the same time I have a view of
myself in history as something which has been created by the past and
conditioned by the present" (Ziegler and Bigsby 195).[24]

In her success with accepting chaos and multiplicity and at reinte-
grating the Other, Martha contrasts sharply with Jack, her occasional
lover, who fundamentally fails to disarm the self-hater. Jack's formative experiences mold him into a sexual fascist. His violently abusive father (who
beat his sons and raped his daughters, "just once, all three of them" [*FGC*
55]) passes on a heritage of controlling brutality. The "tactics of domination" provoke in Jack the paradoxical defensive postures of detachment
and assimilation, or becoming the enemy (Foucault 102). The war, which
reenacts on a global scale the "fact" of Otherness and domination, forever
kills any chance he may have had of reversing his alienation. When seriously wounded and bleeding his life into the sea, Jack holds off exsangui-
nation and the sharks purely by means of physically channeled will. Left
permanently in "awe of . . . the flesh," with an eating disorder, and in
terror of being drowned or devoured, Jack displaces his fears—loss of
control, dissolution, and death—onto the bodies of women, where they
can be contained and regulated at a distance.[25] What begins as sexual ec-
stacy and the idealization of women erodes into perverse fantasies of
sexual enslavement and naked manipulation of the "male-command-and-
female-submission" type (*FGC* 386). Jack accomplishes his chosen work,
"break[ing] in girls for a brothel," through an insidious "process of deg-
radation" that becomes his only pleasure (408). The splitting off and
denial of the female Other (and the flesh) becomes the mainstay of Jack's
survival because for him women paradoxically (but typically) embody both
the voracious sharks who would consume him and the mortality of his
own flesh, which has betrayed him.[26]

Jack's "breaking down" techniques, widely institutionalized for their
usefulness in maintaining certain hierarchies, are "identical with those
used in torture; and in certain armies, and some religious orders . . . ? The
common factor in all these is that a part . . . of the person manipulated has
to be made an accomplice of the person who manipulates" (*FGC* 412).
Thus follows the victims' cooperation, attained through complex mechanisms of power that employ not only repressive coercion but also more insidious methods of "ideological normalisation."[27] Jack's fate, like that of
Thomas Stern, dramatically illustrates Lessing's analysis of history's continuous reprising of multiform oppression and eruptions of violence. As
Martha observes, "If a dictator wishes to control a party, or a country . . .
if any power-seeker anywhere wants to create a manipulated group—he,

she, has to embody the self-hater" (*FGC* 523-24). "Did Hitler," Martha wonders, "plug in to [the] hater?" (513). Sexual politics and geopolitics, Lessing demonstrates, often manifest the same violent phenomena and consistently share the same "techniques and procedures of power," which "ascend" from local sites (such as the family and individual gender relations) to more extensive ones as they are "colonised, utilised . . . transformed, displaced, [and] extended . . . by forms of global domination" (Foucault 99).

Martha's excursion into madness represents only one of her several experimental forays into nontraditional modes of acquiring the "new knowledge" essential to survival. Barbara Hill Rigney, Jean Pickering, and others have explored at length Lessing's use of madness, particularly her Laingian notion of schizophrenia. Lessing depicts schizophrenia, on the one hand, as a strategic response to the "appalling state of alienation called normality" and, on the other, as not a breakdown but a "breakthrough [to] . . . liberation and renewal" (Rigney 74, 83), or even a "mode of insight and prophecy" (*FM* 229). Although Lessing was undoubtedly influenced by Laing's antipsychiatry, her use of madness can also be understood as a necessarily extreme means of shedding the inhibitions of rationalism by embracing its apparent opposite. Unlike Lynda, from whom Martha learns the technique, Martha contains her willed bouts of madness, calling on reason to do so. Clearly Lessing here advocates the use of reason and so-called madness in concert, each modifying and compensating for the excesses of the other. Once again, not either/or, but, rather, both/and. In this sense, madness signifies not reason's opposite, but simply a different "wave length" or register of perception (*FGC* 380). By bringing the madwomen out of hiding, by returning to them their voices, by giving them a messianic role, and by transforming an incapacity into a potential capacity, moreover, Lessing provides an alternative to Lynda's paradigmatic madwoman's tale, in which she is silenced, incarcerated, and reduced to a "nothing-but" (213).[28] In this way, Lessing calls into question not only our culture's entire history of madness as the "female malady," but also invalidates the feminine madness/masculine rationality opposition on which assumptions about madness rest (as figured by the Celia/Caz split in Smith's *The Holiday;* see also *FM*).

This blending, balancing strategy consistently characterizes Martha's approach to self-education. When she looks to Rosa Mellendip's spiritualism, for example, she ultimately finds it

> self-satisfied [and] stagnant, the mirror and shadowside of the ortho-
> dox scientific world which was also . . . self-satisfied, stagnant. One

was a rationalism which had once been useful, a patterning of habit-thoughts already outdated by what was happening on its own outposts. . . .

Elsewhere was the sense of sharp change. . . . But not in the backwaters of "rationalism" which was the official culture, and not in the mirror of the official culture. [*FGC* 485]

In her search for the "knowledge of interconnectedness," however, Martha explores many diverse forms of marginalized, subjugated, or alien (to Western rationalism) knowledges: dreams, religions from Rosicrucianism to Zen, "Yoga . . . witchcraft, magic, astrology . . . vampirism," and so on, all of which, Martha decides, potentially speak the "same psychological truths" (486, 488). But before acknowledging this, "she had to fight off the distaste, a reluctance, implanted in her by her environment" (489). Lessing has often spoken out against the invidious limitations of traditional education, which she believes merely indoctrinates one into "an amalgam of current prejudice" (*GN* Preface in *SPV* 37) and locks one into a "dreadful system of thought" (quoted in Driver 19)—a system crippled by "false dichotom[ies] rooted in the heart of our culture" and giving rise to destructive comparison, competition, and commodification (*SPV* 35). We learn, she continues, "submission to authority." While children think of themselves as "free . . . with a free will and a free mind," on the contrary, each is "a prisoner of the assumptions and dogmas of his time, which he [*sic*] does not question, because he has never been told they exist" (35). The choices individuals think they have are themselves already determined by preestablished "patterns of feeling and thinking" (36). Those who resist such intellectual straitjacketing ironically become even further "divided against themselves" (35). Martha's search for both new knowledge and new ways of knowing combines a proto-Derridean impulse to deconstruct mutually reinforcing binarisms with what Annis Pratt calls the act of "unvention"—"tapping a repository of knowledge lost from Western culture but still available" to those with the necessary imagination (178).

Lessing *names* marginalized and suspect areas of lore and understanding (yoga, witchcraft, astrology, and so on), to which the general reader reflexively responds with varying degrees of distrust, aversion, and scorn. In this way she sets into action precisely the process of cultural reproduction she is attempting to expose and undermine. This strategy promotes self-consciousness in her readers, who find themselves automatically responding in the resisting, dismissive, and negating fashion Lessing would have us recognize and reconsider. Thus, as Foucault has argued, we become part of, but also resistors to, those cultural mechanisms which function in two ways: to maintain current power relations with as little stress to those relations as possible, and to contain the inevitable and continually renewed resistance that those relations manufacture. Accordingly, this vast normalizing network of cultural mechanisms tirelessly works to invalidate, co-opt, or neutralize those registers of understanding, those discourses, that deviate from or de-authorize dominant belief systems. These cultural mechanisms, Lessing reminds us, "were always exactly the same, whether political, religious, psychological, philosophic." Dragons guarded the entrances and exits of each layer in the spectrum of belief, or opinion" (*FGC* 489).[29] But these dragons can be slain, or at any rate, deconstructed, Lessing indicates, if we could only hit upon a workable technique.

By depicting two male characters who do stumble on promising methods but who subsequently fail to translate their radical epistemological forms into new ontological arrangements, Lessing indicates that any widespread epistemic shift first surfaces in individuals (men as well as women), who may nevertheless then find it impossible for one reason or another to complete the metamorphosis. Although inspired to explore that "unknown territory" of fresh insights and altered states of being, Mark Coldridge and Thomas Stern cannot finally cross the border into the waiting frontier. Instead of the saviors they aspire to be, they stand as tragic exemplars of the immense difficulty of refashioning the contours of heart and mind into shapes previously unimaginable and persistently alien to the "reality" that surrounds from without and within.

As Lisa Hogeland has pointed out, Mark's study becomes a model of a feminist epistemological process.[30] In this transformed space, many "kinds of knowing" (Wilshire)—reason, emotion, fact-gathering, and intuition—combine with an ethic of responsibility and care. The study altogether sheds its convention-bound form, assuming diverse functions: a hideaway where Mark broods in isolation; a bedroom where Mark and Martha cling together in mutual release, or simply talk; an office where they work together on various literary projects; a forum where friends, family, and visitors gather to discuss, share, celebrate—to connect. The versatility and openness of Mark's study—alternately an individual and communal space—would perhaps seem unremarkable if it were not for the concurrent evolution of the space itself. Out of his need to "see what was . . . *really* happening" in a world set on self-destruction, Mark tries to confront facts without the usual overlay of presuppositions, ignoring "nationalisms or politics" (*FGC* 282, 283). The study comes to serve as an "unconstituted committee," similar to Woolf's Outsiders' Society. On one wall Mark designates sites of the tangible production of destruction—missile sites and nuclear weapon facilities, armament and poison chemical manufacturers, war research institutions, areas contaminated by fallout, radioactive waste, and pollution, and so on. The other wall constitutes the first wall's "almost metaphysical" counterpart, its "markers denoting War, Famine, Riots, Poverty, Prisons." The juxtaposition and mutual referentiality of these two walls emphasize the fusion of the local and the global as well as the complex, intermeshing network of cause and effect that connects them.

Partners in revolutionary cartography, Mark and Martha together gather the information necessary for this preliminary charting of reality from the perspective of basic survival. Eventually they paper over every surface, including the ceiling, with facts—hard to ferret out facts which seemingly extend well beyond the walls' explicit parameters and which have little or no apparent relevance to one another. When even a "fifth wall" (the ceiling) proves inadequate, an additional, "hinged" wall is added (414). "The study no longer looked anything like a room" (413); indeed, with nothing but gravity to distinguish between walls and ceiling, with the addition of several "walls" which are not walls, the study no longer has a recognizable shape or purpose. It no longer denotes enclosure and exclusion but, rather, expansion and inclusion. More, in their category-defying arrangement of supposedly unconnected facts, Mark and Martha modify not only the shape of their epistemological space, but the manner in which the constituent parts fit together. Tagged by color-coded and multiform symbols, records of such ostensibly disparate bits of information as Lynda's dreams, recent scientific revelations, notes from a madwoman's journal, and data from space research coalesce into surprising new patterns of understanding which surpass so-called pure reason and uncover crucial new ways of making sense. The privileged and the marginalized, the rational and the irrational, the personal and the political, emotion and intellect, male and female, the one and the many—all these distinctions are erased in response to a shared and urgent conviction that "there's something we ought to be doing" about the world's dance with death (*FGC* 380).

As close as Mark comes to achieving an epistemological breakthrough, however, his allegiance to specific habits of mind prevents him from changing the shape of his future or the world's. Although rare in his ability both to sense fundamental but disguised interconnections and (as we shall see) to demythologize war, the ancient dragons of reason and nostalgia prove his undoing. Martha's newly tapped abilities to "plug into" a communally shared consciousness and to communicate telepathically provide a new source of understanding. But Mark turns away in revulsion, perceiving not an additional, legitimate mode of knowing, but a "nasty mixture of irony and St. John of the Cross and the *Arabian*

Nights" (*FGC* 613). Dismissing her accomplishment as self-delusional in-dulgence in wishful thinking and avoidance of hard reality, Mark relies on strictly rational and orderly plans, carefully enumerated in his *Memoran-dum to Myself*, for the realization of his safe harbor. His logic ironically progresses with military precision as he plans to salvage, by the conven-tional means of seeking provisional shelter, as many people as possible from the impending apocalypse. The word *provisional* is key here, for he seeks only to postpone, to palliate, and thus, finally, to accommodate the future—not to subvert or to transform it. His approach derives from a familiar "failure of the imagination," for unlike Martha, Mark cannot conceive that "there is another way to live" and in his heart of hearts "be-lieved in nothing but a recurring destruction" (*FGC* 132, 133). In self-fulfilling prophecy, his City in the Desert, that archetypal symbol of peace and harmony (which with perfect irony enters history only with its demise), materializes as nothing more than a refugee camp in a not-so-very-new order even more dysfunctional and tyrannical than the one it fol-lowed.

Furthermore, Mark looks back on this previous order through the sepia-tinted lens of nostalgia, thus reinvesting his failed marriage with the glow of romance and his once disabused patriotism with the rekind-led warmth of hearth and home, of love for England. Embittered and without hope, Mark confronts the paradox of his regression with self-conscious irony and confirms a root connection of which he remains sadly unaware: "Loving a country is like loving a person, it's all moonshine and anguish. . . . Yet the word England, England makes me ache, makes me stretch out my arms. . . . What I have felt has always been absurd. Lynda, and then Lynda, and then Lynda. Lynda and England. And now it is still Lynda and England" (*FGC* 610, 613). In the end Mark can extricate him-self from neither the plot of heterosexual romance nor a reflexive nation-alism as he succumbs to the Logic of History's twin stories and, therefore, to the nightmare of existential repetition.

Mark's more liberating methods have a prototype in the papers of Thomas Stern (in *Landlocked*), which comprise a puzzling pentimento of patchwork commentary and multiple discourses.[31] Paradoxically, Thomas's methods of seemingly random juxtaposition and apparently incoherent overlay promote understanding even as they problemetize it. His heavily annotated text, a multivocal fusion of "sense and nonsense" (*Ll* 272)—an admixture of Polish folksongs, family recipes, Yiddish jokes, how-to ar-ticles, and fables—denies categorization by genre, ignores rhetorical con-vention, negates order based on opposition, and refuses any hierarchy of discourse. As in Mark's study, unexpected reciprocal connections pop into view; paradox and undecidability are the rule. Stories of African villages at first seem "embedded" in the Polish text, but Martha soon observes that the converse is equally true, that "slap in the middle of Africa, [came] Poland" (*Ll* 271). Neither the stories about Africa nor those about Poland, a distinction which becomes meaningless, take priority but, rather, are indistinguishably part of each other, supplementing and modifying one other. Moreover, the life stories of the Africans, told mostly in the form of death stories (obituaries), move backward and forward in time, with total disregard for linear chronology. Instead, the recursive narrative movement shifting to and fro among ancestors, children, parents, and animals—all accorded equal importance—arises from associative processes, based on kinship ties, emotional affiliation, or empathy. Other unexpected connections are pointedly ironic. Thomas's recollection of a beating received at the hands of his father, for example, leads to his observation that the "mud-smeared savages" among whom he was living "don't beat their children" (*Ll* 271). Finally, the "notes, comments, scribbled over and across and on the margins of the original text, in red pencil" expand Thomas's linguistic space and even further radicalize the form of his text (*Ll* 269). Although "hard to decipher [they] were in themselves *a dif-*

ferent story or, at least, made of the original a different story" (emphasis added). In short, Thomas has revised traditional historical narrative, thus confounding expectations and demanding reconceptualization—precisely as Lessing does.

While his papers model alternative and revelatory modes of perception, however, they also tell a tale of Thomas's failure to close the gap between instinct and rational self-awareness and thus to rupture the circularity of history, to break the cycle of conflict. Ironically, the red-penciled meta-discourse, while flouting discursive conventions and traditional boundaries, illuminates mostly the bitterness, frustration, and self-hate that feed it. "'Vermin, vermin,' said the red pencil, 'the world is a lump of filth crawling with vermin!! . . . Swine. Murderers. Apes. . . . Kill. Kill, my comrades'" (*Ll* 271). The connections on which Thomas focuses to the exclusion of others are those that indict all humanity for unrelieved suffering and eruptions of violence. His epistemological breakthrough is subsumed and frustrated by unmitigated identification with his enemy, blinding rage, paralyzing despair and, most ironically, an "acquiescence in suffering" (272). When Mark recreates Thomas fictionally, the "mode of being" Martha once saw in Thomas's face but could not name achieves a tragic clarity (*Ll* 203). As a survivor of the death camps, who unequivocally rejects his heritage "of patience, of tolerance, of endurance," as a soldier whose one need is to strike back, Thomas/Aaron perversely becomes "a man seeking death . . . the mirror image of his parents and his ancestors; and his future, like theirs, was planned as death in a holocaust" (*FGC* 438). Immured in the quicksand of hatred, oppression, and retaliation,

Thomas, like Mark, cannot imagine a different "mode of being" and thus, despite his great urgency and need, cannot escape the exceedingly tenacious Logic of History.

While Mark and Thomas—would-be saviors with conspicuously Biblical names—cannot script a new ending for their lives, as Lessing's creations they are characters in familiar stories retold without the glossy patina of Judeo-Christian mythologizing. Casting Mark in the basically interchangeable roles of the good Samaritan, the romantic hero, and the crusading philanthropist, Lessing demonstrates that compassion, generosity, and even active intervention—good deeds—though laudable, prove futile if we cannot re-vision the stories we use to make sense of our lives. Thomas's messianic impulse takes the contrasting but equally familiar forms of avenging angel and avatar of justice. But his history and his stories challenge both the bellicose eye-for-an-eye code of the Old Testament and the passive turn-the-other-cheek ethic of the New. Lessing's story further suggests that the sins of humanity cannot be washed clean with blood (literal or figurative). Blood only begets more blood. Unlike the Biblical Martha, who asked Jesus to raise her brother Lazarus from the dead, Lessing's Martha places her faith in neither the Father nor the Son, but in a human capacity for self-transformation.[32] Having discountenanced these traditional stories of salvation, Lessing nonetheless refuses the "luxury of despair, the acceptance of disgust," which she derides as a form of "betrayal" and "cowardice" ("SPV" 11-12). We must, it seems, save ourselves in a fashion heretofore unimagined. If the old stories have deluded, failed, and entrapped us, let us reimagine them. Gifted with an abundance of "imagination, of sympathy," Lessing persistently does just that. Indeed, Martha seems to be speaking for her creator when she declares, "Those who could had a responsibility for those who could not" (*FGC* 492).

As we have seen, while Lessing was spinning out her epic tale, she was relentlessly exposing the skull beneath the skin of storytelling as we know it, disclosing its role in cultural reproduction and "normalization" of the individual. Clearly, her paradoxical notion that fiction, though inevitably a "lie," can also illuminate "truth" asserts itself throughout *Children of Violence*. Even while privileging one standard literary discourse (classic realism) and ostensibly adopting it, she was freely adapting it. And while she seemed to be reweaving the paradigmatic plots of war and romance, she was unravelling them, "forc[ing] a way through" their narrative borders and demonstrating their potential for timely evolution (Sinfield 226). Like Martha, who believes we must work through our "debts" (past mistakes), Lessing returns to the past, reconfiguring her life and the "history" through which she lived, in order to arrive at a newly imagined future.

Claire Sprague and Virginia Tiger speak, for example, of the "total eradication of the marriage plot" in the volume "ironically entitled *A Proper Marriage*" (7).[33] The revision becomes even more extensive in *The Four-Gated City,* in which Martha finally eschews romantic idealism, turning away from male as redeemer to herself and to "possibilities" that lie "elsewhere" than in men (*FGC* 287). Moreover, as Sprague has elsewhere noted, even the notion of the couple gives way to a triad, thus breaking free of dualistic constraints, in the mutually nurturing and constantly shifting relationship shared by Martha, Mark, and Lynda.[34] The one conspicuous flaw in their arrangement remains Mark's inability to abrogate, as Martha has, storybook romance. Like the couple, the family has similarly been displaced by community, whose ties arise from an ethic of care and have nothing to do with institutionalized relationships or legal contracts.

Similarly, (as others have demonstrated) Lessing has refashioned the female Bildungsroman, the realistic subgenre she names at the close of *The Four-Gated City* in order to call attention, it seems, to just how boldly she has flouted its conventions. The shift from couple to community also marks a movement from a single protagonist to what critics have variously called a group, transpersonal, or collective protagonist. The point of view in this final novel of the series appropriately broadens and destabilizes, thus allowing once objectified characters such as Mrs. Quest and Frances Coldridge their own interiority. Furthermore, Martha's maturation actually subverts traditional female growth patterns, leading Martha away from the telos of marriage, motherhood, and integration into society as a contributing (that is, culturally reproductive) member. One could therefore argue that *Children of Violence* ultimately makes for an anti-bildungsroman. Indeed, Molly Hite asserts that the series' conclusion "transform[s] what had appeared to be a five-volume bildungsroman . . . into an experimental narrative that culminates in a repudiation of the assumptions of personality [realist notions of a unified, discrete subject] and history that make the bildungsroman possible" (26).[35] Following this view, *Children of Violence,* like *The Golden Notebook,* becomes another "self-consuming artifact," the final volume's incongruent new directions, its ultimate lack of center, and its fantastic conclusion breaking through realism's boundaries and refuting its underlying assumptions.[36]

Lessing's concurrent task of demythologizing war would have proved somewhat easier if World War II, the "last good war," hadn't been so readily and comfortably "absorbed in myth," particularly the ur-myth of good versus evil (*FGC* 16). Even Martha can say that in the war against fascism "one's head and one's heart moved together. By and large and for better or worse, she, and everyone she knew, had been able to identify with their country, their side: and now, with . . . all the accounts done, they could still say, Yes, we were right, fascism was worse than anything"

(*FGC* 190).[37] And it was worse than anything. Except never breaking the habit of war at all; except the unimaginable horrors of nuclear Armageddon. So Lessing dares to put World War II into a broader perspective, positing that fighting wars even for the best causes does not make any war good, that this war was part of a larger pattern of escalating violence and civil tyranny, that the "causes" of the war extended well beyond Hitler's fanaticism, and most disconcerting of all, that the Allies's victory did not much change the overall scheme of things.

Mark, a World War II veteran, exposes the secret acquiescence, even collaboration, that Lessing sees behind the regret, the outrage, and the protest that greet every outbreak of war. According to Mark, though we claim to condemn war, to resist it however we can, without acknowledging the fact to ourselves we sanction it, even promote it. Politicians, the public, the press may act as if they believed war were preventable, even as if they were actively engaged in preventing it, but quite to the contrary, wars are "organised, planned for, expected" (*FGC* 125). Underlying this hypocrisy, he continues, lurks the unconscious conviction "that war was bound to happen, that nothing could have prevented it, and that forms of war would erupt again."

His self-fulfilling prophecy is born out in the Appendix to *Four-Gated City,* in which Lessing depicts the prelude to and aftermath of the next war, a "Catastrophe" so inevitable that it assumes an agency of its own and begins without apparent volition. She foresees increasingly diffuse, ubiquitous, and authoritarian mechanisms of power organized and dispersed under the "nasty amalgam" of government, religion, social conformity, human regimentation, "official science [and] . . . art," and (of course) the military (*FGC* 568). Motivated by the demands of late international capitalism, regulated by the omnipresent gaze of the social panopticon, and fueled by a flood of rhetoric and social unrest, Lessing's future takes the ugly shape of a "'Fascist' regime," the "iron heel" she elsewhere predicts.[38] Significantly, her dystopia resembles a high-tech version of Burdekin's fascist state in *Swastika Night, sans* the Hitlerian iconography. Lessing's fears for the future therefore appear to bring this study full circle. She follows the trajectory established by the narrative and metaphysical Logic of History in all its circularity, ending, it would seem, back where she—and we—began.

With thirty additional years of history from which to extrapolate, Lessing asserts that fascism, which has become the twentieth-century signifier for authoritarian oppression, will never be laid to rest until we can accomplish our own rebirths. In her defiant revision of the war story and history's final chapter, Joseph and the other "new children," born out of the Catastrophe with fully developed telepathic capacities to "see" and "hear" what others cannot, represent an evolutionary breakthrough that will short-circuit the cyclic trap that has metaphysically and historically circumscribed humanity, the children of violence. Born with the "knowledge of what the human race is in this century," the children "include that history in themselves and . . . have transcended it" (*FGC* 608). Thus, they need not reenact ancient roles in outworn plots or succumb to the "nightmare repetition." Metaphorically, they embody realized human potential for that "new knowledge," the transformed ways of seeing and being, that will redeem the future.

The appearance of these "*new* children" of violence in the Appendix of *The Four-Gated City* effects an ironic reversal of the series' defining title and leads to a reconsideration of the sequence as a whole. Thus, telling a different story of war, Lessing makes of the *original* a different story as well. Rather than merely inscribing acquiescence and/or simple protest, *Children of Violence* asserts the potential for active transformation and, if by fiat, denies the telos of history as we have known it. Just as this quintessential child of violence willfully imagines her own miraculous rebirth into a peaceful, harmonious new age, against all experience to the contrary she inscribes *truly* new life out of the ashes of Armageddon. Along with Anna, Lessing (like Woolf and Bowen's Pepita) wants to believe that "If people can imagine something, there'll come a time when they'll achieve it" (*GN* 276). But she finally leaves it to her readers to ponder the potential efficacy of her "different story." "If the words come," she would have us ask, "the reality will afterwards?"

Coda

As Time Goes By

In the Prologue to *A Rumor of War*, a nonfiction account of his experiences as a marine in Vietnam, Philip Caputo explains, "I have tried to describe accurately what . . . the Vietnam War was like for the men who fought it" (xx). Like many other combatants, Caputo wants to "warn men against war, by telling them the truth about it." Unlike most of his forebrothers-in-arms, however, he professes the apparent futility of his literary caveat: "It might, perhaps, prevent the next generation from being crucified in the next war. But I don't think so" (xxi). Caputo's pessimism seems sadly justified, for *A Rumor of War* tells the "same old story" of war with tragic fidelity. Despite sincere efforts to dispel the romantic myths of war and the consequent "compelling attraction of combat," his own perceptions and the very language in which they are formulated reproduce the persistently masculinist, quasi-fascist, and violently sexual discourse of war.

A "boyhood diet of war movies and blood-and-guts novels," Caputo admits, had filled his head with notion of war as "the ultimate adventure" (6). Thus, he joined the Marines in order "to prove something—my courage, my toughness, my manhood." He endured the "tortures" of basic training, he explains, out of fear of "emasculating" failure and contamination with "the virus of weakness" (10, 11). In class he uncritically absorbed the Marine Corps "mythology"—tales of larger-than-life heroics and glorious, self-validating victories. Succumbing to the "psychology of the mob, of the *Bund* rally," he became oblivious to the depravity of the ritual battle cry, "Gung ho! Gung ho! Pray for war!" (12). Once in the war, "a diminished capacity for compassion" and "an ineradicable streak of *machismo* bordering on masochism" become the price he pays to acquire "military virtues" (21, 27). Enclosed in a cycle of self-fulfilling expectation, the new initiate and his comrades classically conclude after each battle, "We've been under fire, we've shed blood, now we're men" (120). Like William Broyles, his fellow veteran turned writer, and like Alun Lewis, Keith Douglas, and countless others before them, Caputo experiences both the "addictive" intensity of war and its homosocial "intimacy . . . where the communion between men" is even more "profound . . . [than that] between lovers" (xvii).

Even more glaringly than in World War II, war's role in the cultural infusion of male identity with sexual violence flares into relief in the eroticized imagery Caputo uses to express the intense emotions of combat. The "thrill" of successful command during the heat of battle induces "an ache as profound as the ache of orgasm" (254). The interplay of "courage" and the "fear that has aroused it . . . produces a tension almost sexual in its intensity" (278). Another Vietnam vet, Mark Baker, unambiguously takes this metaphoric logic to its chilling conclusion: "A gun is power. To some people carrying a gun constantly was like having a permanent hard on. It was a pure sexual trip every time you got to pull the trigger" (*Nam* 206). For some, then, the conflation of military action and deadly phallic assault requires no camouflage. And (to appropriate the military idiom of Vietnam) women, as much as "gooks," were the fucking enemy: Baker reports that American soldiers who killed women after having sex with (raping) them were called "double veterans" (quoted in Wilden 169). Susan Brownmiller pertinently observes that the repeated gang rape of a Vietnamese woman included "individual acts of superfluous cruelty," the function of which was to establish "a masculine pecking order" (102).

While testifying to a defining link between combat and manhood, sexual violence and male potency, Caputo also records the paradoxically corresponding threat of diminished masculinity (likewise identified by the combatants and cultural historians of World War II). Fighting boredom and fear more often than the human enemy, marching endless miles of booby-trapped terrain, and constantly dreading "emasculat[ion]" by land mines, the Vietnam warriors often "felt more like victims than soldiers" (273). It is no wonder, then, that they "lusted after battle" (68), in which their compensatory role, active and empowering, was potentially that of virile executioner rather than hapless, helpless victim.

Seemingly unfazed by the psychosexual dynamic of his war story and oblivious or indifferent to its ominous implications for the protracted "fight for love and glory," Caputo nevertheless makes a germane observation. Although well versed in the literature of war, including "Wilfred Owen's poetry about the Western Front," in retrospect he reluctantly concludes, "I had learned nothing" (76). Although repeatedly "warned against war" by veterans of both World War II and Vietnam, he confesses, "None of us wanted to listen. . . . So I guess each generation is doomed to fight its wars, to endure the same old experience, suffer the loss of the same old illusions, and learn the same old lessons on its own" (77). Caputo's realization gives proof to its own historical accuracy. With ill-boding redundancy, his Vietnam war story echoes the twentieth century's tragically ironic first-person narratives of war as conventionally told by the men who lived them.

   Although the terrible explosions over Hiroshima and Nagasaki seemed to mark—and require—a decisive transition from one era of geopolitics to another, the psychosexual rhetoric of the war story simply escalated in proportion to war's kill potential. Nuclear arms had raised the stakes, with notable results: On the one hand, the sexually-encoded language of martial destruction as male sexual prowess became even more insistent and exaggerated. On the other, the discourse of high-tech war paradoxically co-opted the power of human procreativity, thus obfuscating the deadliness of nuclear arms even while asserting their singularly male omnipotence. From its "conception," marked by the "birth" of Little Boy and Fat Man, nuclear strategic doctrine has been rife with seemingly inconsistent metaphors of procreation, phallic aggression, and male sexual insecurity. Carol Cohn reports that the atomic and hydrogen bombs were known, respectively, as "Oppenheimer's" and "Teller's bab[ies]": deadly "male progeny" of previously inconceivable explosive potency ("Nuclear Language" 58). As Cohn notes, such "imagery confounds humanity's overwhelming technological power to destroy nature with the power to create . . . [and] converts . . . destruction into . . . rebirth." This attempt to disguise with doublespeak the catastrophic origins of the nuclear arms race and the policies that propel it brings to mind, among other legacies of World War II, the grotesque Auschwitzean motto "Work Makes One Free" and, of course, the Orwellian critique of the manipulation of language as a totalitarian means and end.

   Cohn decodes and attempts to disarm the doublespeak of "techno-strategic discourse" by "deconstructing" its gendered logic ("Emasculating" 161). The language of nuclear war and policy derives its power and validity from two ostensibly incompatible but in truth complementary aspects of masculine identity, according to Cohn. On the one hand, "Its public legitimacy stems in part from its apparent adherence to the highest standards of one ideal version of masculinity—the coolly objective, rationally calculated mind." On the other, "its 'felt truthfulness' and its power as a motivator come from the ways it taps into much more emotional masculine identity issues"—specifically, fears of emasculation and the promise of sexual domination. Thus, in the parlance of defense intellectuals, countries "lose their virginity" when they explode their first nuclear bomb ("Sex and Death" 696); military strategists search for "penetration aids," desire the "nicest holes" for their missiles, and call for bombs that deliver "more bang for the buck"; disarmament equals emasculation; megatonnage delivers an "orgasmic whump" and total war is known as "wargasm" ("Nuclear Language" 54, 55). Even the era of euphemistically "kinder and gentler" rhetoric has not deterred the United States Marines from openly defining warfare in terms of sexual assault. A 1989 graduation photo of a platoon and its training officers features men holding up several declamatory signs, one depicting a "naked woman" and another a "skull and crossbones" accompanied by the motto "kill, rape, pillage, and burn."[1] As Barbara Ehrenreich reluctantly concludes in an essay inspired by Operation Desert Shield (soon to become Desert Storm, the war with Iraq), the "warrior culture" seems here to stay.[2]

Does this mean, then, that the disclosures, the probing analysis, the experimental alternatives of the British women writing the Second World War fell on deaf ears? Did the ground in which they planted their seeds prove too hostile, too impoverished to nurture their ideas? Not exactly. Despite the apparently immutable nature of the militarist nation-state and equally recalcitrant states of mind and the war story, their strategic interventions have not proved altogether ephemeral. As Cohn's linguistic enterprise begins to suggest, the questions they raised in order to strip bare the shared infrastructure of domestic fascism and war continue to inform debate among feminist war and peace analysts of every stripe. The enormous scope of feminist theory relevant to any exploration of gender vis-à-vis war and peace necessarily subsumes war as an exclusive focus of analysis. Nonetheless, British women writing about World War II time and again accurately identified key nodes of theoretical inquiry and interventionist praxis that remain at the heart of a loosely bound network of antiwar intervention to this day. Knowingly or not, a significant number of feminists and/or pacifists, theorists and/or activists have built on the foundation established by the revisionary stories of World War II, including their general critique, specific points of analysis, suggested methods, and implied goals.

The volubly debated issue of women's and feminism's perennially vexed relation to peace remains as "complex and ambivalent" as ever (Carroll 6).[3] In a consideration of the historical and theoretical connections between feminism and pacifism, for example, historian Berenice A. Carroll acknowledges the ideological contradictions and historical "tension[s] between the women's peace movement and the organized feminist movement" (6). She nevertheless finds "a compelling logic" for the "integration of feminism and pacifism on an intellectual level" (6, 18) based on (among other things) the "interconnections among *patriarchy*, domination, and war," and a "shared concern with the elimination of *violence* in both 'private' and 'public' spheres" (19). Calling for non-essentialist analysis that does not "founder on the realities of women's multifarious non-maternal, non-nurturant behaviours," Carroll not only reflects the personal and political tensions felt and explored by Woolf and her sister writers, but seems to catalog the implicitly feminist issues that inform their narratives:

> (a) the emergence of patriarchy and war together in the history of "civilization" (coinciding also with the emergence of class or caste societies, slavery and racism); (b) the male monopoly of "legitimate" or state violence and its functions in maintaining the powerlessness and subordination of women; (c) the patriarchal character of military exploitation of women in service roles and prostitution; (d) the role of mass rape in warfare; and (f) the promotion of war and battle "heroism" as proofs of "masculinity" in patriarchal propaganda. [20]

The "full and careful analysis" Carroll calls for has its fictional counterpart in the "other" war stories catalyzed by World War II.

Carol Cohn's stated goal of "emasculating America's linguistic deterrent" demonstrates one of the several forms this evolving antimilitarist project has taken. Behind her firm academic voice speaks the still resonant chorus of her literary foremothers. The first stage of Cohn's enterprise is "to describe, analyze, and explore the effects of technostrategic discourse"—the present-day justification for the necessity of continuing war's story without meaningful revision. Like Woolf and Lessing, she objects to this discourse because it dangerously impairs human consciousness: it has "colonized our minds and . . . subjugated other ways of understanding relations among states, the women, men, and children who live in them, and the planet itself" ("Emasculating" 154). Thus, Cohn wishes to "break its stranglehold on our . . . imaginations," to "render this discourse 'impotent and obsolete'" by "expos[ing] its limits and distortions, its underlying assumptions and values, and the vast gaps between what it claims to do and what it actually does" (155). Finally, again reiterating Woolf and Lessing, she writes of her desire to "foster the development of more . . . humane ways of thinking . . . to open some new space and make some new connections" (155). As if in response to British women's altered war narratives and to Carroll's call for an appropriate theoretical articulation, Cohn captures the efficacy of the story behind these "other" stories in her claim that "destabilizing and interrupting patriarchal discourse"—in particular the discourse of war—is essential for "establishing new paradigms . . . and for creating systems of knowledge based on different values and interests."

To be sure, a notable portion of feminist war and peace analysis remains (like Smith's Pompey Casmilus) locked into the conceptual dualisms that define war and its traditional telling. Nevertheless, other approaches define themselves by, and self-consciously employ, the deconstruction/reconstruction methods implicit in or actively encouraged by many of the war stories we have considered. In her theoretical examination of *Sexism and the War System*, for example, Betty Reardon reasons that dualistic thinking "has negatively exaggerated and manipulated the difference between men and women and kept us playing the war game for most of history" (93). Like Woolf, Nancy Huston, and others who believe that marginalization facilitates conceptual flexibility, Reardon calls for a "feminine mode of transformation" (32). The advantage of the so-called feminine—that is, holistic and reciprocal—mode is that it tends to "transcend polarization" by rendering more permeable the borders "between science and philosophy, fact and value, the individual and the community, the family and the state, the public and the private spheres, citizens and nurturers, and male and female social roles" (92). As Pompey Casmilus belatedly intuits and Martha Quest finally knows, power must be redefined as the "capacity to change . . . ourselves and our environment"; and that capacity must entail a movement away from "competition, alienation, and fragmentation" toward "cooperation, complementarity, and integration" (Reardon 91-92). In short, then, as the British women's literature of World War II collectively suggests, bringing an end to the "fundamental symbiosis between sexism and the war system" (2) ultimately requires the dissolution of boundaries, the making of new combinations, the unfettering of the human imagination, and the writing of a new plot.

Rather like the narrator of the utopian conclusion of *The Four-Gated City*, some theorists (too) optimistically perceive this re-vision as well under way. French philosopher Elisabeth Badinter, for example, identifies "negative complementarity"—"One" as the "reverse of the Other"—as the "source of a kind of war between the sexes. . . . Having learned from experience that complementarity carries with it the germ of inequality and oppression," however, the "lesser" halves of the human dualism have set out to "undermine its foundations" (150). The resulting change—including the "blurring" of sex roles—"engenders a resemblance that puts an end to this war." The One has thus *become* the Other, Badinter boldly claims, carefully explaining that this paradoxical mutuality does not entail complete and stable co-identification but, rather, signifies "that the One *participates* in the Other . . . that they are at the same time similar and dissimilar" (149).

This simultaneous recognition of difference and mutuality, the fluid closure of gaps, epistemological and ontological flexibility, active acceptance of paradox—these are the salient characteristics of the feminist peace politics embodied in women's projects such as the Women's Pentagon Action and extolled by Ynestra King in her Afterward to *Rocking the Ship of State: Toward a Feminist Peace Politics* (Harris and King). Significantly, this contemporary politics is grounded in both the "truthtelling of art" and the enabling necessity of theory, thus effecting precisely the mergence of (re)presentation and (re)cognition that the literature we have been studying is concerned with. Similarly, the enterprise King describes combines theory and practice, reason and emotion, political savvy and naïvete, and opposition and reconciliation. This cooperative endeavor privileges neither "traditional femininity" nor "radical feminist militance"; on the contrary, it "challenges that basic dualism" and blends the two perspectives, drawing on the strengths and efficacy of both (285). The disparate members of this "hodgepodge of organizations and political actions" likewise challenge the "whole idea of culture against nature" (285). They posit deep, intimate connections between "the militarization of culture" and an "antivitalist cultural ideology" (284) that (re)creates the many "forms of oppression and dominance" their agenda actively resists: "hunger, violence, racism, sematophobia, imperialism, and the devastation of nature" (289). Claiming greater affinity with "art than science," King and her associates strive to generate a perspective and methods that are at once "critical and exemplary," deconstructive and "reconstructive/utopian" (281, 288). "All is connectedness," proclaims the Unity Statement of the Women's Pentagon Action, written by Grace Paley (287). As King explains, the purpose of this organization, like other groups that share its philosophy, is not merely to promote disarmament and peace, but to stimulate the "imagination," "to devise a formula for connecting human beings with what is most deeply feeling and most deeply alive in themselves," and, ultimately, to "transform the social and economic structures that oppress human beings and are killing the planet" (282).

King's notes toward a feminist peace politics provide an appropriate (non)closure for this consideration of British women's revisions of the classical war story, but not (or not simply) because her position represents a point along a linear trajectory of thought. A simple progression ultimately proves an inadequate and misleading formulation of both feminist war/peace theory and of my enterprise. To be sure, interventionists like those of the Women's Pentagon Action are in some sense the "other" story of war come to life because in many ways they enact the conflicted, multifaceted confrontation with a militarist, masculinist world view limned by the literary women of World War II. Indeed, King claims that "unlike Cassandra, and all the women who have been silenced"—women whose war stories have been unheard, forgotten, ignored, or dismissed—"we have reached a historical moment when we can and must be listened to" (295). But while this moment may seem the result of what has come before, it is also a regeneration, a renewal; similarly, our reconsideration of these tales of past wars indicates both a return and a departure. For it is only through the historical, theoretical, and experiential contingencies of our own perceptions and experience that we are able to travel back to the future, to create possibilities for a *new* plot by revisiting the old one.

As the editors of *Arms and the Woman* observe, "the meaning of war changes as the narrative is revised. . . . As an object of discourse . . . its meaning . . . changes as culture codifies that meaning differently" (*AW* 19). Thus, the illuminating cultural and discursive instability of World War II—the singular "clarifying moment" of the war against fascism—enabled those receptive to a new and elusive "truth about war" to revise the "same old story" and to "change" (clarify, broaden) the meaning of war in the process. In similar fashion, on the fiftieth anniversary of that war, the advantage of our feminist, poststructuralist, post-Vietnam perspective and experience enables us to reconstruct and continue their revisionary efforts. Indeed, we unavoidably repeat their writerly act, reading and (re)writing their "meaning" both as (apparently) codified in the war era and as modified by ours. Thus, we not only reincarnate the once-silenced Cassandras, we amplify their voices for the present and broadcast them into a yet to be determined future.

And so I return now to the two commentators I relied upon to establish a rhetorical framework for my inquiry: to the British officer who recognized the Second World War as yet another chapter in a wretchedly immutable "historical story," and to Dorothee Sölle, who asked the tellers of war tales, "Is there no other way?" Adding my voice to theirs, I have suggested to "those who have passed the tale down, written it down, recited it, and believed it" (Reardon, *Sexism* epigraph) that "the meaning of war [can] change as the narrative is revised" (*AW* 19). In the spirit of Woolf, Lessing, and the rest, who would write a different story, Denise Levertov captures the formidible challenge of this endeavor in her meditation on "Making Peace"(1987):

> A voice from the dark called out,
> "The poets must give us
> imagination of peace, to oust the intense, familiar
> *imagination of disaster.* Peace, not only
> the absence of war."
> But peace, like a poem,
> is not there ahead of itself,
> can't be imagined before it is made,
> can't be known except
> in the words of its making,
> grammar of justice,
> syntax of mutual aid.
> A feeling towards it,

dimly sensing a rhythm, is all we have
until we begin to utter its metaphors,
learning them as we speak.
                                    A line of peace might appear
if we restructured the sentence our lives are making,
revoked its reaffirmation of profit and power,
questioned our needs, allowed
long pauses. . . .
                           A cadence of peace might balance its weight
on that different fulcrum; peace, a presence,
an energy field more intense than war,
might pulse then,
stanza by stanza into the world,
each act of living
one of its words, each word
a vibration of light—facets
of the forming crystal.

Notes

1. See, for example, Lionel Tiger, *Men in Groups*. Like Broyles, Tiger argues that aggression and sexuality are profoundly linked and, furthermore, finds aggression in males analogous to childbearing in females. For a dissenting response, see Theodore Roszak's introductory remarks in "Why Men Need a Boys' Night Out."

2. And occasionally in a man's; see in particular Frank Tilsley, *Little Tin God* (1939).

3. The works of H.D., Kay Boyle, Gertrude Stein, Harriette Arnow, Muriel Spark, Sylvia Townsend Warner, and Olivia Manning, for example, often reveal a similar awareness of the "politics of gender . . . in the politics of war" (J. Scott 26). See, for example, H.D.'s *Trilogy,* Manning's *Balkan* and *Levant Trilogies,* Arnow's *The Dollmaker,* and Spark's *The Girls of Slender Means.*

4. The phrase "to tell the truth about the war" is originally from Sassoon's *The Memoirs of George Sherston,* but has been widely used, for example by Herbert Read, who survived the war with "a resolve / to tell the truth without rhetoric / the truth about war and about men / involved in the indignities of war" (quoted in Rutherford 77).

5. This is particularly true in cinema, for example, *Memphis Belle, Hope and Glory, Empire of the Sun, For the Boys,* and *Shining Through.*

1 DISCERNING THE PLOTS

1. Although this story is drawn from a narrow cultural tradition, other western myths (classical Greek, Roman, Norse) have numerous stories with analogous plots.

2. Sedgwick attributes this notion to Jean Baker Miller, *Toward a New Psychology of Women,* 1976.

3. Roszak's examples of the hyper-masculinist political rhetoric of the nineteenth and early twentieth centuries are revealing. Theodore Roosevelt declared, "The nation that has trained itself to a cancer of unwarlike and isolated ease is bound . . . to go down before other nations which have not lost *the manly and adventurous virtues*" (quoted in "The Hard and the Soft" 92). An earlier comment by an influential Spanish political philosopher and statesman, Juan Donoso-Cortés, is even more explicit: "When a nation shows a civilized horror of war, it receives directly the punishment of its mistake. God changes its sex, despoils it of its

common mark of virility, changes it into a feminine nation, and sends conquerors to ravish it of its honor" (quoted in "The Hard and the Soft" 92).

4. For Paul Fussell, this sign manipulation merely represents a move to undercut the "pomposity implied by official acronyms . . . by providing unexpected meanings" (*GWMM* 259). Since World War II, such meanings (rape as military action) have become less unexpected. For a thorough account of the sexually assaultive rhetoric of the war in Vietnam and its cultural representations, see Susan Jeffords, *The Remasculinization of America*.

5. For a more detailed discussion of this point, see Pierson, "'Did your mother wear army boots?'"

6. Catherine Marshall was an active feminist who helped plan The Hague International Woman's Conference (which disregarded national boundaries in the interest of peace) during the war, opposed conscription, and worked for the Women's International League for Peace until the late 1930s, when "the evil she saw in Nazism led her to modify her absolute pacifist stance" (Kamester and Vellacott 20).

7. Charles Kay Ogden, a scholar of Magdalene College, Cambridge, was also editor of *Cambridge Magazine* and wrote for *Common Cause* (official organ of the NUWSS) and *Jus Suffrigii* on various subjects, such as women's rights, birth control, and antimilitarism. Mary Sargant Florence, an active feminist and pacifist, was also a prominent artist.

8. Not all who wrote war-related fiction of this era were of like mind in this matter. Martin Ceadel reports that the "ability of women to prevent war" became a popular literary theme as World War II approached. He cites, for example, Maboth Moseley's *War Upon Women* (1934), in which women prevent war by refusing to have children; George Cornwallis-West's *The Woman Who Stopped War* (1935), in which a pacifist becomes the mistress of an arms dealer in order to bankroll the women's peace movement; and Eric Linklater's *The Impregnable Women* (1938), in which women declare an "international sex-strike" to prevent war (quoted in Ceadel 178). While these novels give Ceadel a good chuckle, I.F. Clarke takes them more seriously, arguing that *The Woman Who Stopped War* shows the "masculine world . . . to be morally bankrupt" (174). *The Impregnable Woman,* he continues, though a Lysistrata-like comedy, questions the "validity of the wholly male world of politics and warfare" (176).

9. See Paul Smith, *Discerning the Subject,* for a useful discussion of the difference between humanist and poststructuralist notions of the "self" or "subject" and the implications of such theorizing for resistance to dominant ideologies.

10. In *My Early Life* (1930), Churchill made a similar observation: "War, which used to be cruel and magnificent, has now become cruel and squalid. In fact it has become completely spoilt. It is all the fault of Democracy and Science. . . . [W]e now have entire populations, including women and children, pitted against one another in brutish mutual extermination" (quoted in Calder 90).

11. In addition to Paul Fussell and Gilbert and Gubar on World War I fiction, see Cadogan and Craig, Parfitt, Tylee, Higonnet et al., and Cooper, Munich, and Squier, and especially Marcus ("Corpus/Corps/Corpse") and Longenbach.

12. Paul Fussell, on the contrary, notes that not only was sex, a traditional "anodyne" to various discomforts and unpleasantnesses, in "short supply," but that on the whole attitudes were rather puritanical (96, 105): "sex before marriage was regarded as either entirely taboo or gravely reprehensible" (*Wartime* 106). This observation does not tally, however, with the sexual permissiveness most chroni-

clers find characteristic of the war era, nor with wartime statistics recording notable increases in both venereal disease and "illegitimate" births.

13. Of course, some women *were* eager to return to the "normalcy" of their prewar lives. As Calder points out, adding fulltime factory work to their usual responsibilities "was hardly emancipation" (401). Alice Coats's sardonic "The 'Monstrous Regiment'" articulates a different perspective on restoration of the status quo. The poem's narrator takes for granted women's ability to step into men's jobs, but rues the men's absence:

> What hosts of women everywhere I see!
> I'm sick to death of them—and they of me.
>
> . . . .
>
> Mechanics are supplanted by their mothers;
> Aunts take the place of artisans and others;
> Wives sell the sago, daughters drive the van,
>
> . . . .
>
> Postman and milkman—all are ladies now.
> Doctors and engineers—yes, even these—
> Poets and politicians, all are shes.
>
> . . . .
>
> All, doubtless, worthy to a high degree;
> But oh, how boring! Yes, including me. [Reilly 29-30]

14. Angus McBride's color plates in Cassin–Scott's *Women at War* reveal how the British view of the female stereotype varied depending on the woman's nationality. The British and American women in uniform are without exception drawn as slender, attractive, highly professional, and noticeably feminine (stylish, made-up, well-coifed, soft). The facial features of the uniformed German women, though not unattractive, are more severe, in some cases suggesting androgyny. And some are shown smoking cigarettes. The Russian women, drawn as downright plain and less curvaceous, appear decidedly masculine. The one whose features are coarsest carries a revolver on her hip and a machine gun in her hand.

15. In this light, professional propagandist Cecil King's comments about Churchill as the personification of England are especially ironic: "Churchill *is* wartime England—England with all its age, its waning virility. . . . He has no contribution to make to our future, but he personifies our present and our past" (quoted in Kendall 91-92). Scholars agree that World War II marked America's replacement of Britain as the dominant Western power.

16. *The Grand Canyon* (1942) is a "cautionary tale" meant to warn against the "terrible consequences" of an "undefeated Germany"; it depicts what might happen if Germany were to defeat Britain and to strike a peace bargain with the United States. The Germans, of course, betray America. The novel is an interesting comment on how real the possibility of defeat seemed in England in 1941, when the story was conceived.

17. In America Carrie Chapman Catt and the NAWSA responded in similar fashion (see Elshtain, *Women and War* 113-14). As in England, however, a minority of feminists, including, for example, Jane Addams, opposed the war.

18. From *King Edward, the Kaiser and the War* by Edward Legge.

19. For further discussion of the possible origins of the reciprocal development of patriarchy and militarism, see Gerda Lerner, Ruby Rohrlich, and Marvin

Harris. The latter's argument seems to me an example of the inability to question one's masculinist assumptions and how they determine one's interpretation of the past (ironically, a problem that Harris explains away in his essay).

20. In this essay, White considers the constitutive role of the "dominant figurative mode of language" in defining both substance and meaning in narrative. He argues that to a great extent, the interpretation of any event is "immanent in the very language which the historian must use to *describe*" it, and that this in turn imposes the *form* of the resulting narrative ("Historical Text" 94).

21. For a dissenting discussion of the "patriarchal myths of scarcity and competition" prevalent in theories of evolution, see Gross and Averill.

22. Campbell does mention a third point of view, one "neither affirming nor denying war as life, and life as war, but aspiring to a time when wars should cease" (199). Such eschatological myths (e.g., the Christian prophecy of Christ's Second Coming) are predicated on a wholly transformative "cosmic crisis" preceded by great wars and initiating an atemporal, otherworldly state of static perfection. Of course, this represents the culmination of yet another master plan/narrative—one that discounts human agency.

23. Charles Johnson's *Oxherding Tale* (1982), although not a war narrative, is an excellent example of a male writer's ideological/narrative struggle to escape the metaphysical logic of hierarchical dualisms, most notably in terms of race and gender. Joseph Heller's *Catch-22,* on the other hand, demonstrates that experimental, non-realist narrative form guarantees neither resistance to the "same old story" on all levels or cognizance that any meaningful escape from our ontological catch-22 is possible.

24. Paul Fussell has obviously read Manning's *Balkan* trilogies and Bowen's *The Heat of the Day,* both of which he mentions. And although he has also read Woolf's *Between the Acts* (and, presumably, *Three Guineas*), he lists Woolf among those who "had little to say about the war" (*Wartime* 133).

2 Inscribing An/Other Story

1. Hynes briefly mentions a few essays or book reviews by Virginia Woolf, Rosamund Lehmann, Storm Jameson, and Elizabeth Bowen, but none of their fiction.

2. Hynes's two foremost examples are Auden and Isherwood's *Ascent of F6* and Graham Greene's *Journey without Maps.*

3. Of the futuristic novels of the 1930s and 1940s, the majority specifically oppose fascism; these include Storm Jameson's *Then We Shall Hear Singing* (1942) and Vita Sackville-West's *The Grand Canyon* (1942). For additional discussions of prophetic novels of World War II, see Martin Ceadel and I.F. Clarke.

4. For a discussion of "cognitive estrangement," see Darko Suvin, 4-11.

5. Daphne Patai, the scholar who rescued *Swastika Night* from oblivion, has discovered that after 1930 Burdekin, who had already published six novels, began writing under the name Murray Constantine. See Patai, "Orwell's Despair, Burdekin's Hope: Gender and Power in Dystopia" and the afterword in *The End of This Day's Business* (one of Burdekin's two other novels currently in print). This companion text to *Swastika Night* depicts an extremely "ambiguous utopia" (to borrow a phrase from Ursula K. LeGuin) in which women have become dominant and men are kept submissive and compliant by means of various—and quite familiar—psychosocial manipulation. Burdekin thus depicts this role reversal as prob-

lematic despite what she imagines would be its clear advantages, such as the establishment of permanent peace and a classless society.

6. As Patai explains, Weininger was a proto-fascist ideologue who characterized women as passive, submissive pure negation, as obsessed with sexuality, and as an obstacle to men's morality. In true fascist fashion, he disparagingly contrasted women and Jews with men and Aryans. According to Weininger, "the woman of the highest standard is immeasurably beneath the man of the lowest standard" (quoted in Intro., *SN* viii).

7. As in, for example, Walter M. Miller, Jr.'s *A Canticle for Leibowitz* (1959) and Margaret Atwood's *The Handmaid's Tale* (1985).

8. See Dale Spender (163-182) for a discussion of the politics of naming within the specific contexts of sexuality and of God as male. For a broader sampling of various aspects of the feminist critique of language, see Cameron.

9. See Nancy Huston, "The Matrix of War: Mothers and Heroes," for a relevant discussion of the historic misconception that attributes the "specifically female and somewhat terrifying power" of procreation exclusively to males, specifically in terms of the "symbolic equivalence between childbirth and war" (160, 161). For German military theoretician Clausewitz (and many others), the male appropriation of giving birth logically (if metaphorically) extends to the patriarchal state: "War develops in the womb of State politics; its principles are hidden there as the particular characteristics of the individual are hidden in the embryo" (quoted in Huston, "Matrix" 167).

10. In addition to de Beauvoir, see Sheila Rowbotham. For discussion of the political and social position of women in Britain during and after the war, see Vera Douie, Denise Riley, and Elizabeth Wilson.

11. Richard J. Evans, in *Comrades and Sisters: Feminism, Socialism and Pacifism in Europe, 1870-1945,* and Maria-Antoinetta Macciochi, in "Female Sexuality in Fascist Ideology," attempt to account for "the problem of women's 'consent to' fascism" (Macciochi 67) from different perspectives. Evans suggests sociohistorical explanations while Macciochi takes a psychological and semiotic approach, arguing (in Jane Caplan's words) that "women have . . . been the willing accomplices of fascist regimes" because "the system of signs and unconscious representations which constitute the 'law' of patriarchy is invoked in fascist ideology in such a way that women are drawn into a particular supportive relation with fascist regimes" (61).

12. In *The End of This Day's Business* Burdekin reiterates this point, but in reverse, for in a matriarchal society, it is the men who fail to develop psychologically and intellectually. Her point once again is that no one gender should be—or even feel—superior to another.

13. Woolf's extended procreation metaphor (*Room of One's Own* 106-8) regarding artistic creativity reflects this notion: The effect of "unmitigated masculinity . . . upon the art of poetry" will be the creation of a "horrid little abortion," shortlived "monsters." Without androgyny of the mind "the intellect seems to predominate and the other faculties of the mind harden and become barren" (107). "Some collaboration has to take place in the mind between the woman and the man [in each individual] before the act of creation can be accomplished. Some marriage of opposites has to be consummated" (108).

14. For elaboration of this point, see Patai's comparison of *Swastika Night* and *Nineteen Eighty-Four* in "Orwell's Despair, Burdekin's Hope: Gender and Power in Dystopia" and her book-length study *The Orwell Mystique: A Study in*

Male Ideology. Orwell's *Coming up for Air* (1939), in which he manifests his own misogyny-tainted anxieties about war-induced social change and impending totalitarianism, is particularly instructive in this regard.

15. "*Danse macabre*" is from Jean Bethke Elshtain's "Women as Mirror and Other: Toward a Theory of Women, War, and Feminism," to which I am indebted for its lucid discussion of the reciprocal, even symbiotic nature of the phallocentric oppositional (dominance/submission) paradigm. Elshtain rightly insists that cultural notions of male and female "require one another, feed one another, are a neat dualistic match, a deadly *danse macabre* with each as Other to the other" (40). Both Elshtain's and Burdekin's (implied) argument have much in common with Dinnerstein's in *The Mermaid and the Minotaur.*

16. Joan W. Scott charts a path through the still thorny thicket of the equality and difference issue in "Deconstructing Equality-Versus-Difference: Or, the Uses of Poststructuralist Theory for Feminism."

17. In 1920 Harriet Stanton Blatch, writing about the Great War, pointed to the "dangers of war for the survival of democratic forms": "the most soul-killing reaction of war is the denial of the right to think and to express thought freely" (quoted in Elshtain, "Women as Mirror" 40). As Gordon Wright (*The Ordeal of Total War*) reminds us, Tocqueville made a similar observation: War endangers the usual liberties of democratic nations, intensifying "the traditional balance between authority and liberty" as the central government must "borrow such authoritarian techniques as [are] necessary for survival and victory" (243). War's impact on "social structures," Wright adds, "may be even deeper and more durable" than Tocqueville realized, for civilian values are partially replaced by military ones and a "more hierarchical set of relationships" is imposed (244). Paul Fussell makes this point exactly in his fascinating analysis of the widespread and tenacious ramifications (social, political, artistic, psychological, and cognitive) of World War II (*Wartime*).

18. According to Calder, pacifism was more generally tolerated during the Second World War than during the First but harder to justify because of the blatant evils of Nazism. During World War II 59,192 people claimed conscientious objector status, four times as many as in World War I, and more than half agreed to take up "approved work" as a substitute for military service. Besides the Society of Friends, the Peace Pledge Union (to which Vera Brittain belonged) was the only large pacifist organization.

19. Angus Calder reports that Lord Vansittart, chief diplomatic adviser to the British government, gave a series of talks on the Overseas Service of the BBC, in which he propagated race hatred of the Germans, conveniently "ignoring the origin of the 'Anglo-Saxons' themselves" (490). He characterized Germans as historically "brutal butchers," identified "envy, self-pity, and cruelty" as their fundamental traits, labeled them a "predatory and bellicose" breed, and claimed that Hitler gave them what they "liked and wanted." The attitude that "ALL GERMANS ARE GUILTY" (a newspaper headline) became known as "Vansittartism," which "at least in its cruder forms," Calder adds, "was the creed of a vocal minority" (491).

20. For firsthand autobiographical material, see Kay Dick, "Talking to Stevie."

21. Smith attended secretarial school because she could not afford her first choice, the London School of Journalism, and because the headmistress of her secondary school thought her "an unsuitable candidate for university" (Barbera

and McBrien 40). Smith agreed that she was not ready for the distractions of higher education, but apparently later "regretted her lack of a university education" (40).

22. Rebecca West's "Indissoluble Matrimony" (1914), a World War I story of near-murderous domestic discord that similarly invokes, in James Longenbach's words, the "rhetoric of military confrontation" ("Women and Men of 1914" 99) bears comparison with "Sunday at Home." Ironically, considering Wyndham Lewis's position on women and modern art, West's story was originally published in the first issue of *Blast* (20 June 1914).

23. Barbera and McBrien view this relationship as I do but within a narrower context and without elaborating on its broader implications.

24. On Vera Brittain and pacifism, see Muriel Mellown and Lynne Layton.

25. Paul Fussell argues that the Battle at Somme marked an abrupt shift from innocence into the disillusioning "knowledge of good and evil" for the fighting men of the Great War, a rift in consciousness which has subsequently permanently modified Western perceptions of war (*GWMM* 29).

26. In her review of de Beauvoir's *The Second Sex*, Smith takes the author to task for a similar betrayal: "Miss De Beauvoir has written an enormous book about women and it is soon clear that she does not like them and does not like being a woman" (quoted in Barbera and McBrien 191).

27. Woolf similarly ruminates on the difficulty of this change in *A Room of One's Own*, asking, "When the guns fired in August 1914, did the faces of men and women show so plain in each other's eyes that romance was killed?" (15).

28. It is interesting to note that, rather than dressing as a male, Smith was noted for her child-like clothing and general appearance (Barbera and McBrien 3), perhaps an idiosyncratic manifestation of her ambivalence about donning the costumes of fully developed femininity.

29. For a discussion of the increasing militarization of women's lives in various capacities see Cynthia Enloe, *Does Khaki Become You?*

30. A poem entitled "Who Shot Eugenie?" (1950) less ambiguously expresses Smith's concern that the sanctioned violence of war all too insidiously infects one's consciousness and fatally poisons relations with others, even those whom we do not consider enemies. The speaker complains that military duty dehumanizes and alienates:

> How blank is the heart when on service bent
> Empty of all but official content
> So inappropriate is all individual consideration
> So impossible in the individual a communal realization
> Of states', peoples', any group-mind's preoccupation,
> That a girl in the service of her country at war
> Must have a mind as blank as a wall
> Apt only to carry
> The terms of her commission and hurry.

The speaker and her riding companion, Eugenie, "were old campaigners" out of whom the "heart" and the "virtue" had drained. This foreshadowing nevertheless leaves the reader unprepared for the poem's tragic, enigmatic conclusion, which suggests that murderous agency in this case must be deflected onto warring "ways without ending." After a harrowing night scarred by dreams in which nature itself is a "hostile" agent "deploying and advancing with the power of death," the speaker awakens to find that

> . . . Eugenie was dead,
> Shot, with a bullet through her head.
> Yet every chamber in her revolver was full to plenty
> And only in my own is there one that is empty.
>   [*Selection* 124-25]

31. As Elaine Showalter has noted, while the "image of the madwoman" has evolved historically to coincide with the "shifting definitions of female insanity," the "feminine nature of Ophelia's insanity" has consistently "contrasted with Hamlet's universalized metaphysical distress" (*FM* 10, 11). And although in "modern literature and art, the schizophrenic woman stands for the alienation and fragmentation of the age"—as she surely does in *The Holiday*—Showalter reminds us that even modern stories of female madness tend to "operate as ways of control-ling and mastering feminine difference itself" (19, 17). In her Ophelia-like act of self-immolation, however, Celia calls attention to the disabling trap such notions of feminine difference entail. More, if one considers the trilogy as a whole, Smith has appropriated the story of female madness and recoded it *as* metaphysical distress. Ironically, then, Smith adopts/adapts a classic madwoman plot in order to chal-lenge its conventional significance.

32. See Theweleit, *Male Fantasies* vol. 2 for a fascinating discussion of the reconstruction of the male body into impenetrable steel or other such hard sub-stances as a psychological defense mechanism for the maintenance of the inviolate self (especially against the female and the masses). As Anson Rabinbach and Jessica Benjamin explain in their Foreword, Theweleit demonstrates that "in this world of war the repudiation of one's own body, of femininity, becomes a psychic compul-sion which associates masculinity with hardness, destruction, and self-denial" (xiii).

3 DOUBLE-VOICED DISCOURSE

1. For a detailed account of Ireland's neutrality and Bowen's activities in Ireland during the war, see Robert Fisk, *In Time of War.*

2. Bowen's grandfather's name was Robert, the family name she chose for the spies (Robert Kelway and Robert Harrison) in *Heat of the Day.* Unlike the an-guished Robert Kelway, Robert Bowen, a Victorian patriarch who never ques-tioned England's greatness nor his own authority, became a content and successful man. However, the grandfather's nickname is not the only clue Bowen leaves that suggests the unpleasant consequences of his sternly autocratic personality for others. She admits that his children feared him, and she describes his wedding bed as "broad . . . as a battlefield" (*BC* 321).

Another model for Robert Kelway was Bowen's friend and lover, Charles Ritchie, a Canadian diplomat who remained friends with Bowen even after his mar-riage. He reports that she told him, "I would like to put you in a novel. . . . You probably wouldn't recognize yourself" (quoted in Ritchie 132). Although cer-tainly not a spy himself, Ritchie kept Bowen informed about espionage in diplo-matic circles, a topic that apparently fascinated her.

3. Although Glendinning similarly characterizes Bowen's writing as "full of tension," she finds Bowen unambiguously true to traditional values and, like

Cadogan and Craig, sees no hint of rebellion in Bowen's writing (xiii).

4. As Barbara Brothers explains, "'the big-house' tradition for Bowen was the embodiment of an authority . . . outside the self which provided the self a refuge and which also acted as a curb upon the intense power of the ego" (138).

5. Bowen traces the breakdown of Irish society to the introduction of democracy into the arrangement between Anglo-Irish landlords and their Irish tenants. She poignantly tells the disturbing story of Big George, the "benevolent" yet "despotic" landowner who lost his senses when his tenants turned on him by failing to vote for his chosen man. "It was democracy . . . that sent Big George mad," Bowen claims (*BC* 258). For Bowen democracy seems to have been part and parcel of the disastrous shift from cohesive, orderly "Society" to a fragmented and dangerously unfettered "period of Personal Life" (259).

6. For a more detailed study of Bowen's "Vision of Historical Process," see Lassner, who argues that Bowen "saw the immediate terrors of World War II as part of a cycle of wars in which the present recreates the infinitely regressing, un-resolved fears of the past" (quoted from an unpublished paper).

7. See *The Resisting Reader*, in which Judith Fetterly defines "immascula-tion" as the socialization of women "to think as men, to identify with a male point of view, and to accept as normal and legitimate a male system of values, one of whose central principles is misogyny" (xx).

8. All the page references to Bowen's short stories are from *The Collected Stories of Elizabeth Bowen*.

9. For a highly relevant discussion of Bowen's "profound ambivalence toward her own powers of authorship," see Harriet S. Chessman, who argues that Bowen's ambivalence toward story-making "involves a sense of her betrayal of her own gender" (70). From Bowen's fiction, Chessman continues, "emerges . . . the problematic of how women can produce their own stories, as subjects, without being 'appropriated to and by the masculine'" (71). I take up similar questions later in this chapter.

10. See Elshtain, *Women and War*. In her essay "The Protected, the Protector, and the Defender," Judith Hicks Stiehm identifies a similar dichotomy, the "protected" and the "protector," a distinction she argues is false for two rea-sons: in and since World War II the civilian population has had "little immunity" to war's violence (369); second, the (male) protectors can easily become predators whose victims are the so-called protected. Vietnam provides an all too graphic ex-ample of both these notions.

11. Angus Calder reports that there were more British civilian than military casualties in the first three years of the war (43,000 killed in 1940 and 1941). These numbers exclude the millions of civilian casualties in Europe and Asia throughout the war.

12. Similarly, in "Threnody for Young Soldiers in Action" (1947), Juliette de Bairacli-Levy asks, "How can I for such a sacrifice atone?" and decides that "Only my life would be fair sacrifice" (Reilly 8).

13. See Douglas A. Hughes, "Cracks in the Psyche," for an elaboration of this point of view.

14. Some feminist critics have taken exception to Gilbert and Gubar's read-ing of World War I's literature. Jane Marcus, for example, in "Asylum of Antaeus" writes that the argument (originally published by Gilbert in *Signs*) "confirms the status of the male canon of war literature . . . [and] argues that [male modernists'] vision of women as blood-thirsty vampires who gloat over men's death and derive

pleasure and profit from war is correct" (136). In "Maleness Run Riot" Claire Tylee chides Gilbert for her "vehement" tone and accuses her of "fudging the cultural distinctions of class . . . age" and nationality, thus obscuring the fact that, rather than experiencing "exuberance" and "sexual glee," rather than being liberated by the war, women were in their own way as dehumanized and traumatized as men (199). Tylee finds Gilbert guilty of misreading women's "sardonic humour" and compassionate irony as "aggressive satisfaction at the injury done to young men" (209). While I find that in their strenuous objections Marcus and Tylee sometimes misrepresent Gilbert's argument as a whole, they also point to another (and perhaps complementary) register of women's responses to the war.

15. For a sampling of the original terms of this debate and its renewal vis-à-vis World War II, in addition to Brittain's *Lady into Woman* see Minns, Priestley (*British Women Go to War*), Goldsmith, and Sutherland. Many of these early arguments are marked by biological essentialism.

16. According to Cadogan and Craig, the notion that women voters were "responsible for many social ills that they had failed to remedy" was "commonplace" but tended to fade as the war went on, giving way to an "equally unrealistic" "tone of adulation" (189, 190).

17. The "myth of Dunkirk" (as so romantically rendered in the film *Mrs. Miniver*, for example) played a significant role in the popular perception of the war. Calder reports that 225,000 of 250,000 British men were rescued (and all materiel abandoned). A subsequent headline—"Bloody Marvelous"—indicates how completely this "miserable blunder" was mythologized into "an epic of gallantry" (Calder 108; Priestley, *PS* 27). As Robert Hewison comments, the transmutation of "the defeat of Dunkirk into a moral victory" reflected England's desperate "need for myth" (*Under Seige* 47). According to Calder, however, the troops felt quite differently about their ignominious withdrawal. "Savagely wounded in their pride," they bitterly criticized the planners, officers, and the RAF for inadequate air coverage (109).

18. In *Revolutions of Our Time: Fascism*, Schüddekopf reports that Mussolini, who proclaimed "authority, discipline and hierarchy, instead of liberty, equality and fraternity as the proper scale of human values," was nostalgic for the earlier phase of his career, when "he was given firm commands to obey": "That was the life," Mussolini mused. "I shall abdicate. . . . For who is going to give me orders now!" (84, 157).

19. For a discussion of Lawrence's fascist-leaning fiction, including *Kangaroo*, see Nixon.

20. Roderick Rodney's name is notable for its emphatic masculine hardness and its slightly varied doubling of the patronymic.

21. Although other readers (Heath, Watson, and Dorenkamp, for example) have noted the affinity between Kelway and Harrison, I can find no mention of their link with Roderick.

22. Bowen's fears for her ancestral home materialized in 1959, when (for financial reasons) she was forced to sell Bowen's Court, which was then demolished for its timber. While she did have to abandon her home, which for her embodied the very essence of the Anglo-Irish tradition, at least (in Bowen's words) "It was a clean end. Bowen's Court never lived to be a ruin" (quoted in Glendinning 234).

23. Gilbert and Gubar note that for wounded "dehumanized" men nurses embody the ancient nurturing, healing power of maternal women, which can "recall [men] to life" (*Sexchanges* 286). Theweleit similarly argues that for incipient

Nazis the notion of the "white nurse" as a "pure mother figure . . . a type . . . diametrically opposed to the castrating woman" was essential to men's "psychic security system" (vol. 1, 91 and 125).

24. Louie's use of the newspapers significantly contrasts with her friend Connie's approach, which suggests the kind of reading strategy encouraged by Woolf and later feminists, such as Judith Fetterly and Adrienne Rich: "Connie's reading . . . was for the most part suspicious"; in "rereading . . . everything," she "read[s] between the lines" (153).

25. See, for example, (in addition to Watson) Blodgett and Lee.

26. "The Disinherited" has a fascinating and highly relevant subplot in which an ex-soldier feels compelled to write to the woman who was his lover and whom he has murdered—smothered in her bed with a pillow, as if to quell and displace those male fears of asphyxiation at a woman's hands articulated in "The Cat Jumps." The murderer writes, "I was a fool to love you the way I did. . . . I saw you had bought me up. . . . A war gentleman after the war, you'd have liked me then in the war" (*CS* 394, 395). But now, apparently, she merely uses him, a soldier turned commodity, thus reversing the usual gender configuration. Unable to bear this demotion, he kills her, the perceived cause of his humiliation.

27. Interestingly, Bowen's Magdela suggests H.D.'s Mary of Magdala in Book III ("The Flowering of the Rod") of *Trilogy*, which, like Bowen's wartime writing, grew out of firsthand experience of the London Blitz. In this revisionary poem H.D. refashions the Christian myth of Mary Magdalene, called Mary of Magdala, who evokes in the Magus Kaspar a vision of "the drowned cities of prehistory," of "what the sacrosanct legend / said still existed, / . . . the lands of the blest, / the promised lands, lost" (156, 153-54).

As we shall see, this vision is hauntingly similar to Pepita's in "Mysterious Kôr," but H.D.'s treatment is even more optimistic. For unlike Arthur, who is not quite persuaded to share Pepita's vision, Kaspar, as Rachel Blau DuPlessis argues in *Writing beyond the Ending,* actually experiences a "conversion to anti-patriarchal thinking" (120). Thus, through her characters Stella Rodney and Pepita, Bowen participates in the same sort of revisionary mythmaking more fully realized by H.D. And Bowen's Magdela senses the possibility of precisely the sort of forthcoming transfiguration posited by Mary of Magdala, who confidently declares both her symbolic status and her transformative power: "I am Mary—O, there are Marys a-plenty, / (though I am Mara, bitter) I shall be Mary-myrrh" (135).

28. The emphasis most readers put on Bowen's obvious conservatism obscures the (admittedly) muted oppositional discourse that runs throughout her wartime writing. Alan Sinfield, for example, rather single-mindedly argues that the purpose of *The Heat of the Day* "is to entertain the thought that vulgarity dwells with the democratic victors of 1945, and civilisation with fascism" (17).

"The Happy Autumn Fields" (1944) is often used to document Bowen's supposed preference for a sort of feudal golden age, but the Victorian family life of which the story's protagonist dreams is just as marred by loss, dislocation, and death as is her war-weary reality. Space precludes extensive discussion of this evocative and artful story here, but it is well worth reconsideration.

29. For discussion of this dilemma, see Chessman, who argues (à la Irigaray) that Bowen unconsciously fears that as a woman she is unavoidably positioned outside discourse (see note 9, this chapter). On a mundane rather than a linguistic level, the difficulty of breaking free of the old order, especially when haunted (like Aunt Fran) by guilt, is the subject of another of Bowen's wartime stories, "Pink May."

30. Interestingly, the headstone of Bowen's tyrannical grandfather ("Old Mussolini") reads, "Here we have no abiding city, but we seek one to come" (*BC* 377).

31. See note 27, this chapter, for comparison of "Mysterious Kôr" and "The Flowering of the Rod," Book III of H.D.'s *Trilogy.*

4 Re-Plotting the War(s)

1. Over thirty years ago Joan Bennett noted that war was one of the "two forms of human misery that most haunt" Woolf's books (70). Echoes of wartime misery reverberate painfully through *Jacob's Room, Mrs. Dalloway, To the Lighthouse, The Waves,* and *The Years* in addition to *Between the Acts,* where it finally becomes the central focus.

2. In "Nature and History in *The Years,*" James Naremore writes that "the late thirties left [Woolf] uncertain whether the world was moving in the direction of greater unity or greater totalitarianism. Therefore her typical ambivalence over the life process . . . was doubled and intensified by a more immediate ambivalence about history. This uneasiness gives *The Years* its remarkably complex tone" (244). This observation is equally pertinent to *Between the Acts.*

3. In "The Asylum of Antaeus," Jane Marcus notes that Cavell's observation "Patriotism is not enough" is "inscribed in small letters at the base of the statue," while the ostensibly "opposite sentiment 'For King and Country'" is writ large at the statue's top, thus essentially "denying Cavell's radical pacifism and imaging her for [the state's] own ends" (135).

4. In a letter (vol. 6, no. 3695) to Ethyl Smith dated 1 March 1941, Woolf writes "this is the worst stage of the war" (*L* 475).

5. There is, of course, a lighter side both to Woolf's wartime responses and to *Between the Acts.* Herbert Marder has observed that readers tend to choose up sides, "read[ing] the novel either as a celebratory hymn or as a kind of dirge for Western civilization" (466). Although this evaluation is somewhat too polarizing, several readings of *BA,* in contrast to those I allude to in the text, do tend toward the optimistic. See, for example, Nora Eisenberg, "Virginia Woolf's Last Word on Words" and Renée Watkins, "Survival in Discontinuity—Virginia Woolf's *Between the Acts.*" Others, for example, B.H. Fussell in "Woolf's Peculiar Comic World: *Between the Acts,*" explore the novel's usually overlooked comic elements.

6. In "The Leaning Tower" Woolf defines tower dwellers as those male writers who perceive the world from the necessarily skewed perspective of their masculine cultural privilege, a perspective that she argued had become increasingly problematic and inadequate for the changing times.

7. For an example of the prewar pessimism with which Woolf had to contend, see *Barbarians at the Gate* (1939), Leonard Woolf's disheartened analysis of the political dissolution of Western civilization, threatened from without by totalitarianism and from within by the inadequacies of bourgeois liberalism. The extreme position to which fear of this war drove some of Woolf's associates is dramatically illustrated by a passage from Clive Bell's pacifist pamphlet *Warmongers:* "A Nazi Europe would be, to my mind, heaven on earth compared with Europe at war . . . the worst tyranny is better than the best war" (quoted in *L* 293 fn.).

8. Woolf discusses this topic in "Women and Fiction" (1929), which sheds light on her narrative choices, the profound difficulty of her ambition to level

gender-coded novelistic discourse, and her initial academic relegation to minor writer status:

> [W]hen a woman comes to write a novel, she will find that she is perpetually wishing to alter the established values—to make serious what appears insignificant to a man, and trivial what is to him important. And for that, of course, she will be criticized; for the critic of the opposite sex will be genuinely puzzled and surprised by an attempt to alter the current scale of values, and will see in it not merely a difference of view, but a view that is weak, or trivial, or sentimental, because it differs from his own.
> [*CE* 2:146]

Woolf's deviation from and implied critique of dominant forms of narrative were not only puzzling to male critics but understandably alarming, if at root, as DuPlessis claims, "All forms of dominant narrative . . . are tropes for the sex-gender system as a whole" (*WBE* 43).

9. Zwerdling also discusses this point, noting that Woolf's attachment to England is not "mindless patriotism," but "a different kind of feeling for one's country—a love for its history, its idiosyncratic culture and traditions, a passionate attachment to the land itself" (312). He concludes, however, that *BA* "seems to affirm the continuity of English cultural tradition."

10. While living at Rodmell (in April 1940), Woolf was invited to write a village pageant. She never did so, though seemingly intrigued by the possibilities, which emerged so brilliantly in *BA*. She had seen (or read) other pageants of this sort, including E.M. Forster's patriotic offering, "England's Pleasant Land" (1940). For a discussion of the cultural and biographical sources of the pageant in *BA*, see Jane Marcus, "Some Sources for *Between the Acts*."

11. In "History, Pattern, and Continuity in Virginia Woolf," Werner J. Deiman argues that Woolf's (apparently unequivocal) "reverence" for historical continuity and (unattenuated) "love" for the tradition she inherits leads her, in *BA*, to "[affirm], however cautiously . . . the inevitability of the historical cycle" (54, 64). While I agree with Deiman's conclusion that Woolf believed in the possibility of a "new historical 'moment,'" it was not the "timeless . . . pattern of history [which] offered redemption from time and affirmed . . . a continuum into the future," but the possibility of *breaking* that pattern (66). Like Zwerdling, Deiman does not consider Woolf's profound ambivalence nor her antipathy for the patriarchal nature of England's history and traditions.

12. For a relevant discussion of "Woolf's appeal for spiritual regeneration" in *BA* and other works, see Herbert Marder, "Virginia Woolf's 'Conversion': *Three Guineas*, 'Pointz Hall' and *Between the Acts*."

13. Furthermore, Zwerdling finds that the "forces of dispersal," rather than mergence, predominate and "mov[e] with the power of historical inevitability" (320).

14. Appropriately, this passage brings to mind "Flying Over London," in which Woolf describes an imagined plane ride that enables her to see London and its environs from a dual perspective. When the plane soars at great heights, she can see the "River Thames . . . as the Romans saw it, as Paleolithic man saw it" (*CE*, vol. 4 168); but as the plane swoops down near the ground, with the aid of bi-

noulars the myriad detail of London's congested urban landscape periodically returns to view. Thus, "one had to change perpetually air values into land values" (171). Woolf's fictional flight, with its constantly shifting perspective, yields a metaphor for her "view" of England in *BA*, in which she ultimately sees tradition and continuity from multiple vantage points—through the imagined recollection of the past and the reality of the present as well as through (so to speak) a wide-angle lens and a microscope. Indeed, this imaginary flight serves admirably as an explanatory model for the complex flights of imagination that shape her fiction in general.

15. In *Writing beyond the Ending,* Rachel Blau DuPlessis explores women writers' efforts to extricate themselves from the romance plot, which "separates love and quest, values sexual asymmetry, including division of labor by gender, is based on extremes of sexual difference, and evokes an aura around the couple itself. In short, the romance plot, broadly speaking, is a trope for the gender system as a whole" (5).

16. In *Jacob's Room,* Jacob writes an essay while at the university that asks, "Does History consist of the Biographies of Great Men?" (39)—for Woolf a rhetorical question to which her novels continually reply.

17. I owe this useful metaphor to Margaret R. and Patrice L.-R. Higonnet, who use the double helix configuration to image the steady but always dynamic relation of men's and women's intertwined roles within various cultures.

18. For a more detailed discussion of the individual playlets, their sources and significance, see James Naremore, *The World without a Self* and B.H. Fussell, "Woolf's Peculiar Comic World: *Between the Acts.*"

19. Jane Marcus reminds us that Isa, both Irish and female, fills the role of a colonized subject in a double and mutually validating sense. In the nineteenth century "patriarchal domestic tyranny" became the rhetorical "basis for colonial imperialism"; in a neat reversal, England was dubbed "the mother country" (a phrase coined by James Stephen, Woolf's grandfather) ("LSM" 72). Women, in their relations with colonial subjects and servants, enforced the terms of the very "master-servant" paradigm that kept them in domestic bondage. Fitzjames Stephen (Woolf's uncle) apparently did not hesitate to make the disciplinary significance of this system, which infantilized women, the working class, and colonials alike, quite explicit: "women and the working class must be kept down forcefully in order to show the colonies how rebellion will be treated" (quoted in "LSM" 84).

20. See Jane Marcus, "Liberty, Sorority, Misogyny," for a detailed discussion of the "sister swallow" motif and the salience of the Procne/Philomela myth to the novel as a whole.

21. In *Writing beyond the Ending,* DuPlessis devotes three chapters to the study of Woolf's evolution as a writer seeking alternatives to the romance plot.

22. In an essay that explores the significance of evolutionary theory for Woolf, specifically the "idea of pre-history," Gillian Beer notes that (especially in *BA*) "the prehistoric is seen not simply as part of a remote past, but as contiguous, continuous, a part of ordinary present-day life" (102). In addition, "pre-history implies a pre-narrative domain" (103); "pre-history is anterior to knowledge. It lies beneath the *polarisations* and *emplotments* of knowledge" (106, emphasis added). Thus could Woolf conceive of an epistemological and narrative shift rooted in pre-history ("a time before" in Woolf's words) but manifest in the present/future.

23. Many readers have explored the link between Woolf's politics and aesthetic practice. In addition to DuPlessis, see, for example, Jane Marcus, "'No more horses'" and Diane Filby Gillespie, "Political Aesthetics." James Naremore, among

others, has recognized that Woolf's "program for modern fiction was an aestheticism which was also deeply political" ("Nature and History in *The Years*" 242). (Apropos to my reading of *Between the Acts*) Woolf admits in "The Artist and Politics" that, despite her aversion to explicit didacticism, the war has forced writers "to take part in politics" in order to work for their "own survival" and "the survival of [their] art" (*CE*, 2:232).

24. DuPlessis's reading of *The Years* (in *WBE*) reveals how neatly it prefigures *Between the Acts* in its preoccupation with the dissolution of boundaries.

25. I am indebted to Patricia Waugh's lucid study of postmodernism and feminism, which articulates modern women writers' concern with "dissolution and mergence" and the "construction of identity *in relationship*" (17, 10). Waugh's argument helped me to clarify my own.

26. Naremore points to the "bubble and stream" passage as crucial to all of Woolf's work, explaining that it conveys her preoccupation with the "synthesis of extremes" and, more specifically, the need "to develop a human consciousness and a manner of writing which is able to express" both "a world of pure unity . . . [and] a world of pure individuality" at once ("Nature and History" 259).

27. In "Towards a Woman's Poetics," Josephine Donovan similarly argues that a "contextual and relational" epistemology is the crucial foundation of a woman's poetics (107).

28. To be sure, this passage also signifies Isa's penchant for romantic escapism—manifest in her imagined love affair with Mr. Haines, her secretive poetry, and her rather self-pitying wish that "the waters should cover [her]" (103). But whatever impatience one may feel with her desire to withdraw must be tempered by acknowledgment of her untenable state of mind, for she is cursed with a consciousness of the inadequacy of her position but remains powerless (in her estimation) to change it.

29. Several readers have noted La Trobe's rather *too* "masculine"—that is, authoritative, controlling, possessive—personality. Gillespie, for example, finds that in La Trobe's desire to "master and possess," to "capture and coerce" her audience, she "both parodies and reflects the values of male dominated society and art" ("Miss La Trobe" 41, 42). Nevertheless, La Trobe does ultimately relinquish her power; thus, Gillespie concludes, La Trobe embodies the "artist's struggle against masculine values" (45). Gillespie's argument becomes even more relevant to mine when one considers Ruotolo's observation that Woolf at times depicts La Trobe in distinctly military terms: the "commander" (or "Admiral" or "General") orders her "troops" about (*BA* 62). Yet, as Ruotolo adds, "Sensing, perhaps, that she must relinquish all pretense of leadership before her design can grow in the minds of others, La Trobe undercuts . . . her own arrangement" (218). This, of course, is Woolf's own paradoxical predicament.

30. Gilbert and Gubar demonstrate that "many feminist modernists [e.g., Stein, Barnes, and Woolf, to name but a few] were concerned" with the notion of "third-sexed beings," defiant deviations from "the paradigms of dominance and submission enforced by the hierarchies of gender" (*Sexchanges* 363, 364). Such beings of indeterminate or fluid gender, Gilbert and Gubar continue, were symbolic of the women artists' desire to "restore a primordial, gender-free chaos." This observation is of particular relevance to the prehistoric scene that ends *Between the Acts* and opens La Trobe's nascent drama.

31. For DuPlessis, "breaking the sentence severs dominant authority and ideology. Breaking the sequence is a critique of narrative, restructuring its orders

and priorities precisely by attention to specific issues of female identity and its characteristic oscillations" (x). Thus, as others have noted, in *Room* Woolf provides a model for escaping and undermining "conventional literary ideology."

32. Marcus, for example, refers to the dissolution of "the individual and the authorial voice" into a "collective voice" in *The Years* ("Some Sources" 1). Similarly, Patricia Waugh observes that "[f]rom *The Waves* onwards, Woolf experiments increasingly with the articulation of a more radically 'collective' concept of subjectivity" (*FF* 123). DuPlessis speaks of Woolf's "communal" or "choral" protagonist (in both *The Years* and *BA*), the use of which "makes the group, not the individual, the central character." As a result, she adds, "[t]he novel can suggest the structures of social change in the structure of narrative" (*WBE* 163).

33. As DuPlessis astutely observes, "Woolf constructed [*BA*] so that the choral protagonist may include both vanguard outsiders" and uncritical insiders (and everyone in between, I would add). "In keeping with this dialogic stance," she continues, "the text does not privilege its own ideological position" (*WBE* 174).

34. See Sallie Sears, "Theater of War," for an excellent discussion of the radical form of the pageant, especially its "progressively daring technical innovations" (225-27).

35. Ruotolo similarly comments that the "boundaries of [La Trobe's] text are expanded" by "things extrinsic to the text" and that, ultimately, the pageant becomes a "collaborative venture" (219, 221, 227).

36. As P. Waugh explains in a narrower context, "Woolf has . . . fictionally embodied the recognition that differentiation is not necessarily separateness, distance, and alienation from others, but a form of *connection* to others" (11).

37. Rachel Bowlby makes some pertinent remarks about the sheep passage: "The 'trained' as opposed to the wandering, cartwheeling mind is here firmly snubbed, as reducing every question to fit its ready-made answer. And in the same gesture, the 'pen'—for Gilbert and Gubar the instrument and symbol *par excellence* of masculine literary authority—is punned into . . . a tame retreat to which the sheep returns in blind obedience" (38).

38. For a relevant discussion of "Anon," see Eisenberg, "Virginia Woolf's Last Words on Words."

39. Although our arguments differ substantially, Deiman also describes Woolf's "projection . . . into an indefinite future which pervades . . . *Between the Acts*" as a "leap of faith" (66).

5 A Different Story

1. The *Children of Violence* series includes *Martha Quest* (1952), *A Proper Marriage* (1952), *A Ripple from the Storm* (1958), *Landlocked* (1958), and *The Four-Gated City* (1969). The first two novels of her later science fiction series (*Canopus in Argos*)—*Shikasta* (1979) and *The Marriage between Zones Three, Four, and Five* (1981)—likewise demythologize and rescript the war/romance plots. Although other considerations preclude their inclusion here, they attest to Lessing's continued preoccupation with this vital task.

2. American writers have recently been contributing to this tradition. See, for example, Marge Piercy, *Gone to Soldiers* (1987), Bobbie Ann Mason, *In Country* (1985), and Sherri Tepper, *The Gate to Women's Country* (1988).

3. For two literary/cultural histories (with dissimilar perspectives) of postwar Britain, see Hewison, *In Anger: British Culture in the Cold War* (1981) and Sinfield, *Literature, Politics, and Culture in Postwar Britain* (1989).

4. Of her experiment with mescaline, Lessing has said, "I took one dose out of curiosity, and that's enough. . . . It was the most extraordinary experience" (Newquist 58).

5. Muriel Spark's "The First Year of My Life" is remarkably similar to Lessing's dream-vision, though its ironic obverse. A baby born during the last year of World War I silently narrates the horrors of the war and refuses to smile—that is, to sanction the state of the world by socially engaging it. Ironically, the infant finally smiles when she hears former Prime Minister Asquith's asinine claim that since the war "All things have become new. In this great cleansing and purging it has been the privilege of our country to play her part" (268). Her wry response to this blind absurdity sets the darkly sardonic tone that from that point on mediates the tragic gap between the child's insightful perceptions and the official view.

6. Lessing's somewhat controversial opinion in this matter is supported by Andrew Rutherford, who in *The Literature of War: Five Studies in Heroic Virtue* (1978) argues that the Great War poets' antiwar position was much more complex and ambivalent than is usually recognized. In the poetry of Owen, Sassoon, Graves, and so on, he discerns "an assertion of heroic manhood in an otherwise meaningless universe" (93). He identifies and describes various forms of heroic literature from both world wars and the Cold War (the spy as hero) to support his contention that the notion of stoic, courageous male heroism, though somewhat redefined, remains a staple in war literature (and thus in the popular perception of war).

7. Of her father Lessing has said, "[H]e was lucky not to have been killed a dozen times over. But the war did him in nevertheless: he lost his leg, and was psychologically damaged. He went into the fighting . . . optimistic, and came out with what they then called shell shock . . . minus a leg and inwardly in torment" ("Impertinent Daughters" 55-56).

8. As Claire Sprague has observed, "Alfred's amputated leg suggests the castration that in fact defines his life. . . . The soldier/father is . . . as much a victim figure as the nurse/mother" (*Rereading* 60, 61).

9. See also "The Fate of Chivalry and the Assault upon Mother," in which P. Fussell argues that "after the shocks and disillusionments of the Great War, satiric assaults upon Mother began to recommend themselves to the new post-war audience" (206)—as part of the turn against chivalry in general and specifically because of the way mothers had been implicated in the willing "sacrifice" of their sons as cannon fodder. In America such assaults reached textual apotheosis in Philip Wylie's *Generation of Vipers* (1942).

10. Paul Fussell comments that this "essentially feudal language . . . was not the least of the ultimate casualties of the war. But its staying power was astonishing. As late as 1918 it was still possible for some men who had actually fought to sustain the old rhetoric" by employing such phrases as "the good fight" and "keeping the faith" (*GWMM* 21-23). World War II soon developed its own idiom, which Fussell discusses with his usual élan in *Wartime*.

11. The phrase "sacred witness" is Elshtain's, who identifies one of women's dual roles in war as that of mirror "reflecting [the warrior's] bloody glory back" ("Women as Mirror" 32). She thus reiterates Woolf's designation of women as "magnifying mirrors" essential to war. The other function Elshtain discusses (equally pertinent to Martha's realization) is that of the Other.

12. Documenting the strong strain of homoeroticism of the Great War, especially among those educated in public schools, P. Fussell quotes J.B. Priestley, who remembers that many upper-class men off to war "hailed with relief . . . a wholly masculine way of life uncomplicated by Woman" (*GWMM* 273-74).

13. In *Rereading Doris Lessing,* Sprague argues that the "major political issues" of *RS* are "not war and socialism . . . but racism and sexism," adding that "[p]ersonal and political destinies . . . are densely interwoven" (132, 133). She concludes that this novel thus expresses Lessing's most "forthright" feminism (135).

14. To be fair, Jimmy and a few other men side with the women on this point.

15. Nancy Huston identifies and discusses the familiar wartime role of "sexual cheerleader" in "Tales of War and Tears of Women" (225).

16. This phrase is from Lessing's admiring review of Kurt Vonnegut's *Mother Night,* the main theme of which she identifies as coming to grips with the fact that in one way or another everyone shares responsibility for the Nazi horrors.

17. For an analysis of "the realist novel as an ideologically complicit form whose conventions are bearers of ideology" (Greene 85), see Roland Barthes, *S/Z* and Catherine Belsey, *Critical Practice.*

18. The phrase "racist voyeurism" is Jenny Taylor's, from "The Deconstruction of a Colonial Radical."

19. The one exception, entitled "The Romantic Tough School of Writing," parodies not only the kind of "hard masculine" writing to which this title refers, but also the literary convention (so prominent in postwar British fiction) of hyper-masculinist (and violent) male bonding into which women tragically intrude, luring pure-hearted, big-fisted men "to death and the framehouse funeral" (*GN* 541).

20. Saul's aggressive "I, the naked ego," which is also "I against women" would seem the identical twin of "the straight dark bar," the insistent "I" remarked by Virginia Woolf, that lies "across the page" of a certain representative Mr. A's writing (*Room* 103). For Woolf, the "dominance" of this "I," whose arid and lifeless shadow obscures all else, betrays Mr. A's "self-conscious virility," which in his fiction has taken the intrusive and artless form of "protesting against the equality of the other sex by asserting his own superiority" (*Room* 104, 105). As we have seen, Woolf associated such irruptions of self-conscious virility with fascism.

21. In "Her Story of War: De-Militarizing Literature and Literary Studies," Lynne Hanley also points to this passage in *The Golden Notebook,* but she attributes the "convergence" of love and war to war's having "invaded and shaped [Anna's] emotions" (22). That is, rather than seeing gender relations and war as twin manifestations of particular ways of seeing and being, she argues that "the combat zone invades the protected zone of intimate relations between men and women, forcing those relations to conform to the law of the battlefield." However, Hanley later calls this dichotomy into question, arguing that "the prevention of war would seem to require . . . the reconstruction of the prevalent form of the relation between the sexes in western culture, so as to erode the boundaries between male and female, white and black, the abstract and the concrete, the professional and the personal" (23).

22. Stanley E. Fish, *Self-Consuming Artifacts: The Experience of Seventeenth-Century Literature.* Jeanette King similarly argues that there is "no conclusion to *The Golden Notebook* because the end of the novel directs us immediately back to its beginning, making us feel that we need to re-read the whole novel differently in order to grasp its meaning" (53). She also notes that the novel "succeeds in resisting the hierarchization of discourse which determines the relationship of center to margin," adding that "there is no single originator of meaning" (52, 53).

23. In *Feminine Consciousness in the Modern British Novel,* Sydney Janet Kaplan discusses Lessing's assertion of the "possibility of freedom" in the pur-

poseful development of an "expanded consciousness which is not particularly 'masculine' or 'feminine' but human." She also notes Lessing's related "attempts to awaken humans who have not yet evolved into an understanding of their individual selves as merely parts of a whole . . . part of . . . the Cosmic Harmony" (171, 172). Kaplan later argues (in "Passionate Portrayal of Things to Come") that Lessing "intensif[ies] her exploration of states of consciousness by incorporating into the realistic novel elements usually ascribed to genres of fantasy, romance, and science fiction" (2). Kaplan calls the holistic type of consciousness Lessing describes in this later fiction "transpersonality" (6).

24. King argues that in the *Canopus in Argos* series, in particular in *Shikasta,* Lessing's notion of subjectivity seems even more radical than she herself admits: "The belief in individuality," King writes, "is shown to be based on spurious ideas of difference which are simply ideological constructs without real foundation" (75). Although Lessing's novels offer plenty of evidence in support of King's conclusion, they just as often belie it. On this point, King may be taking Lessing further into total constructivism than she actually ventures.

25. Once again Theweleit's analysis of male fear of and animosity toward women's bodies is highly relevant. As Rabinbach and Benjamin explain in the Foreword to *Male Fantasies,* vol. 2, in the proto-fascist literature and iconography of post–World War I Germany, Theweleit finds that "fear and revulsion of the feminine manifests itself in the incessant invocation of metaphors of an engulfing fluid [e.g., sea water, blood] or flood." Obversely, the male body is figured as "a mechanism for eluding the liquid, for incorporating or repelling undesired emotions, thoughts, longings." These fascists specifically eschew being identified with "a sensuality that is responsive to other beings" (xix). In Jack's case, sensuality or eros is channeled into a mechanism of domination and diminution.

26. Drawing on the work of object-relations theorists (Melanie Klein and Dorothy Dinnerstein in particular), Patricia Waugh explains that "women . . . carry not only the affiliative and domestic human ties"—which Jack has rejected—"they also carry the deep human ambivalence about the flesh and mortality (about that which cannot be ultimately controlled)" (75).

27. The phrase "ideological normalisation," while not a concept original with Foucault, is from *Power/Knowledge.* I would like to acknowledge my general indebtedness to Foucault's theories of the nature and function of power as articulated throughout this collection of essays.

28. On realist representation of female madness, which renders the madwoman (and, ultimately, all women) the invisible, objectified, and mastered Other, see Shoshana Felman, "Women and Madness: The Critical Phallacy."

29. Lessing seems in agreement with Foucault, who postulates that "power isn't localized in the State apparatus and [consequently] . . . nothing in society will be changed if the mechanisms of power that function outside, below and alongside the State apparatuses, on a much more minute and everyday level, are not also changed" (*P/K* 60).

30. See *An Edge of History,* in which Hogeland argues that Lessing's emphasis on "feminist process, even without an ideological connection to feminism per se, reveals her implicit feminism" (vi). Hogeland is of course responding to Lessing's expressed dismissal of feminism as too narrowly focused on the (admitted) subordination of women.

31. In "'Without Contraries Is No Progression': Lessing's *The Four-Gated City,*" Sprague argues that Thomas Stern's "chaotic" notes (along with the writing

of other "mad" characters) articulate the "chaos . . . behind" Mark's *A City in the Desert*. Such "anti-memoirs," she continues, serve as a "reminder of the questionable truth" of the published—that is, normalized—representation of Martha's parabolic four-gated city.

32. Alluding to the significance of Martha's Biblical name, Catherine Stimpson finds that Lessing's Martha "personifies the principle of activity and faith, and the conviction that history might be redeemed and changed" (183). This is so, but only because the modern Martha does not rely on the kind of faith that purportedly raised Lazarus from the dead.

33. DuPlessis similarly notes that in *A Proper Marriage* Lessing discredits the romance plot.

34. See Sprague, *Rereading Doris Lessing,* and DuPlessis, *Writing beyond the Ending,* for example.

35. Belsey more broadly argues that "classic realism" (of which the bildungsroman is a prime example) "performs . . . the work of ideology, not only in its representation of a world of consistent subjects who are the origin of meaning, knowledge and action, but also in offering the reader, as the position from which the text is most readily intelligible, the position of the subject as origin both of understanding and of action in accordance with that understanding" (67).

36. Lessing's readers have construed her treatment of the bildung differently: Mona Knapp argues that Lessing deliberately exploits a seemingly outmoded form, adding, however, that "the process of education . . . seems, at the end . . . to have totally disoriented the heroine, rather than propelling her toward her right place [!] in life" (39, 47). Betsy Draine claims that, working with a form "under pressure" of its substance, Lessing "orchestrates a double *Bildung*—the intertwined development of individual and society" (41). And Ellen Cronan Rose, who analyzes *Children of Violence* from within the framework of Eriksonian development, finds the series a "flawed bildungsroman" because in creating a heroine who "neither rejects society nor is reclaimed by it, but recreates it," Lessing "fail[s] to obey the rules of the genre" (66, 68). For Rose, then, the series is flawed because it depicts a pattern of psychological development that intentionally deviates from specifically androcentric patterns (such as Erickson's "Eight Ages of Man") and, further, because Lessing "cheats" by "sidestepping reality."

37. Lessing experienced more ambivalence about the war than does Martha. In a 1969 interview she said, "I supported England and the USA in the fight against Germany and Japan, but I was nauseated by the bombing of Dresden, and I was disgusted by our own propaganda. I was split down the middle" (Raskin 65).

38. Lessing has said (1969) that she considers *The Four-Gated City* "true prophecy. I think that the 'iron heel' is going to come down" (Raskin 70). "Iron heel" possibly alludes to Jack London's futuristic dystopia *The Iron Heel* (1908), in which the proletariat masses of the world organize to prevent a world war, only to be crushed by a totalitarian, capitalist oligarchy. Whether or not Lessing was familiar with London's novel, the parallels are striking. The two writers, both socialists, would certainly have differed on one point in particular, however: London's hero, the people's leader, bears the conspicuously virile name of Earnest Everhard.

CODA: AS TIME GOES BY

1. "Senator Outraged by Marine Slogan," *The* (Bloomington, IN) *Herald-Telephone* (4 Oct. 1989): A6.

2. "The Warrior Culture," *Time* (15 Oct. 1990): 100.

3. In addition to Carroll, see, for example, Dorothy Thompson, "Women, Peace and History: Notes for an Historical Overview," Janet Radcliffe Richards, "Why the Pursuit of Peace Is No Part of Feminism," and Elizabeth Douvan and Linda Kaboolian, "Women and Peace."

Works Cited

Adorno, Theodor W. "Freudian Theory and the Pattern of Fascist Propaganda." *The Essential Frankfurt School Reader.* Ed. Andrew Arato and Eike Gebhardt. New York: Continuum, 1990. 118-29.

Althusser, Louis. "Ideology and Ideological State Apparatuses (Notes towards an Investigation)." Trans. Ben Brewster. *Lenin and Philosophy and Other Essays.* New York: Monthly Review P, 1972. 127-86.

Arnow, Harriette. *The Dollmaker.* New York: Avon, 1972.

Badinter, Elisabeth. *The Unopposite Sex: The End of the Gender Battle.* Trans. Barbara Wright. New York: Harper and Row, 1989.

Bailey, Leslie. *BBC Scrapbooks.* Vol. 1 *1896-1914.* London: Allen and Unwin, 1966.

Baker, Mark. *Nam: The Vietnam War in the Words of the Men and Women Who Fought There.* New York: Morrow, 1981.

Barbera, Jack, and William McBrien. *Stevie: A Biography of Stevie Smith.* New York: Oxford U P, 1987.

Barthes, Roland. *S/Z.* Trans. Richard Miller. New York: Noonday P, 1974.

Beard, Mary R. *Women as Force in History.* New York: Macmillan, 1946.

Beer, Gillian. "Virginia Woolf and Pre-History." *Virginia Woolf: A Centenary Perspective.* Ed. Eric Warner. New York: St. Martin's P, 1984. 99-123.

Belsey, Catherine. *Critical Practice.* London: Methuen, 1980.

Bennett, Joan. *Virginia Woolf: Her Art as a Novelist.* 2d ed. Cambridge: Cambridge U P, 1964.

Bikman, Minda. "A Talk with Doris Lessing." *New York Times Book Review* (30 March 1980): 24-27.

Blodgett, Harriet. *Patterns of Reality: Elizabeth Bowen's Novels.* Paris: Mouton, 1975.

Bloom, Harold. *The Anxiety of Influence.* New York: Oxford U P, 1973.

Booth, Wayne. "Freedom of Interpretation: Bakhtin and the Challenge of Feminist Criticism." *Critical Inquiry* 9 (1982): 145-76.

Bowen, Elizabeth. *Bowen's Court.* New York: Knopf, 1942.

———. "The Cat Jumps." 1929. *Collected Stories* 362-70.

———. *The Collected Stories of Elizabeth Bowen.* Introd. by Angus Wilson. New York: Vintage, 1981.

———. *Collected Impressions.* London: Longmann, Green, 1950.

———. "The Demon Lover." 1941. *Collected Stories* 661-66.

———. "The Disinherited." 1934. *Collected Stories* 375-407.

———. "Do Women Think Like Men?" *The Listener* (30 October 1941: 593-94.

———. "Eire." *The New Statesman and Nation* 21 (12 April 1941): 382-83.

———. "The Happy Autumn Fields." 1944. *Collected Stories* 671-85.

———. *The Heat of the Day.* 1949. Harmondsworth, England: Penguin, 1962.

———. "I Died for Love." *Choice: Some New Stories and Prose.* Ed. William Sansom. London: Progress, 1946. 129-37.

———. "I Hear You Say So." 1945. *Collected Stories* 751-57.

———. "In the Square." 1941. *Collected Stories* 609-15.

———. "A Love Story 1939." 1939. *Collected Stories* 497-511.

———. "The Mulberry Tree." *Mulberry Tree* 13-20.

———. *The Mulberry Tree: Writings of Elizabeth Bowen.* Ed. Hermione Lee. London: Virago, 1986.

———. "Mysterious Kôr." 1944. *Collected Stories* 728-40.

———. "Notes on Writing a Novel." 1945. *Modern Literary Criticism: An Anthology.* Ed. Irving Howe. Boston: Beacon, 1958. 50-64.

———. "On writing 'The Heat of the Day.'" *Now and Then: A Journal of Books and Personalities* 79 (1949): 11.

———. *Pictures and Conversations.* New York: Knopf, 1975.

———. "Pink May." 1942. *Collected Stories* 712-18.

———. "Preface to *The Demon Lover* (American ed.)." *Collected Impressions.* London: Longmann Green, 1950. 47-52.

———. "Preface to *The Last September.*" *Seven Winters and Afterthoughts* 197-204.

———. "The Roving Eye." *Seven Winters and Afterthoughts* 69-73.

———. *Seven Winters: Memoirs of a Dublin Childhood* and *Afterthoughts: Pieces on Writing.* New York: Knopf, 1962.

———. "She." Radio broadcast. *Seven Winters and Afterthoughts* 228-37.

———. "Songs My Father Sang Me." 1944. *Collected Stories* 650-60.

———. "Summer Night." 1941. *Collected Stories* 583-608.

———. "Unwelcome Idea." 1940. *Collected Stories* 573-77.

Bowlby, Rachel. *Virginia Woolf: Feminist Destinations.* Oxford: Basil Blackwell, 1988.

Brittain, Vera. *Lady into Woman: A History of Women from Victoria to Elizabeth II.* New York: Macmillan, 1953.

Brothers, Barbara. "Pattern and Void: Bowen's Irish Landscapes and *The Heat of the Day.*" *Mosaic* 12 (1979): 129-38.

Brownmiller, Susan. *Against Our Will.* New York: Simon and Schuster, 1975.

Broyles, William, Jr. "Why Men Love War." *Esquire* (November 1984): 55-65.

Burdekin, Katharine. *The End of This Day's Business.* Ca. 1937. Old Westbury, N.Y.: Feminist P, 1989.

———. *Swastika Night.* 1937. Old Westbury, N.Y.: Feminist P, 1985.

Cadogan, Mary, and Patricia Craig. *Women and Children First: The Fiction of Two World Wars.* London: Gollancz, 1978.

Calder, Angus. *The People's War, Britain 1939-1945.* New York: Pantheon, 1969.

Cameron, Deborah, ed. *The Feminist Critique of Language: A Reader.* London: Routledge, 1990.

Campbell, Joseph. *Myths to Live By.* New York: Viking, 1972.

Camus, Albert. *Neither Victims nor Executioners.* 1946. Trans. Dwight Macdonald. Philadelphia: New Society, 1986.

Caplan, Jane. "Introduction to Female Sexuality in Fascist Ideology." *Feminist Review* 1 (1979): 59-66.

Caputo, Philip. *A Rumor of War.* New York: Ballantine, 1977.

Carroll, Berenice A. "Feminism and Pacifism: Historical and Theoretical Connections." *Women and Peace: Theoretical, Historical and Practical Perspectives.* Ed. Ruth Roach Pierson. London: Croom Helm, 1987. 2-28.

Cassin-Scott, Jack. *Women at War 1939-45.* Colour plates by Angus McBride. London: Osprey, 1980.

Ceadel, Martin. "Popular Fiction and the Next War, 1918-1939." *Class, Culture and Social Change: A New View of the 1930s.* Ed. Frank Gloversmith. Atlantic Highlands, N.J.: Humanities P, 1980. 161-84.

Chamberlin, E.R. *Life in Wartime Britain.* London: B.T. Batsford, 1972.

Chessman, Harriet S. "Women and Language in the Fiction of Elizabeth Bowen." *Twentieth-Century Literature* 29 (1983): 69-85.

Cixous, Helene. "Laugh of the Medusa." Trans. Keith Cohen and Paula Cohen. *Signs* 1 (1976): 875-93.

Clarke, I.F. *Voices Prophesying War 1763-1984.* London: Oxford U P, 1966.

Cohn, Carol. "Emasculating America's Linguistic Deterrent." Harris and King 153-70.

———. "Nuclear Language and How We Learned to Pat the Bomb." *Exploring Language.* Ed. Gary Goshgarian. 5th ed. Glenview, Ill.: Scott, Foresman, 1989. 52-67.

———. "Sex and Death in the Rational World of Defense Intellectuals." *Signs* 12.4 (1987): 687-718.

Cooper, Helen, Adrienne Auslander Munich, and Susan Merrill Squier, eds. *Arms and the Woman: War, Gender, and Literary Representation.* Chapel Hill: U of North Carolina P, 1989.

———. "Arms and the Woman: The Con[tra]ception of the War Text." *Arms and the Woman.* 9-24.

Craig, Patricia. *Elizabeth Bowen.* New York: Viking Penguin, 1986.

Croft, Andy. "Worlds without End Foisted upon the Future—Some Antecedents for *Nineteen Eighty-Four.*" *Inside the Myth—Orwell: Views from the Left.* Ed. Christopher Norris. London: Lawrence and Wishart, 1984. 183-216.

de Beauvoir, Simone. *The Second Sex.* 1949. Rpt., trans. and ed. H.M. Parshley. New York: Vintage Books, 1989.

Deiman, Werner J. "History, Pattern, and Continuity in Virginia Woolf." *Contemporary Literature* 15 (1974): 49-66.

de Lauretis, Teresa. *Technologies of Gender: Essays on Theory, Film, and Fiction.* Bloomington: Indiana U P, 1987.

Dick, Kay. "Talking to Stevie." *Ivy and Stevie: Conversations and Reflections.* London: Duckworth, 1971. 35-60.

Dinnerstein, Dorothy. *The Mermaid and the Minotaur: Sexual Arrangements and Human Malaise.* New York: Harper Colophon, 1976.

Donovan, Josephine. "Towards a Woman's Poetics." *Feminist Issues in Literary Scholarship.* Ed. Shari Benstock. Bloomington: Indiana U P, 1987. 98-109.

Dorenkamp, Angela G. "'Fall or Leap': Bowen's *The Heat of the Day.*" *Critique* 10 (1968): 13-21.

Douglas, Keith. *Alamein to Zem Zem.* Ed. Desmond Graham. Oxford: Oxford U P, 1979.

Douie, Vera. *The Lesser Half.* London: Women's Publicity Planning Assoc., n.d.

Douvan, Elizabeth, and Linda Kaboolian, "Women and Peace." *Feminist Re-Visions.* Ed. Vivian Patraka and Louise A. Tilly. Ann Arbor: U of Michigan P, 1983. 283-307.

Draine, Betsy. *Substance under Pressure: Artistic Coherence and Evolving Form in the Novels of Doris Lessing.* Madison: U of Wisconsin P, 1983.

Driver, C.J. "Profile: Doris Lessing." *The New Review* (London) (November 1974): 17-23.

DuPlessis, Rachel Blau. *Writing beyond the Ending: Narrative Strategies of Twentieth-Century Women Writers.* Bloomington: Indiana U P, 1985.

Eagleton, Terry. *Criticism and Ideology: A Study in Marxist Literary Theory.* Atlantic Highlands, N.J.: Humanities P, 1976.

Ehrenreich, Barbara. "The Warrior Culture." *Time* (15 October 1990): 100.

Eisenberg, Nora. "Virginia Woolf's Last Words on Words: *Between the Acts* and 'Anon.'" Marcus, *New Feminist Essays* 253-66.

Elshtain, Jean Bethke. "Feminist Discourse and Its Discontents: Language, Power, and Meaning." *Feminist Theory: A Critique of Ideology.* Ed. Nannerl O. Keohane, Michelle Z. Rosaldo, and Barbara Gelpi. Chicago: U of Chicago P, 1981. 127-45.

———. *Women and War.* New York: Basic Books, 1987.

———. "Women as Mirror and Other: Toward a Theory of Women, War and Feminism." *Humanities in Society* 5 (1982): 29-44.

Enloe, Cynthia. *Does Khaki Become You?: The Militarization of Women's Lives.* London: Pluto P, 1983.

Evans, Richard J. *Comrades and Sisters: Feminism, Socialism and Pacifism in Europe, 1870-1945.* New York: St. Martin's P, 1987.

Felman, Shoshana. "Women and Madness: The Critical Phallacy." *Diacritics* 5 (1975): 2-10.

Fetterly, Judith. *The Resisting Reader: A Feminist Approach to American Literature.* Bloomington: Indiana U P, 1978.

Fiedler, Leslie A. "Images of the Nurse in Fiction and Popular Culture." *Literature and Medicine* 2 (1983): 79-90.

Fish, Stanley E. *Self-Consuming Artifacts: The Experience of Seventeenth-Century Literature.* Berkeley: U of California P, 1972.

Fishburn, Katherine. *Doris Lessing: Life, Work, and Criticism.* Fredericton, New Brunswick, Canada: York P, 1987.

———. *The Unexpected Universe of Doris Lessing.* Westport, Conn.: Greenwood P, 1985.

Fisk, Robert. *In Time of War: Ireland, Ulster, and the Price of Neutrality 1939-45.* Philadelphia: U of Pennsylvania P, 1983.

Flax, Jane. "Political Philosophy and the Patriarchal Unconscious: A Psychoanalytic Perspective on Epistemology and Metaphysics." Harding and Hintikka 245-81.

Fleishman, Avrom. *Virginia Woolf: A Critical Reading.* Baltimore: Johns Hopkins U P, 1975.

Ford, Ford Maddox. *Parade's End.* 1924-28. Rpt. New York: Vintage, 1979.

Foucault, Michel. *Power/Knowledge: Selected Interviews and Other Writings.* Ed. Colin Gordon. New York: Pantheon, 1980.

Fussell, B.H. "Woolf's Peculiar Comic World: *Between the Acts.*" *Virginia Woolf: Revaluation and Continuity.* Ed. Ralph Freedman. Berkeley: U of California P, 1980. 263-83.

Fussell, Paul. "The Fate of Chivalry and the Assault upon Mother." *Thank God for the Atom Bomb and Other Essays.* New York: Ballantine, 1988. 186-210.

———. *The Great War and Modern Memory.* London: Oxford U P, 1975.

———. *Wartime: Understanding and Behavior in the Second World War.* New York: Oxford U P, 1989.

Gilbert, Sandra M. "Costumes of the Mind: Transvestism as Metaphor in Modern Literature." *Critical Inquiry* 7 (1980): 391-417.

Gilbert, Sandra M., and Susan Gubar. *Madwoman in the Attic: The Woman Writer and the Nineteenth-Century Literary Imagination.* New Haven, Conn.: Yale U P, 1979.

———. *Sexchanges.* Vol. 2 of *No Man's Land: The Place of the Woman Writer in the Twentieth Century.* New Haven, Conn.: Yale U P, 1989.

Gillespie, Diane Filby. "Political Aesthetics: Virginia Woolf and Dorothy Richardson." Marcus, *Feminist Slant* 132-51.

———. "Virginia Woolf's Miss La Trobe: The Artist's Last Struggle against Masculine Values." *Women and Literature* 5 (1977): 38-46.

Gilligan, Carol. *In a Different Voice: Psychological Theory and Women's Development.* Cambridge, Mass.: Harvard U P, 1982.

Glendinning, Victoria. *Elizabeth Bowen.* New York: Avon, 1977.

Goldsmith, Margaret. *Women at War.* London: Lindsay Drummond, n.a. (ca. 1942).

Green, Henry. *Caught.* 1943. Rpt. London: Hogarth P, 1965.

Greene, Gayle. "Doris Lessing's *Landlocked:* A New Kind of Knowledge." *Contemporary Literature* 28 (1987): 82-103.

Gross, Michael, and Mary Beth Averill. "Evolution and Patriarchal Myths of Scarcity and Competition." Harding and Hintikka 71-95.

Gubar, Susan. "Blessings in Disguise: Cross-Dressing as Re-Dressing for Female Modernists." *Massachusetts Review* 22 (1981): 477-508.

———. "This Is My Rifle, This Is My Gun: World War II and the Blitz on Women." Higonnet, et al. 227-59.

H. D. *Trilogy.* New York: New Directions, 1973.

Haggard, H. Ryder. *She. Collected Novels.* Secaucus, N.J.: Castle, 1987. 139-286.

Hamilton, Edith. *Mythology.* 1940. Rpt. Boston: New American Library, 1953.

Hanley, Lynne. "Her Story of War: De-Militarizing Literature and Literary Studies." *Radical America* 20 (1986): 17-28.

———. *Writing War: Fiction, Gender, and Memory.* Amherst: U of Massachusetts P, 1991.

Hardin, Nancy Shields. "The Sufi Teaching Story and Doris Lessing." *Twentieth Century Literature* 23 (1977): 314-26.

Harding, Sandra, and Merrill B. Hintikka, eds. *Discovering Reality.* Boston: D. Reidel, 1983.

Hardwick, Elizabeth. "Elizabeth Bowen's Fiction." *Partisan Review* 16 (November 1949): 1114-21.

Harris, Adrienne, and Ynestra King, eds. *Rocking the Ship of State: Toward a Feminist Peace Politics.* Boulder, Colo.: Westview P, 1989.

Harris, Marvin. "Why Men Dominate Women." *Columbia* 4 (1978): 9-13, 39.

Harrison, John R. *The Reactionaries: A Study of the Anti-Democratic Intelligentsia.* New York: Schocken Books, 1967.

Hartsock, Nancy. "Masculinity, Heroism, and the Making of War." Harris and King 133-52.

Hartsock, Nancy C.M. "Prologue to a Feminist Critique of War and Politics." *Women's Views of the Political World of Men.* Ed. Judith Hicks Stiehm. Dobbs Ferry, N.Y.: Transnational, c. 1984. 121-50.

Heath, William. *Elizabeth Bowen: An Introduction to Her Novels*. Madison: U of Wisconsin P, 1961.

Hewison, Robert. *In Anger: British Culture in the Cold War 1945-60*. New York: Oxford U P, 1981.

———. *Under Siege: Literary Life in London 1939-1945*. London: Weidenfeld and Nicolson, 1977.

Higonnet, Margaret R., and Patrice L.-R. Higonnet. "The Double Helix." Higonnet, et al. 31-47.

Higonnet, Margaret R., Jane Jenson, Sonya Michel, and Margaret Collins Weitz, eds. *Behind the Lines: Gender and the Two World Wars*. New Haven, Conn.: Yale U P, 1987.

Hite, Molly. "Doris Lessing's *The Golden Notebook* and *The Four-Gated City*: Ideology, Coherence, and Possibility." *Twentieth Century Literature* 34 (1988): 16-29.

Hogeland, Lisa Marie. "An Edge of History: The Implicit Feminism of Doris Lessing's *The Four-Gated City*." Stanford: Humanities Honors Program, 1984.

Holtby, Winifred. *Women in a Changing Civilization*. London: Bodley Head, 1934.

Howard, Michael. *The Causes of War*. 2d ed. Cambridge: Harvard U P, 1983.

Howe, Florence. "A Conversation with Doris Lessing (1966)." Pratt and Dembo 1-19.

Hughes, Douglas A. "Cracks in the Psyche: Elizabeth Bowen's 'The Demon Lover.'" *Studies in Short Fiction* 10 (1973): 411-13.

Huston, Nancy. "The Matrix of War: Mothers and Heroes." *Poetics Today* 6 (1985): 153-70.

———. "Tales of War and Tears of Women." Stiehm, *Women and Wars* 271-83.

Hynes, Samuel. *The Auden Generation: Literature and Politics in England in the 1930s*. London: Bodley Head, 1976.

Isherwood, Christopher. *Lions and Shadows: An Education in the Twenties*. New York: New Directions, 1977.

Jaffe, Don. "Poets in the Inferno: Civilians, C.O.'s and Combatants." *The Forties: Fiction, Poetry, and Drama*. Ed. Warren French. Deland, Fla. Everett/Edwards, 1969. 33-61.

Jeffords, Susan. *The Remasculinization of America: Gender and the Vietnam War*. Bloomington: Indiana U P, 1989.

Kamester, Margaret, and Jo Vellacott, eds. *Militarism versus Feminism: Writings on Women and War* by Catherine Marshall, C.K. Ogden and Mary Sargant Florence. London: Virago, 1987.

Kaplan, Carey, and Ellen Cronan Rose, eds. *Doris Lessing: The Alchemy of Survival*. Columbus: Ohio U P, 1988.

Kaplan, Sydney Janet. *Feminine Consciousness in the Modern British Novel*. Urbana: U of Illinois P, 1975.

———. "Passionate Portrayal of Things to Come: Doris Lessing's Recent Fiction." *Twentieth-Century Women Novelists*. Ed. Thomas F. Staley. Totowa, N.J.: Barnes and Noble, 1982. 1-15.

Keegan, John. *The Face of Battle*. New York: Vintage, 1977.

Keller, Evelyn Fox, and Christine R. Grontkowski. "The Mind's Eye." Harding and Hintikka 207-24.

Kendall, Alan. *Their Finest Hour: An Evocative Memoir of the British People in Wartime 1939-1945.* London: Wayland, 1972.

King, Jeanette. *Doris Lessing.* London: Edward Arnold, 1989.

Knapp, Mona. *Doris Lessing.* New York: Ungar, 1984.

Kokopeli, Bruce, and George Lakey. "More Power than We Want: Masculine Sexuality and Violence." McAllister 231-40.

Lassner, Phyllis. *The Short Fiction of Elizabeth Bowen.* Boston: G.K. Hall, 1991.

Lauter, Estella. *Women as Mythmakers: Poetry and Visual Art by Twentieth-Century Women.* Bloomington: Indiana U P, 1984.

Lawrence, D.H. *Kangaroo.* 1923. Rpt. New York: Viking P, 1964.

Layton, Lynne. "Vera Brittain's Testament(s)." Higonnet, et al. 70-83.

Lee, Hermione. *Elizabeth Bowen: An Estimation.* London: Vision, 1981.

Leed, Eric J. *No Man's Land: Combat and Identity in World War I.* Cambridge: Cambridge U P, 1979.

Lerner, Gerda. *The Creation of Patriarchy.* Women and History 1. New York: Oxford U P, 1986.

Lessing, Doris. *The Four-Gated City.* 1969. Rpt. New York: Plume, 1976.

———. *Going Home.* London: Michael Joseph, 1957.

———. *The Golden Notebook.* 1962. Rpt. New York: Bantam, 1979.

———. "Impertinent Daughters." *Granta* 14 (1984): 51-68.

———. "In the World, Not of It." Schlueter 129-38.

———. *Landlocked.* 1958. Rpt. New York: Plume, 1970.

———. *Martha Quest.* 1952. Rpt. New York: Plume, 1970.

———. "My Father." Schlueter 83-93.

———. Preface to *The Golden Notebook.* Schlueter 23-44.

———. *A Proper Marriage.* 1952. Rpt. New York: Plume, 1970.

———. *A Ripple from the Storm.* 1958. Rpt. New York: Plume, 1970.

———. "A Small Personal Voice." Schlueter 3-22.

———. "Vonnegut's Responsibility." Review of *Mother Night,* by Kurt Vonnegut. Schlueter 139-42.

Levertov, Denise. "Making Peace." 1987. Rpt. *Women on War: Essential Voices for the Nuclear Age.* Ed. Daniela Gioseffi. New York: Simon and Schuster, 1988, 326-27.

Longenbach, James. "The Women and Men of 1914." Cooper, Munich, and Squier 97-123.

Macciochi, Maria-Antoinetta. "Female Sexuality in Fascist Ideology." *Feminist Review* 1 (1979): 67-82.

Macdonald, N.P. *What Is Patriotism?* London: Thornton Butterworth, 1935.

Macdonald, Sharon, Pat Holden, and Shirley Ardener, eds. *Images of Women in Peace and War.* Madison: U of Wisconsin P, 1988.

Manning, Olivia. *The Balkan Trilogy.* 1960, 1962, 1965. Rpt. New York: Penguin, 1988.

———. *The Levant Trilogy.* 1977, 1978, 1980. New York: Penguin, 1988.

Marcus, Jane. "The Asylums of Antaeus: Women, War, and Madness—Is There a Feminist Fetishism?" *The New Historicism.* Ed. H. Aram Veeser. New York: Routledge, 1989. 132-51.

———. "Corpus/Corps/Corpse: Writing the Body in/at War." Cooper, Munich, and Squier 124-67.

———. "Liberty, Sorority, Misogyny." *The Representation of Women in Fiction.* Ed. Carolyn G. Heilbrun and Margaret Higonnet. Baltimore: Johns Hopkins U P, 1983. 60-97.

———. "'No more horses': Virginia Woolf on Art and Propaganda." *Women's Studies* 4 (1977): 265-90.

———. "Some Sources for *Between the Acts.*" *Virginia Woolf Miscellany* 6 (1977): 1-3.

———, ed. *New Feminist Essays on Virginia Woolf.* Lincoln: U of Nebraska P, 1982.

———, ed. *Virginia Woolf: A Feminist Slant.* Lincoln: U of Nebraska P, 1983.

Marder, Herbert. "Virginia Woolf's 'Conversion': *Three Guineas,* 'Pointz Hall' and *Between the Acts.*" *Journal of Modern Literature* 14 (1988): 465-80.

Marwick, Arthur. *The Home Front: The British and the Second World War.* London: Thames and Hudson, 1976.

Mason, Bobbie Ann. *In Country.* New York: Harper and Row, 1985.

McAllister, Pam. *Reweaving the Web of Life: Feminism and Nonviolence.* Philadelphia: New Society, 1982.

Mellown, Muriel. "One Woman's Way to Peace: The Development of Vera Brittain's Pacifism." *Frontiers* 8 (1985): 1-6.

———. "Reflections on Feminism and Pacifism in the Novels of Vera Brittain." *Tulsa Studies in Women's Literature* 2 (1983): 215-28.

Miller, Betty. *On the Side of the Angels.* 1945. Rpt. New York: Penguin/Virago, 1986.

Miller, Jean Baker. *Toward a New Psychology of Women.* Boston: Beacon P, 1976.

Minns, Raynes. *Bombers and Mash: The Domestic Front 1939-45.* London: Virago, 1980.

Moi, Toril. *Sexual/Textual Politics: Feminist Literary Theory.* London: Methuen, 1985.

Moore, Madeline. *The Short Season between Two Silences: The Mystical and the Political in the Novels of Virginia Woolf.* Boston: Allen and Unwin, 1984.

Naremore, James. "Nature and History in *The Years.*" *Virginia Woolf: Revaluation and Continuity.* Ed. Ralph Freedman. Berkeley: U of California P, 1980. 241-62.

———. *The World without a Self: Virginia Woolf and the Novel.* New Haven, Conn.: Yale U P, 1973.

Nathan, Peter. *The Psychology of Fascism.* London: Faber and Faber, 1943.

Newquist, Roy. "Interview with Doris Lessing." Schlueter 45-60.

Newton, Judith. "Making—and Remaking—History: Another Look at Patriarchy." *Tulsa Studies in Women's Literature* 3 (1984): 125-41.

Nixon, Cornelia. *Lawrence's Leadership Politics and the Turn against Women.* Berkeley: U of California P, 1986.

Ong, Walter. *Fighting for Life: Contest, Sexuality, and Consciousness.* Ithaca, N.Y.: Cornell U P, 1981.

Ortner, Sherry B. "Is Female to Male as Nature Is to Culture?" *Women, Culture, and Society.* Ed. Michelle Zimbalist Rosaldo and Louise Lamphere. Stanford: Stanford U P, 1974. 67-88.

Orwell, George. *Coming up for Air.* 1939. London: Secker and Warburg, 1971.

———. "My Country Right or Left." *The Penguin Essays of George Orwell.* New York: Penguin, 1984. 139-44.

Parfitt, George. *Fiction of the First World War: A Study.* London: Faber, 1988.

Patai, Daphne. Introduction to *Swastika Night* by Katharine Burdekin. iii-xv.

———. *The Orwell Mystique: A Study in Male Ideology.* Amherst: U of Massachusetts P, 1984.

———. "Orwell's Despair, Burdekin's Hope: Gender and Power in Dystopia." *Women's Studies International Forum* 7 (1984): 85-95.

Pickering, Jean. "Marxism and Madness: The Two Faces of Doris Lessing's Myth." *Modern Fiction Studies* 26 (1980): 17-30.

Piercy, Marge. *Gone to Soldiers.* New York: Fawcett, 1987.

Pierson, Ruth Roach. "'Did your mother wear army boots?': Feminist Theory and Women's Relation to War, Peace and Revolution." Macdonald, Holden, and Ardener 205-27.

Playne, Caroline E. *Society at War, 1914-1916.* Boston: Houghton Mifflin, 1931.

Pratt, Annis. *Archetypal Patterns in Women's Fiction.* Bloomington: Indiana U P, 1981.

Pratt, Annis, and L.S. Dembo, eds. *Doris Lessing: Critical Studies.* Madison: U of Wisconsin P, 1974.

Priestley, J.B. *British Women Go to War.* London: Collins, n.d.

———. *Postscripts.* London: William Heinemann, 1940.

Quinn, Antoinette. "Elizabeth Bowen's Irish Stories—1939 to 1945." *Studies in Anglo-Irish Literature.* Ed. Heinz Kosok. Bonn: Bouvier Verlag Herbert Grundmann, 1982. 314-21.

Rabinbach, Anson, and Jessica Benjamin. Foreword. *Male Fantasies,* vol. 2, by Klaus Theweleit. ix-xxv.

Raskin, Jonah. "Doris Lessing at Stony Brook: An Interview." Schlueter 61-76.

Reardon, Betty. "Militarism and Sexism: Influences on Education and War." *Women, Militarism, and Disarmament.* Ed. Birgit Brock-Utne, Julianne Traylor, and Solveig Aas. Oslo: International Peace Research Institute, 1986.

———. *Sexism and the War System.* New York: Teacher's College P, 1985.

Reilly, Catherine, ed. *Chaos of the Night: Women's Poetry and Verse of the Second World War.* London: Virago, 1984.

Richards, Janet Radcliffe. "Why the Pursuit of Peace Is No Part of Feminism." *Women, Militarism, and War: Essays in History, Politics, and Social Theory.* Ed. Jean Bethke Elshtain and Sheila Tobias. Savage, Md.: Rowman & Littlefield, 1990. 211-26.

Rigney, Barbara Hill. *Madness and Sexual Politics in the Feminist Novel.* Madison: U of Wisconsin P, 1978.

Riley, Denise. "Some Peculiarities of Social Policy Concerning Women in Wartime and Postwar Britain." Higonnet, et al. 260-71.

Ritchie, Charles. *The Siren Years: Undiplomatic Diaries 1937-1945.* London: Macmillan, 1974.

Rohrlich, Ruby. "State Formation in Sumer and the Subjugation of Women." *Feminist Studies* 6 (1980): 76-102.

Rose, Ellen Cronan. *The Tree outside the Window: Doris Lessing's Children of Violence.* Hanover, N.H.: U P of New England, 1976.

Roszak, Theodore. "The Hard and the Soft: The Force of Feminism in Modern Times." Roszak and Roszak 87-104.

———. "Why Men Need a Boys' Night Out." Roszak and Roszak 38-50.

Roszak, Theodore, and Betty Roszak, eds. *Masculine/Feminine: Readings in Sexual Mythology and the Liberation of Women.* New York: Harper and Row, 1969.

Rowbotham, Sheila. *Woman's Consciousness, Man's World.* New York: Penguin, 1973.

Rubenstein, Roberta. *The Novelistic Vision of Doris Lessing: Breaking the Forms of Consciousness.* Urbana: U of Illinois P, 1979.

Rubin, Gayle. "The Traffic in Women: Notes toward a Political Economy of Sex." *Toward an Anthropology of Women*. Ed. Rayna Reiter. New York: Monthly Review P, 1975. 157-210.

Ruotolo, Lucio P. *The Interrupted Moment: A View of Virginia Woolf's Novels*. Stanford: Stanford U P, 1986.

Rupp, Leila J. *Mobilizing Women for War: German and American Propaganda 1939-1945*. Princeton, N.J.: Princeton U P, 1978.

Rutherford, Andrew. *The Literature of War: Five Studies in Heroic Virtue*. New York: Barnes and Noble, 1978.

Sackville-West, Vita. *The Grand Canyon*. Garden City, N.Y.: Doubleday, 1942.

Sarton, May. "Elizabeth Bowen." *A World of Light: Portraits and Celebrations*. New York: Norton, 1976.

Sassoon, Siegfried. *The Complete Memoirs of George Sherston*. Garden City, N.Y.: Doubleday, 1937.

Schlueter, Paul, ed. *A Small Personal Voice: Essays, Reviews, Interviews*. New York: Knopf, 1974.

Schüddekopf, Otto-Ernst. *Revolutions of Our Time: Fascism*. New York: Praeger, 1973.

Schweik, Susan. "Writing War Poetry Like a Woman." *Critical Inquiry* 13 (1987): 532-56.

Scott, Joan W. "Deconstructing Equality-Versus-Difference: Or, the Uses of Poststructuralist Theory for Feminism." *Feminist Studies* 14 (1988): 33-49.

———. "Rewriting History." Higonnet, et al. 212-30.

Scott, Peggy. *They Made Invasion Possible*. London: Hutchinson, n.d.

Sears, Sallie. "Theater of War: Virginia Woolf's *Between the Acts*." Marcus, *Feminist Slant* 212-35.

Sedgwick, Eve Kosofsky. *Between Men: English Literature and Male Homosocial Desire*. New York: Columbia U P, 1985.

Showalter, Elaine. *The Female Malady: Women, Madness, and English Culture, 1830-1980*. New York: Penguin, 1985.

———. "Rivers and Sassoon: The Inscription of Male Gender Anxieties." Higonnet, et al. 61-69.

Silver, Brenda. "*Three Guineas* Before and After: Further Answers to Correspondents." Marcus, *Feminist Slant* 254-76.

Sinfield, Alan. *Literature, Politics and Culture in Postwar Britain*. Berkeley: U of California P, 1989.

Smith, Paul. *Discerning the Subject*. Theory and History of Literature 55. Minneapolis: U of Minnesota P, 1988.

Smith, Stevie. "The Ambassador." Smith, *Selection* 114.

———. *The Holiday*. 1949. Rpt. New York: Pinnacle, 1979.

———. *Me Again: Uncollected Writing of Stevie Smith*. Ed. Jack Barbera and William McBrien. London: Virago, 1981.

———. "Mosaic." Smith, *Me Again* 105-7.

———. *Novel on Yellow Paper*. 1936. Rpt. New York: Pinnacle, 1982.

———. "On the Side of the Angels" (review of Vera Brittain's *Testament of Experience*). Smith, *Me Again* 193-94.

———. *Over the Frontier*. 1938. Rpt. London: Virago, 1980.

———. *Stevie Smith: A Selection*. Ed. Hermione Lee. London: Faber and Faber, 1983.

———. "Sunday at Home." Smith, *Me Again* 44-49.

———. "Who Shot Eugenie?" Smith, *Selection* 123-25.

Spark, Muriel. "The First Year of My Life." *The Stories of Muriel Spark*. New York: Dutton, 1985.

———. *The Girls of Slender Means*. New York: Perigee, 1963.

Spender, Dale. *Man Made Language*. 2d ed. London: Routledge and Kegan Paul, 1985.

Sprague, Claire. "Doris Lessing Redefines the Front: The (Un)Common Places of War." *Revista Canaria de Estudios Ingleses* 17 (November 1988): 53-65.

———. *Rereading Doris Lessing: Narrative Patterns of Doubling and Repetition*. Chapel Hill: U of North Carolina P, 1987.

———. "'Without Contraries Is No Progression': Lessing's *The Four-Gated City*." *Modern Fiction Studies* 26.1 (1980): 99-116.

Sprague, Claire, and Virginia Tiger, eds. *Critical Essays on Doris Lessing*. Boston: G.K. Hall, 1986.

Squier, Susan. *Virginia Woolf and London*. Chapel Hill: U of North Carolina P, 1985.

Stamberg, Susan. "An Interview with Doris Lessing." *Doris Lessing Newsletter* 8 (1984): 3-4, 15.

Stiehm, Judith Hicks. "The Protected, the Protector, the Defender." Stiehm, *Women and Wars* 367-76.

———, ed. *Women and Men's Wars*. London: Pergamon P, 1983.

Stimpson, Catharine R. "Doris Lessing and the Parables of Growth." *Doris Lessing*. Ed. Harold Bloom. New York: Chelsea House, 1986. 183-200.

Sutherland, Mary. "Women and the War." *Victory or Vested Interest?* Ed. Fabian Society. London: Routledge, 1942.

Suvin, Darko. *Metamorphoses of Science Fiction: On the Poetics and History of a Literary Genre*. New Haven, Conn.: Yale U P, 1979.

Taylor, Jenny. "The Deconstruction of a Colonial Radical." Sprague and Tiger 37-43.

Tepper, Sheri S. *The Gate to Women's Country*. New York: Bantam, 1988.

Theweleit, Klaus. *Male Fantasies*. Vol. 1 *women floods bodies history*. Trans. Stephen Conway. Minneapolis: U of Minnesota P, 1987.

———. *Male Fantasies*. Vol. 2 *Male bodies: psychoanalyzing the white terror*. Trans. Erica Carter and Chris Turner. Minneapolis: U of Minnesota P, 1989.

Thompson, Dorothy. "Women, Peace and History: Notes for an Historical Overview." *Women and Peace: Theoretical, Historical and Practical Perspectives*. Ed. Ruth Roach Pierson. London: Croom Helm, 1987. 29-43.

Tiger, Lionel. *Men in Groups*. New York: Marion Boyars, 1984.

Tilsley, Frank. *Little Tin God*. London: Collius, 1939.

Torrents, Nissa. "Doris Lessing: Testimony to Mysticism" (interview). *Doris Lessing Newsletter* 4 (1980): 1, 12-13.

Tylee, Claire. *The Great War and Women's Consciousness: Images of Militarism and Womanhood in Women's Writings 1914-64*. Iowa City: U of Iowa P, 1990.

———. "'Madness Run Riot'—The Great War and Women's Resistance to Militarism." *Women's Studies International Forum* 11 (1988): 199-210.

Vlastos, Marion. "Doris Lessing and R.D. Laing: Psychopolitics and Prophecy." *PMLA* 91 (1976): 245-58.

Watkins, Renée. "Survival in Discontinuity—Virginia Woolf's *Between the Acts*." *The Massachusetts Review* 10 (1969): 356-76.

Watson, Barbara Bellow. "Variations on an Enigma: Elizabeth Bowen's War Novel." *Southern Humanities Review* 15 (1981): 131-51.

Watts, Jane. Introduction. 1980. *Over the Frontier* by Stevie Smith. 5-8.

Waugh, Evelyn. *Unconditional Surrender.* London: Chapman and Hall, 1961.

Waugh, Patricia. *Feminine Fictions: Revisiting the Postmodern.* London: Routledge, 1989.

West, Rebecca. "Indissoluble Matrimony." *The Young Rebecca: Writings of Rebecca West 1911-17.* Ed. Jane Marcus. Bloomington: Indiana U P, 1982.

———. *Return of the Soldier.* New York: Century, 1918.

White, Hayden. "The Historical Text as Literary Artifact." *Tropics of Discourse: Essays in Cultural Criticism.* Baltimore: Johns Hopkins U P, 1978. 81-100.

———. "The Value of Narrativity in the Representation of Reality." *The Content of the Form: Narrative Discourse and Historical Representation.* Baltimore: Johns Hopkins U P, 1987. 1-25.

Wilden, Anthony. *Man and Woman, War and Peace.* London: Routledge and Kegan Paul, 1987.

Wilshire, Donna. "The Uses of Myth, Image, and the Female Body in Re-visions of Knowledge." *Gender/Body/Knowledge: Feminist Reconstructions of Being and Knowing.* Ed. Alison M. Jaggar and Susan R. Bordo. New Brunswick, N.J.: Rutgers U P, 1989. 92-114.

Wilson, Elizabeth. *Only Halfway to Paradise: Women in Postwar Britain 1945-1968.* London: Tavistock, 1980.

Wiltsher, Ann. *Most Dangerous Women: Feminist Peace Campaigners of the Great War.* London: Pandora P, 1985.

Woolf, Leonard. *Barbarians at the Gate.* London: Gollancz, 1939.

Woolf, Virginia. "The Artist and Politics." V. Woolf, *Collected Essays,* 2:230-32.

———. *Between the Acts.* New York: Harcourt Brace Jovanovich, 1941.

———. *Collected Essays.* 4 vols. London: Hogarth, 1967.

———. *The Diary of Virginia Woolf.* Ed. Anne Olivier Bell. 5 vols. San Diego: Harcourt Brace Jovanovich, 1984.

———. "Flying Over London." V. Woolf, *Collected Essays,* 4:167-72.

———. *Jacob's Room.* 1922. New York: Harcourt Brace Jovanovich, 1960.

———. "The Leaning Tower." V. Woolf, *Collected Essays,* vol. 2 162-81.

———. *The Letters of Virginia Woolf.* Ed. Nigel Nicolson and Joanne Trautmann. 6 vols. New York: Harcourt Brace Jovanovich, 1977.

———. *Orlando.* New York: Harcourt Brace Jovanovich, 1928.

———. *A Room of One's Own.* New York: Harcourt Brace Jovanovich, 1929.

———. "Thoughts on Peace in an Air Raid." V. Woolf, *Collected Essays,* 4:173-77.

———. *Three Guineas.* New York: Harcourt Brace Jovanovich, 1938.

———. *The Waves.* New York: Harcourt Brace Jovanovich, 1931.

———. *A Writer's Diary.* Ed. Leonard Woolf. New York: Harcourt Brace, 1953.

———. *The Years.* New York: Harcourt Brace Jovanovich, 1937.

Wright, Gordon. *The Ordeal of Total War 1939-1945.* New York: Harper, 1986.

Ziegler, Heidi, and Christopher Bigsby. *The Radical Imagination and the Liberal Tradition: Interviews with English and American Novelists.* London: Junction, 1982. 188-208.

Zwerdling, Alex. *Virginia Woolf and the Real World.* Berkeley: U of California P, 1986.

Index

DATE DUE

HIGHSMITH #45115